The Pizza BIBLE

The World's Favorite Pizza Styles, from Neapolitan,
Deep-Dish, Wood-Fired, Sicilian, Calzones and Focaccia
to New York, New Haven, Detroit, and More

★★ TONY GEMIGNANI ★★

12-Time World Pizza Champ

WITH SUSIE HELLER AND STEVE SIEGELMAN

Photography by Sara Remington

TEN SPEED PRESS
California | New York

I would like to dedicate this book to three amazing people in my life.

My wife Julie, who is always so supportive of me and my career. Her light feeds my soul making me want to be better. She is simply the best.

Susie Heller, for bringing everyone involved in this groundbreaking book together. Since our first introduction we shared the same vision, excitement and determination. She is a true artist and great friend.

George Karpaty, my best friend and business partner. He fuels my fire that burns within. George is one of the hardest working entrepreneurs I know. He shares my passion and commitment to perfection.

CONTENTS

RESPECT THE CRAFT

Pizza is simple. It's dough, tomato, cheese, and toppings. But as someone who has devoted more than half of my life to it, I can tell you that, like all really great, really simple things, pizza is infinite. I'm still learning, still refining, still trying to make it even better every single day. And what I can tell you for sure is that pizza doesn't come down to just recipes or formulas. It's a craft.

That one word—that's why I wanted to write this book. There are hundreds of pizza books, blogs, and websites filled with thousands of recipes out there. Do we really need another one? I thought about this a lot, and here's where I ended up: when I teach home cooks and certify chefs and *pizzaiolos*, it's less about recipes and more about inspiring people to master the craft of pizza—the techniques, the reasons to choose one ingredient over another, the art of "reading" the dough as you mix, shape, top, and bake it.

Anyone can hand you a pizza recipe, and if that recipe is halfway decent, chances are you can make yourself a perfectly good pizza for dinner tonight in your own kitchen with no special equipment and not much preparation. But that's not where I want to take you. *I want to get you all the way to five-star, killer-pizzeria-quality pizza.* I want you to master any style you love—whether it's Chicago deep-dish or cracker-thin, a big, fluffy Sicilian pan pizza or a classic Neapolitan margherita with that authentic char blistering the edges—right in your own kitchen with whatever oven you've got.

Is that really possible? Can you actually do all that without a real pizza oven? That's the question I get asked most often. Believe it or not, you can. It's not your oven. It's the ingredients and the techniques you use, and I'm going to give you every piece of ingredient and technique advice you'll need to succeed.

But if you truly want to get all the way to rocking restaurant-style pizza at home, there's one thing I'm going to ask you to commit to. It's the motto that runs across the front of my menu, and the three words etched on the door of my restaurants. Hey, I even had it tattooed right onto my hands. *Respect the craft.*

Craft is the difference between good and great. It takes a few extra steps, the right equipment, a little more time, and a fair amount of practice. But if you're up for it, the payoff is golden.

So I'm going to start by asking you to try something a little unusual for a cookbook. I want you to read all the way through page 19 before you try a single recipe. And then I'm inviting you to take a Master Class where we make your first pizza together—and maybe even take that class a few more times before you graduate to trying all the great stuff in the rest of the book and eventually coming up with your own variations and improvisations.

That's what I mean by respecting the craft and getting a handle on the whys and hows behind it. It might sound a little back-to-schooly. But trust me, it'll be fun. And you get to eat the final exam.

Want more information and inspiration? Check out my blog at ThePizzaBible.com.

GEARING UP

Before we start making pizzas, you're going to need to line up some basic equipment and ingredients.

Depending on how well outfitted your kitchen is, the equipment part might call for a bit of initial investment. But all of this stuff lasts forever, and it's going to make a big difference in your pizza making. And besides, gear is fun.

I've pared down the following list to the absolute essentials, just for our Master Class. For other recipes, there will be a few more things you'll want to get, but for now, this is your starter list. Take it to a cookware or restaurant supply store or go online and round up any of the items you don't already have. And be sure to check out my recommendations and sources starting on page 304.

EQUIPMENT CHECKLIST

- ☐ Digital scale with both gram and ounce settings that registers to 0.1 gram
- ☐ Palm scale (sometimes referred to as a pocket scale) that registers to 0.01 grams (optional, but helpful)
- ☐ Stand mixer
- ☐ Immersion blender
- ☐ Prep bowls (a set of nesting glass ones is nice to have)
- ☐ Wet and dry measuring cups and a set of measuring spoons
- ☐ Instant-read thermometer
- ☐ Straight-edged dough cutter
- ☐ Round-edged bowl scraper
- ☐ Half sheet pan (or two quarter sheet pans)

- ☐ Plastic wrap, preferably extra-wide
- ☐ Tape measure
- ☐ Two square or rectangular pizza stones or baking steels (see page 5 before you buy) at least 15 inches square but as wide and as deep as your oven will allow
- ☐ Pizza peel at least 14 and preferably 15 inches square with a short handle
- ☐ Kitchen timer
- ☐ Pastry brush (for drizzling oil)
- ☐ Rocking pizza cutter (or pizza wheel)
- ☐ Large round platters or boards for serving
- ☐ Wide, stiff-bristled, heat-resistant brush and dish towel for cleaning stones or steels

Tools of the Trade

Stones or steels?

Most of my recipes call for two pizza stones or baking steels. Stones have been around for years, and good, large rectangular ones work really well. Baking steels are a relative newcomer, and I've really been happy with the results we've gotten from them as we developed the recipes in this book for home cooks. Steels heat beautifully, cook evenly, and recover their heat more quickly than stones, which is great when you're making multiple pizzas. They're also easier to store than stones. Steels work especially well with the Home-Oven Broiler Method (page 202).

What kind of peel?

You'll need a wooden peel to build your pizzas on and to move them in and out of the oven. Look for one that's at least 14 inches square—15 inches square will give you a little more room to work with. If you're going to be using a wood-burning oven, make sure to buy a peel with a handle that's at least 20 inches long (longer if your oven is large).

In professional kitchens, we usually build pizzas right on the marble work surface. We then slide the topped pizza onto a peel to transfer it to the oven. In my restaurants, we use a thin perforated metal peel (see page 305) that lets you shake off most of the semolina and flour from the underside of the pizza, so it doesn't burn in the oven. These peels are an awesome innovation, but maneuvering a fully loaded unbaked pizza on and off a perforated peel can be tricky because unless you work very quickly, the dough can settle into the holes, causing the pizza to grab. So for home cooks, I recommend building your pizza directly on a wooden peel. Once you get proficient, you can reward yourself with a perforated metal peel and graduate to that.

Dough cutter versus bowl scraper

A dough cutter (sometimes called a bench scraper or dough scraper), which has a straight edge and a flat surface, is used to cut and lift dough; it's also great for cleaning and scraping your work surface. A bowl scraper, which is more flexible and has a rounded edge, is used like you would use a rubber spatula to scrape dough from the bowl. I suggest you have one of each within easy reach whenever you're making dough.

A rockin' way to slice

You can use a traditional pizza wheel, but that wheel has been reinvented in recent years. The better option is a rocking pizza cutter. It looks like a giant mezzaluna, the traditional Italian chopper with a curved blade and a handle on each end. You want to buy a big, heavy one, with a 20-inch blade that will allow you to slice a pizza in one smooth move. To use it, hold the pizza cutter at a 45-degree angle to the cutting board with the lower end over one edge of your pizza. Slam that end of the cutter right through the crust, and then rock the cutter, pressing down very firmly to slice all the way across. Use the same motion again to make as many slices as you want. Once you experience this, you'll never go back to the wheel for cutting a pizza, but you should still keep one on hand for trimming dough.

Pizza stand

When you're having a group over for pizza and you're serving other stuff, it's handy to have a pizza stand, which gets the pie up off the table, leaving you space for everything else. It's especially useful when you're serving a large pizza, like a Sicilian or a Romana.

MASTER CLASS SHOPPING LIST

Here's a list of ingredients you'll use for our class. I've recommended quantities that will give you enough to try the whole process a few times. Also note that I'm leading with easy-to-find consumer brands here, just for the purpose of this class. In my recipes, you'll see that I always recommend you try to use my preferred professional brands.

☐ 1 (3 pounds/1.4 kilograms will be plenty) bag high-gluten flour, preferably King Arthur Sir Lancelot Unbleached Hi-Gluten Flour (or Giusto's High Performer High Protein Unbleached Flour or Pendleton Flour Mills Power Flour, or Tony's California Artisan Flour); for more information on flour, see page 11

☐ 1 (24 ounces/680 grams) bag fine semolina will be enough for several pizzas

☐ Active dry yeast (avoid quick-rise or instant yeast), preferably Red Star brand

☐ Fine sea salt

☐ Diastatic malt (see page 16); you'll need only a small amount—a few teaspoons or about 9 grams per pizza; look for it online or at a local home-brewing supply store

☐ Extra virgin olive oil

☐ 1 (28-ounce/794-gram) can ground tomatoes, preferably 7/11 or DiNapoli

☐ 1 (12-ounce/340-gram) can tomato paste, preferably Contadina or SuperDolce

☐ 1 (28-ounce/794-gram) can whole plum or pear tomatoes, preferably DiNapoli

☐ 12 ounces (340 grams) whole-milk mozzarella cheese (1 pound/453 grams if you want to make two cheese pizzas)

☐ Dried oregano, preferably Greek

☐ Small piece Parmigiano-Reggiano cheese, for shaving

☐ Grated Pecorino Romano cheese, for dusting

☐ 4 ounces (115 grams) sliced pepperoni, or 5 ounces (140 grams) bulk fennel or Calabrese sausage, homemade (pages 54 and 55) or store-bought

☐ 6 thin slices (about 4 ounces/115 grams) prosciutto

☐ 1½ cups (20 grams) arugula leaves

☐ 12 cherry tomatoes, preferably multicolor

☐ 1 head garlic

☐ 1 bunch basil

PART ONE: THEORY

Welcome to Pizza School. It's early in the morning, you're sitting in the empty dining room at Tony's Pizza Napoletana in San Francisco with a baker's dozen of assorted students, and as the sun begins to creep across the tables and you sip your cappuccino, I'm going to start with a quick overview of the fundamental principles that define every pizza I make. And then, we'll get cooking.

SLOW IS THE SECRET

People are always paying me this weird left-handed compliment. They'll come up to me like someone entering a confessional booth, glance from side to side, lower their voice, and say, "You know, Tony, I have to say, I never really *liked* pizza that much. But now that I tried yours, I love it!"

Or they'll say, "Oh man. Your pizza totally brought me back to the stuff I loved as a kid."

I'm not telling you this to brag but to make a point. The people who loved their childhood pizza were probably remembering what they'd get at a local, independently owned pizzeria in their neighborhood. The ones who never really felt the pizza love undoubtedly grew up eating at pizza chains, where the ingredients are cheap and the dough is made factory style—or even literally in a factory.

That kind of pizza is designed to fill you up quickly and inexpensively. My pizza is just the opposite. You can eat a whole pie and not feel overwhelmed with either regret or stomach pain. If you've ever eaten a pizza in Italy, you know what I'm talking about. Each person gets served a big pizza that looks like it could feed a family. You tuck into it with a knife and fork, and the next thing you know, you've eaten the whole thing, no problem.

What we're talking about here is *digestibility*. If a dough is made correctly, it's not just nicely flavored, it's also light and easy to eat. And the key to that is time. Pizza dough is a living thing. The minute you mix yeast with flour and water, it starts eating the simple sugars in that flour, and the longer you let it feed—up to a point—the more it will eat. That's why, from today on, I want you to *make pizza dough that rises in the refrigerator for at least 24 hours—preferably 48 hours.*

You can find all kinds of recipes that put pizza on your table in an hour or less, with no rising and no kneading. They usually use a large amount of quick-rise yeast, activated with a jolt of sugar right at the start. That's like giving your yeast a triple espresso. You can make pizza that way, but it'll be nowhere near as flavorful, as tender, or as digestible. (If you're the kind of person who doesn't like to plan more than a day ahead, check out my frozen dough recipe and strategy on page 49.)

Moisture, warmth, and sugar are what get yeast going. What I do is all about controlling those factors to make the process as slow as possible. I activate the yeast with lukewarm water, then I usually mix flour with some malt (to add a slight amount of sweetness and help with browning—more on that later) and add ice water, which will calm the yeast down when it's incorporated. I mix that very slowly and relatively briefly in a stand mixer, always on the lowest speed setting (rather than in a food processor, which heats up the dough too much). The yeast mixture goes in next and is mixed slowly, again relatively briefly, and then the salt is added, which slows the yeast down even more. Finally, a small amount of oil is mixed in. Then I let the dough rest at room temperature for up to an hour before I refrigerate it for 24 hours or longer. This slow proofing process means you can start with a relatively small amount of yeast and you won't end up with that unpleasant overly yeasty flavor that's typical of a lot of home-baked bread and pizza.

The slower the yeast eats the simple sugars in the flour, the better. And the more the yeast gets to eat, the lighter and more digestible the pizza. Think of it this way: *you're letting the yeast do most of the digesting for you.*

Slow fermentation creates a more complex flavor, too. It's like brewing beer, making wine, or aging cheese. These maturation processes can't be rushed without sacrificing taste. Forget the shortcuts. Pizza, the world's favorite fast food is, in fact, slow food.

WEIGHING IS THE WAY

If this book changes one thing about the way you cook and bake, I hope it's that it gets you comfortable with the idea of weighing ingredients and using metric measurements. Cooks in Europe and most of the rest of the world are lucky because they grow up doing this. An Italian pizza recipe will start with half a kilogram of flour and give you the rest of the measurements in either gram or milliliter (liquid) quantities.

In the United States, where we're used to cups and tablespoons, it's worth making the leap to weighing, especially for baking. As a rule, weighing dry and liquid ingredients is both more accurate and easier than using volume measures. That's why most chefs and professional bakers weigh them. In a pizzeria, you need total accuracy and consistency night after night. And the same goes for home recipes. If you and I both measure a cup of flour and then weigh it, chances are we'll get different weights because one of us packed the cup more loosely or topped it off less accurately than the other. If we're measuring different flours, that adds another layer of potential discrepancies. But as long as you've got an accurate scale, a weight is a weight. If we each weigh 453 grams (by the way, that's a pound) of any flour for a dough recipe, we'll have exactly the same amount.

You'll see that I use both grams and ounces in my recipes. When I measure ingredients for doughs and starters, where precise weights are critical, I go with grams alone. For most other ingredients that are measured by weight, like cheese, for example, I give you ounce measurements because I think they're easier to get your head around. In the grocery store, you won't be shopping for 200 grams of cheese. You'll buy it by the ounce, and it's fine to measure it that way for a recipe. The point is that weighing it at all will give you a more accurate measurement than grating it and measuring it with a cup measure.

So before you read another word, go get yourself a nice digital kitchen scale that can read both grams and ounces with resolution to 0.1 gram (you'll find some recommendations on page 305). To measure ingredients in smaller quantities (yeast, for example), I also recommend buying a digital palm scale that goes to 0.01 gram.

Once you get used to weighing in grams, you'll find that they're easy to work with, and they give you a better sense of proportions because everything is based on factors of ten. Which brings us to . . .

BAKER'S PERCENTAGES

If you've ever seen a professional baking recipe, you know that they're usually based on baker's percentages. This is a handy method of giving a formula by showing the amount of each ingredient not as a fixed quantity (the way a typical cookbook recipe would), but as a percentage of the amount of flour. The flour is the base amount, so it's always at 100 percent. The other ingredients are expressed as percentages of that amount.

So, if I'm making a batch of dough with 500 grams of flour and I add 350 grams of water, the formula would show the flour as 100 percent and the water as 70 percent (because 350 is 70 percent of 500).

I've included baker's percentages for all of the doughs in this book (see page 302). I did that partly for professionals but also for home cooks. That's because once you get used to baker's percentages, you'll find they give you a quick snapshot of a dough. And scaling a recipe up or down is easy because you just pick whatever amount of flour you want to start with and then, for every other ingredient, you multiply the amount of flour by the percentage given for that ingredient in the formula.

Now, back to my example of 500 grams flour. If the formula puts the yeast at 1 percent, then you calculate 1 percent of 500 (multiply 500 by 0.01) and get 5 grams. If you scale the batch up to 10 kilograms (10,000 grams) of flour, then your yeast would be 10,000 multiplied by 0.01 or 100 grams.

There's a handy online tool that professionals use to scale up dough recipes. It's called the Lehmann Pizza Dough Calculator, and it lets you plug in your desired percentages and dough weight and then calculates all your quantities for you. For home cooks, doing the math yourself is pretty straightforward, but I recommend checking out the dough calculator anyway. It'll give you a deeper under-standing and appreciation of the way dough ingredients relate to one another. You can find it, along with other calculating tools, at pizzamaking.com under "dough tools."

HYDRATION

Since most pizza doughs are based on the same basic ingredients—flour, water, yeast, and salt—what makes one kind of dough different from another has a lot to do with the *amount of water relative to the flour*. This is called hydration.

As a general rule, the higher the hydration of your dough, the lighter, puffier, more tender, and more crisp the dough is likely to be. That's right, *more crisp*. You might think more water would make a dough soggier, but (at least up to a point) what it does is create steam that helps the dough expand during baking, giving the crust a crisp exterior while the inside stays moist and soft.

I love that effect, and so do most *pizzaiolos* and bakers. It's why a lot of recipes out there recommend hydration levels way up around 85 percent. But there's a huge trade-off. The higher your hydration, the less workable your dough will be. Above 70 percent hydration, dough becomes

increasingly unmanageable, especially for a home baker. It's soft, wet, and floppy. It tears easily when you handle it. And it can be very hard to stretch and shape into a nice even circle with uniform thickness. That means you'll end up with free-form pizzas that cook unevenly and form holes that leave melted cheese and sauce all over your pizza stone. Some recipe writers call these overhydrated pizzas "rustic." I call them a mess.

That's why most of the doughs in this book come in at between 60 and 70 percent hydration. Now that you know about baker's percentages, you can eyeball any of my dough recipes and instantly see what the hydration level is, just by looking at the percentage number next to the water. Handy, right?

As you get used to working with dough, you can try pushing the hydration a bit higher (by simply adding a little more water during mixing) and see if you like the results. But for now, know that I've set the hydration level of every dough in this book to hit the sweet spot of texture, performance, and workability.

PRO TIP

THE AUTOLYSE METHOD To give breads and pizzas a better crumb and stronger structure, some bakers like to "presoak" their flour in water (for 30 minutes, or even up to 6 to 8 hours to maximize absorption), a technique known as the autolyse method. This gives the flour a headstart on hydrating before you add the other ingredients. The enzymes in the flour begin to break down its starches and proteins, which helps gluten develop. If you're curious to give it a try, here's how: In the bowl of a stand mixer, combine just the flour and water in your dough recipe, mixing on low speed just until combined. Cover the bowl with plastic wrap, and let the mixture sit at room temperature for about 30 minutes, then proceed with your recipe.

INGREDIENTS

You've heard this a thousand times, but when it comes to pizza, it's worth repeating. There just aren't that many ingredients involved, so every single one needs to be the best you can get your hands on. A package of store-bought shredded mozzarella might be convenient, but it's likely to have cellulose added as an anticaking agent, and it probably won't be as flavorful as cheese you grate yourself. That's just one example. Everything from the salt and the malt to the tomatoes and the toppings deserves careful consideration. You'll taste the difference.

I generally like to prepare authentic regional pizza styles—whether American or Italian—using the ingredients traditionally used in those regions. I'll go to just about any length and expense to get those ingredients from the source. That means not just the famous foodie ingredients, like Caputo flour and DOP San Marzano tomatoes from Italy for my Neapolitans, but also Provel, a processed cheese that's the signature ingredient of St. Louis–style pizza. The closer you get to the source, the more your pizzas will taste like unique and original creations.

The good news is that these days you can source virtually any specialty pizza ingredient online, so you have more access than ever to the same stuff the pros use. The bad news is that you may have to buy it in large quantities. But hey, some ingredients store or freeze well, and you can always go in on a purchase with a friend or two and divvy up your haul.

Another great option is to get to know the owner or manager of a good pizzeria in your town. Chances are they'll be happy to sell you any ingredients you need and maybe even special order ingredients and equipment for you.

Meanwhile, if you prefer to explore the pizza world on your own, see my Sources section, starting on page 304, for recommendations and tips on tracking down all the right stuff.

FLOUR

Flour is the heart and soul of a pizza, so it's really important to choose the right one for the job. It all depends on the type of pizza you want to make and the length of time you want your dough to mature.

I'm very much a traditionalist, and that means I like to use the time-honored flour of whatever style of pizza I'm making. I source many types from all over the United States and from Italy to make the regional American and Italian pizzas on my menu as close as I can to what you'd get in those places. In the dough recipes in this book, I give you those specific types, some of which can be challenging to source in small quantities for home cooks, along with recommendations for brands that are easy to find in stores or online in more reasonable quantities.

A lot of cookbooks and websites will tell you that all-purpose flour is good for pizza making. For most pizzas, I disagree. Wheat flour contains gluten, a protein that forms a "gluten network"—a web of protein strands—when you knead and work dough. The higher the gluten in the flour, the stronger that network will be, and the more elasticity it will have. On the next page is a photo of the inside of a dough ball—a surprising visual I always share with my students to give them a sense of the gluten network.

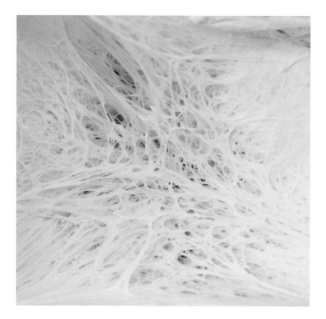

As the yeast releases carbon dioxide, it's that gluten network that traps the gas, causing the dough to stretch and rise. Most of the protein in wheat flour is gluten, so a high-gluten wheat flour is also a high-protein flour.

All-purpose flour typically has 10 to 12 percent gluten (also expressed, with wheat flours, as 10 to 12 percent protein). That's okay for doughs that mature for only a short time. But since I like longer maturation, I prefer stronger, higher-protein flours with more gluten. In my restaurants, I tend to use flours with 12.5 to 13 percent protein for a 36-hour rise, and 13 to 14 percent protein for a 36- to 48-hour rise. These are typically sold as bread flours. But here's the catch: you won't find the protein or gluten content listed on a bag of flour because it tends to vary throughout the year. So instead, it's best to get to know certain brands that can become your go-to flours for different purposes. In the recipes in this book, I always give you a recommended brand or type, as well as some alternative options.

On pages 14 and 15, you'll find a list of the flours I use in this book with their typical protein ranges. For sources, see page 304.

WATER

After flour, water is the second biggest component of pizza dough, so the water you use makes a difference. Very hard water (which has a higher mineral content, mostly calcium and magnesium) can make your dough stiff. Soft water can have the opposite effect, causing your dough to be too "relaxed." Moderately hard water is what you want.

Most tap water is fine for making pizza dough, so follow this simple rule: If your tap water is good to drink, it's good for baking. If it's not, try filtering it, or use purified bottled drinking water (but not mineral water), such as Aquafina.

If you know you're dealing with very hard water, try adding a little less salt to your dough; with soft water, try increasing the salt in the recipe slightly. If your water is very chlorinated, it can impede the performance of your yeast. To find out, just give it a whiff. If it smells a little like swimming pool water, try leaving it open in your fridge overnight and much of the chlorine will dissipate.

YEAST

Yeast is sold in three forms:
- Fresh compressed, which is also known as cake yeast because it's sold in pressed cubes; look for it in the refrigerated dairy section of some grocery stores
- Active dry, typically sold in three-section packets in the baking section of supermarkets
- Quick rise (or instant), also sold in packets in most supermarkets

All three types have had some of the water removed from the yeast cells to keep them in a dormant state. About 30 percent of the water in fresh yeast is removed versus 90 percent or more in active dry and quick rise. The lower the moisture content, the longer the yeast lasts.

Although I use a lot of fresh yeast in my restaurants, for home cooks, I tend to recommend active dry yeast because it's easier to find and less perishable. I like Red Star brand. You'll see that I call for active dry yeast for most of the recipes in this book. The Neapolitan-style pizzas are the exception. For those I use fresh yeast because it's a required ingredient in the officially mandated Associazione Verace Pizza Napoletana recipe. If you want to experiment with fresh yeast, you'll generally want to use two to three times as much as you would active dry yeast.

For pizza, I recommend avoiding quick rise (instant) yeast altogether. It defeats the whole purpose of keeping the proofing process as slow as possible.

Yeast is a living single-celled organism, and it's activated by moisture and heat, so you should store it in the refrigerator. Wrap compressed yeast loosely in plastic wrap so it can breathe. Discard it if you see any discoloration or dry spots. For home cooks, I recommend buying yeast in packets. If you buy it in larger quantities, keep it in a tightly capped Mason jar or other airtight storage container.

Fresh yeast has a shelf life in the fridge of roughly 2 weeks. Dry yeast will last for up 2 months, but you can never be sure how it was stored before you got it, and how that storage might have shortened its lifespan or killed it altogether. So as a rule, of thumb, don't buy much more yeast than you need. It's better to buy your yeast fresh each time you're planning to make pizza and use it up as quickly as possible.

I don't believe in freezing yeast. Freezing causes the moisture in the cells to expand, which can break the cell wall and kill the yeast. Store even factory-sealed packets in an airtight container to keep the yeast fresh. And remember that storing an opened package of yeast in the fridge is a little like putting a lion in a sheep's pen. That yeast is hungry, and it will travel through the air and start fermenting whatever it finds to feed on in your fridge. A lot of us *pizzaiolos* have learned the hard way that an open container of yeast in the walk-in cooler can quickly cause a nearby container of tomato sauce to spoil.

When you're activating fresh or dried yeast, if your water is too hot, you'll risk killing the cells. Never use water hotter than 85°F. I generally go for about 80°F because I like to start the yeast slowly.

STARTERS

Starters are another "secret" that will make a huge difference in your pizzas. Making a dough with a starter is sometimes known as the "indirect method," because the ingredients are combined in more than one phase. A starter (also known as a preferment) is a mixture of flour and water fermented with yeast. That yeast can be the packaged kind, it can be "harvested" from grape skins or other fruits and vegetables, or it can simply be the natural airborne yeast that's floating all around us (as in my Bran Starter on page 175). For most of my starters, I like the control and consistency of good packaged yeast.

A starter can be thick like dough or as liquid as a thin batter. It can even be nothing more than a bit of proofed dough from a previous batch. You may be familiar with the idea of feeding starters to keep them "alive" indefinitely. In my restaurants, we use both starters made in that way and starters we make from scratch every time, the day before we'll be using them. For beginner home pizza makers, I recommend always making starters from scratch the day before you make your dough. It's easier and you'll get more consistent results. Once you become more familiar with preferments, you can experiment with other kinds, like levain or natural fruit–based starters.

With the exception of Chicago deep-dish, Detroit, St. Louis, and Grandma pizzas, I use starter in every kind of dough I make in my restaurants, and I recommend that you do the same. It's an added step, but a little starter will make a noticeable difference, giving your crust a more complex flavor, a wonderfully fresh-baked aroma, a nicer crumb, better texture, and greater digestibility.

I recognize that a starter needs to be prepared at least 18 hours before you make your dough, so when I call for a starter in a recipe in which not using starter will still give you a good result, I give you that recipe with and without starter (with the proportions of the other ingredients adjusted accordingly). For this class, because you're just "getting started," I'm giving you a recipe without starter to keep things a little simpler.

You can find my main go-to starters on pages 46–47.

MY GO-TO FLOUR LIST

FLOUR	DESCRIPTION	% PROTEIN
Power Flour (Pendleton Flour Mills)	• classic pizzeria flour • very strong • universal • my go-to for almost any style other than Neapolitan and Chicago • a western-US flour not seen much on the East Coast • great for long maturation • slightly sweet flavor	13.5%
All Trumps Flour (General Mills)	• classic pizzeria flour • traditional for New York slice pizza • available with or without bromate* • very strong (but without the bromate, much weaker) • slight wheaty flavor • made from a hard red spring wheat	14.2%
Harvest King Flour (General Mills)	• light, nutty, medium-strong • made from a winter wheat	12%
High Performer High Protein Unbleached Flour (Giusto's)	• similar to Power flour • universal • yields a crust with taste and texture on the bready side • made from a dark northern spring wheat	13 – 13.5%
Tony's California Artisan Flour	• I developed this flour (which is available in both professional and home-use packaging) in collaboration with Central Milling • strong • sweet • universal, similar to Power flour • not recommended for Neapolitan	13 – 13.5%
Sir Lancelot Unbleached Hi-Gluten Flour (King Arthur)	• a good pizza flour if no professional flours are available • semistrong • universal • yields a crust with slightly bready flavor and texture	14.2%
Organic High Mountain Hi-Protein Flour (Central Milling)	• strong • sweet, wheaty flavor that's not super dry • slight yellow color • made from 100% dark northern spring wheat	13%
Organic Artisan Type 70 Malted Flour (Central Milling)	• lighter in flavor than High Mountain • sweet, wheaty • slight yellow color • 70% extraction	12.5%
Organic Whole Wheat Medium Flour (Central Milling)	• made from 100% whole wheat with the germ included, which makes the flavor sweeter and promotes quicker fermentation because of the natural sugar in the germ	12.5%

FLOUR	DESCRIPTION	% PROTEIN
Ceresota and Heckers All-Purpose Flour	• perfect for Chicago cracker-thin or deep-dish pizzas • not too bready • great chew • light but pliable • delicate with medium strength	12%
Organic Dark Rye Flour (Central Milling)	• 100% whole-grain, made from a rye variety with a nice blue-green color • great for adding to dough that needs a fermentation kick or doughs with low activity, because its natural sugar content speeds up fermentation • ideal for enhancing starters • fine, no separation, pure	NA
Organic White Khorasan Flour (Central Milling)	• an ancient wheat first used by the Egyptians and now popular in Italy • like durum in its protein strength, hardness, and color, but much sweeter • mixing characteristics more like spelt	14.7–15%
Einkorn Flour (Jovial)	• slightly dense, yellow in color, absorbs a lot of water • better for shorter-maturation doughs	14%
Antimo Caputo 00 Flour (labeled 00 Pizzeria Flour on professional-sized bags)	• ideal for Neapolitan and grilled pizzas • medium strength • consistent • slightly sweet • soft and delicate but pliable	11.5 – 12.5%
Molino San Felice 00 Flour	• ideal for Neapolitan and grilled pizzas • medium strength • sweet • soft and delicate but pliable	11 – 12.2%
Le 5 Stagioni	• A popular Italian pizza flour brand with a range of products for classic Italian, pan and Neapolitan pizzas.	11.5 – 13.5%
Mulino Marino	• Stone-ground 00 and 0 flours from Italy's Piedmont region • Ideal for blending, excellent digestibility	12.5–16%
Molino Pasini	• An Italian flour mill offering a range of products for classic Italian, pan and Neapolitan pizzas.	11 – 13.5%

In addition to these, here are other flours I've had great results with over the years, but which didn't make it into this book. Although I'm not generally a fan of bleached flours, some of these fall into that category.

• King Kaiser (protein: 14%; high gluten; high protein; bleached; western US)
• Balancer (protein: 14%; high gluten; high protein; bleached; eastern US)
• Superlative (protein: 12.6%; malted; bleached; eastern US)
• Kyrol (protein: 14%; high gluten; high protein; bleached; eastern US)
• All Aces (protein: 12%; eastern US)
• Full Strength (protein: 12.6%; bromated* or unbromated; malted; eastern and western US)
• Hi-Rise High-Gluten Flour (protein: 14.5%; eastern US)
• Shawnee Hi-Gluten Pizza Flour (protein: 10.5 – 11.5%; Oklahoma and midwest)
• Perfect Diamond (protein: 13.2 – 13.8%; high gluten; high protein; spring wheat; Illinois and central US)

* A note on bromated flours: Potassium bromate is added to flours to strengthen them. True New York–style pizza dough is generally made with bromated flour. But because potassium bromate (also known simply as "bromate") has been linked to cancer in some studies, I recommend you avoid it.

SALT

I always use fine sea salt in my doughs and in my cooking in general, because I like its intense, clean flavor. Its fine grind is important for making doughs because it dissolves and disperses more quickly and evenly into the dough than coarse sea or kosher salt. Whatever you do, avoid iodized salt, which has a bitter, chemical taste.

It's better to weigh salt rather than measure it because different crystal sizes can give you very different results when using teaspoon or tablespoon measures.

Salt adds more than flavor to pizza dough. It strengthens the gluten network, making dough stronger and more elastic (which is why we typically add up to three times the normal amount of salt for doughs used in pizza-tossing competitions). Extremely humid weather can make dough soft and weak. If that happens, the trick I learned long ago is to increase the salt by 0.5 to 1 percent.

Salt also acts as a preservative and keeps the dough from oxidizing and discoloring. And it slows fermentation because it causes yeast cells to release some of their moisture, which makes them less active. That's why I don't add it right at the beginning with the other dry ingredients. I wait for a few minutes, until the yeast has had a chance to start doing its work.

For garnishing pizzas, I like the large, visible flakes of Maldon sea salt.

OIL AND FAT

Most of my doughs are made with extra virgin olive oil, which helps emulsify the ingredients, creating a smoother texture and a more tender dough. It also helps a bit with browning. The same goes for any fat used in a dough, which might include butter, lard, milk, or eggs. I generally add oil toward the end of the mixing process. If you add it too early, it can form a barrier that can impede the absorption and hydration of the flour. I always tell my students that making dough is like building an engine. You put all the parts together and then you add oil at the end to start it up.

For sautéing and frying, I use pure olive oil (called simply olive oil in recipes), which can withstand higher heat than extra virgin. I use extra virgin—straight up or in homemade flavored oils—for garnishing and finishing pizzas and other foods. I like extra virgin oil that's fruity and not too grassy or peppery, like Filippo Berio or Corto.

MALT

Malt is sometimes called the European baker's secret because it's frequently used in doughs for breads and other baked goods there. It's also a wonderful secret ingredient for baking pizzas in a conventional home oven, which can't reach the temperatures of a pizzeria oven. A small amount of malt added to your dough will help it brown and will give it a subtle nutty-caramel sweetness in lower temperatures. If you're planning to bake your pizza on a grill, in a wood-burning oven, or using the broiler method (see page 202)—all of which can give you temperatures higher than 650°F—you should omit the malt from your dough.

Malt is most commonly made from barley, which has been sprouted and then dried and ground. It contains a sugar called maltose, that not only adds flavor and color but also fuels the yeast in your dough, giving it a stronger rise.

There are two kinds of malt: diastatic and nondiastatic. Diastatic (sometimes labeled low-diastatic) is the one you want for pizza. It contains active enzymes, which give you the added benefit of helping break down some of the starches in your flour, turning them into sugars that feed the yeast. Nondiastatic malt doesn't have those enzymes, and it's added to foods only as a sweetener. Like most bakers, I prefer diastatic malt, which is slower-acting, allowing for longer fermentation. You can find it online (see page 305) or at beer-brewing supply stores.

TOMATOES

Here's my basic tomato philosophy for pizza. The more substantial the pizza and its crust, the heartier the tomato sauce. So, for a big Chicago deep-dish or a thick-crust Sicilian, I'll go with a chunkier, more gutsy sauce. For a classic New York, I'll use a thinner sauce.

You might think that the gold standard of pizza sauce is fresh tomatoes simmerring away for hours. I've got nothing against that idea, assuming you start with outstanding tomatoes. But the fact is that no matter where you live, truly great fresh tomatoes are pretty hard to come by most of the year.

It might surprise you to learn that most pizza sauces, including most of the sauces I use in my restaurants, are made from canned tomatoes and tomato products (like crushed tomatoes and tomato paste) that are simply combined, maybe lightly seasoned and blended with a little olive oil, and then used just like that—no cooking involved. In other words, they're not like a typical red sauce for pasta.

I bring my sauces to room temperature before using them on pizzas, but in most cases, they don't need any actual cooking for two reasons. First, the tomatoes are already "cooked" by the heat and pressure of the canning process, and second, they cook on the pizza as it bakes in the oven. If you simmered them in advance, most sauces would lose their fresh tomato flavor and become overcooked, overly concentrated, or even burned during baking.

For Chicago deep-dish, stuffed, and Detroit-style pizzas, I do give my sauce a quick simmer to warm it, which sacrifices a bit of flavor in favor of a much faster cook time and, as a result, a stronger overall structure. For the rest of the sauces in this book, which are simply made by

MY FAVORITE TOMATO PRODUCTS

TOMATO PRODUCT	PROFESSIONAL BRANDS	SUPERMARKET BRANDS
Whole peeled plum or pear tomatoes	• Stanislaus Valoroso • Stanislaus Alta Cucina	• DiNapoli • Bianco DiNapoli Organic
San Marzano tomatoes *Go with San Marzanos imported from Italy rather than tomatoes grown from San Marzano seeds in the United States or elsewhere. Look for the Italian DOP designation on the can.*	• Strianese • Nina • La Regina di San Marzano	• Strianese
Ground tomatoes	• Stanislaus 7/11 • Stanislaus Tomato Magic • Escalon 6 in 1 • Escalon Christina's Organic Ground Tomatoes in Extra-Heavy Puree	• Escalon 6 in 1 All Purpose • Escalon Christina's Certified Organic in Heavy Puree • DiNapoli Ground Tomatoes in Purée
Tomato paste	• Stanislaus Saporito Super Heavy Pizza Sauce • Stanislaus SuperDolce • Escalon Bontá	• Contadina

blending ingredients and seasoning them without cooking, I recommend that you make them a day ahead so the flavors have time to meld. Store them in the fridge, and then take them out when you take out your dough (usually an hour or two before baking time), so both can come to room temperature.

Whatever you're making, remember this ironclad rule: never put cold sauce on pizza dough. It should always be at room temperature or slightly warm.

The key to great tomato flavor is, of course, to use tomatoes of super high quality. A canned tomato is not a canned tomato. If you don't believe me, try this eye-opener: Buy a few brands of whole canned tomatoes, drain them in a colander, and rinse them off. Once the dark red juice (which often doesn't even come from the tomatoes in the can but is added during canning) is washed away, you might be surprised to see that your juicy red tomatoes are actually paler, yellower, and greener than they look in the can.

I buy sweet, intensely flavorful tomatoes, sauces, and other tomato-based products that have no added sugar or other enhancements to correct their flavor because they don't need them. The ones I buy are grown and packed for foodservice, and they make all the difference in the world. On page 17, I've listed the professional brands I strongly recommend, along with some more readily available supermarket brands.

CHEESE

Whole-milk or part-skim mozzarella cheese is the "anchor" topping for most American pizzas, and getting your hands on a good one is important. For home cooks, I suggest buying block cheese and grating it yourself to avoid the anticaking additives (like cellulose) and performance-enhancing starches and gums often found in pregrated cheese. Grating your own cheese saves you money, too. Grande is the mozzarella brand I've always used, and it's worth going out of your way to find it.

The difference in flavor between a whole-milk and a part-skim mozzarella isn't always that obvious. What's more noticeable is the performance. With its higher fat and moisture content, whole-milk mozzarella holds and reheats better. In my restaurants, I use whole-milk mozzarella for pies that we prebake and reheat by the slice because its higher fat and moisture content makes for better reheating results.

When a recipe calls for sliced mozzarella or other cheeses, there's nothing like having your own meat slicer. My Italian Beef Sandwich alone—(page 109) will make you want to get one. If you don't have a slicer, use a long, sharp knife, and in either case, make sure your cheese is well chilled before you slice. Or, you can ask a deli to slice cheese freshly for you (rather than buying packaged slices, which typically have less flavor).

For recipes that call for fresh mozzarella (*fior di latte*), see pages 139, 205, and 297.

Of course, just as with flour, tomatoes, and toppings, I source the traditional cheese used in whatever type of pizza I'm making—or I get the closest thing I can. And I call for shredded or sliced cheese depending on what's authentic to a given pizza and what will perform best during baking and serving.

THE THEORY OF
PIZZA RELATIVITY

Before we roll up our sleeves and make pizza, I've got to tell you one last thing.

The most important rule about any pizza recipe is that *it's always relative*. The ingredients, their age, the water, the weather, the elevation, your equipment, your oven, how long your dough has proofed—all of these make a difference. So there's no single truth.

Instead, I talk a lot about ratios, ranges, and principles to follow, and I encourage you to go with visual cues. "Read" what's happening to your dough in the mixer, not on the page of any book. "Read" how the cheese and dough are browning as the pizza bakes, rather than simply following the timings in any recipe. It sounds obvious, but I'm bringing it up here because I've even seen a lot of professionals miss the boat on this. Recipes are guidelines, not rules, and you're the boss.

This book covers the major regional pizza styles popular in the United States, as well as several from Italy. And that brings me to the most important part of pizza relativity: When I'm trying to re-create a classic style of pizza, I do everything I can to source the traditional ingredients and to use the time-honored baking techniques, the typical pans, and the right kind of oven. But I'm also all about doing whatever I can to make that classic pizza the best it can be—to make a pizza my customers, my staff, and I love to eat. If that means taking some liberties with tradition or adding some little touches and variations along the way, that's okay by me. I hope this book will inspire you to feel the same way—to try to discover pizzas you love, to make them again and again, to tweak and perfect, to add and subtract. Make them faithful to their origins but, above all, make them your own. That's the real truth. That's the craft of pizza.

PART TWO: PRACTICE

Okay, guys. Let's do this. My Master Class is going to take you through every step of the process. You'll end up with two classic pizzas—one very American and one very Italian—based on a great multipurpose Master Dough that gives you a medium-thick, crispy-chewy crust. If you prefer, you can just buy double the topping ingredients for one of the types and make two of the same pizza.

Stick with my directions exactly the first time so you can get the hang of everything, and then you'll have a good foundation for improvising and trying all the other recipes in the book. For quick reference, you'll also find the entire Master Dough recipe (with and without starter) repeated on page 44 and 48. But for now, follow the more detailed instructions here.

DAY ONE

Equipment you'll need: scale, five prep bowls, instant-read thermometer, stand mixer, rubber spatula, bowl scraper, dough cutter, large mixing bowl, plastic wrap

For this class, I've chosen a dough made without starter that uses a two-phase rising process, which gives you outstanding results. You will end up with two pizzas. You'll need to start making the dough at least 2 days before you want to bake and eat the pizzas. That's counting time to let the dough rise as a single mass (bulk ferment) in a bowl for 24 hours in the fridge and then shape it into balls, which will rise for another 24 hours.

Yes, this is a long process, but it's not much actual work, and the two-step rising technique makes a big difference in how your dough performs and tastes.

Every dough in this book, except Chicago Deep-Dish Dough, follows the basic sequence you're about to go through:

• Weigh out ingredients
• Activate yeast in warm water
• Combine flour and malt (if using)
• Hydrate flour with ice water
• Add yeast and water
• Add starter (if using)
• Add salt
• Add oil or other fat (if using)

You're not just throwing a bunch of stuff in a mixer or food processor and turning on the machine. I follow these steps in this order for specific reasons, which I'll tell you about as we go along. Sticking to this progression makes a difference in the finished pizza, so I want you to get a feel for the sequence and follow it every time.

1. WEIGHING AND MEASURING

All of the ingredients below refer to the ones described on the Master Class Shopping List on page 6. We'll start by weighing each of them separately in its own container or bowl. I recommend doing this because you'll end up with all of your ingredients lined up in front of you and you'll be sure not to forget anything.

A lot of cooks and bakers get used to weighing ingredients in a single bowl simply by zeroing out the scale before adding each new ingredient. If you're not that used to weighing, I'd recommend avoiding this method for now, so you don't risk accidently dumping in a little too much of one ingredient on top of the ones you've already weighed. If you do that, there's no going back. Weighing each ingredient in its own bowl eliminates this risk.

The other advantage to measuring everything individually before you start the mixing is that once you do begin the process, you won't risk interrupting it to search for a spatula, accidentally spill olive oil on the floor, chase the dog out of the kitchen, clean up, and then have to remember where you were with steps and timing. Measure first, and once you start combining ingredients, everything will go like clockwork.

Note that I am asking you to weigh the ingredients in basically the order in which you'll use them. The exceptions are the warm and cold water, which I want you to weigh out last, so they're still at the right temperature when you add them.

4.5 grams active dry yeast

Use a small bowl with a rounded bottom rather than a container with straight sides. That way, there are no "corners" to trap undissolved yeast. Set the bowl on the scale and hit the tare button to zero out the scale. Slowly pour in yeast until the scale registers 4.5 grams. Note that this isn't much yeast; it's not even a whole packet. If you have a palm scale, this is a good time to use it.

453 grams King Arthur Sir Lancelot Unbleached Hi-Gluten Flour (or other flour with 13 to 14 percent protein, preferably All Trumps, Pendleton Flour Mills Power, Giusto's High Performer, or Tony's California Artisan Flour)

Put the bowl of your stand mixer on the scale and hit the tare button to zero it. Gradually spoon in flour until you have 453 grams. (If you're not used to grams, this is about a pound of flour.)

9 grams diastatic malt

Use the same method to measure 9 grams of malt into a small bowl.

9 grams fine sea salt

Weigh out 9 grams of fine sea salt into a separate small bowl.

5 grams extra virgin olive oil

Weigh out 5 grams of olive oil into another small bowl.

225 grams ice water

You want the majority of the water you use in your dough to be ice-cold to slow down the yeast. Grab a quart measure, add a handful of ice cubes and fill with cold water. Put a medium bowl on the scale, zero the scale, and pour the ice water (without the ice) into the bowl until you have 225 grams; discard the remaining water and ice. The temperature of the ice water should be between 38°F and 40°F.

70 grams lukewarm water

You'll need this to activate the yeast. Fill a 2-cup measure about halfway with warm water and use your instant-read thermometer to check the temperature. Add hot or cold water to adjust the temperature to between 80°F and 85°F. Eventually, you'll get a feel for this tepid water temperature, and you can skip the thermometer, but for now, I recommend using it. Put a small bowl on the scale, zero the scale, and pour in the warm water until you have 70 grams.

2. ACTIVATING THE YEAST

This step is next for two reasons: First, it gives the yeast a chance to wake up before you add it to the flour. Second, if there's a problem with your yeast, you'll know right away not to move on to the rest of the process.

Add the 70 grams of lukewarm water to the bowl holding the yeast. Use a small whisk to mix the yeast and water fairly vigorously for about 30 seconds. The yeast should dissolve and the mixture should have a bit of foam on the top. If the granules don't dissolve and you see some floating to the surface, your yeast is dead. Discard the mixture and start over with fresh yeast.

3. MAKING THE DOUGH

Put the mixer bowl with the flour in it on the mixer stand fitted with the dough hook. Add the malt to the flour and turn on the mixer to the lowest speed for a few seconds to combine the flour and malt. (If you don't have a stand mixer, see below for directions on hand mixing.)

With the mixer still on the lowest speed, pour in most of the 225 grams of ice water, reserving about 2 tablespoons. Now, add the yeast mixture to the bowl. Pour the reserved ice water into the yeast bowl and swirl it around to clean off any bits of yeast that may have stuck to the bowl. Add this liquid to the mixer bowl.

No Mixer, No Worries

A stand mixer is really the way to go for making dough. But if you don't have one, here's how to mix dough by hand:

- *Use the same proportions of ingredients in the Master Dough (or any dough). Weigh out the ingredients as directed for the mixer method, putting the flour in a large bowl.*

- *Proof the yeast with the lukewarm water.*

- *Add the malt to the flour and stir well with a sturdy spoon to combine.*

- *Make a well in the middle of the flour-malt mixture and pour in the ice water, reserving about 2 tablespoons.*

- *Stir together the flour and ice water a few times and then add the yeast-water mixture.*

- *Pour the reserved ice water into the yeast bowl, swirl, and add it to the dough (if you are using a starter, it should be mixed in at this point).*

- *Begin using your hands to work the dough. Pull the dough from the sides of the bowl toward the center, pressing down with the palm of one hand. Rotate the bowl a quarter turn from time to time. If the dough looks dry and crumbly or there is unincorporated flour, add a small amount of water (1/2 teaspoon to start).*

- *Continue for about 1 minute, then add the salt and continue to work the dough until it is well combined.*

- *Make a well in the center of the dough and add the oil. As before, work the dough to combine.*

- *Remove the dough from the bowl and knead it (see Kneading the Dough, page 24) for 2 to 3 minutes. The dough will not be completely smooth.*

- *Proceed as directed in the Master Dough recipe.*

Mix the dough for about 1 minute. You'll see most of it come together around the hook. Stop the mixer, use your fingers to pull the dough away from the hook ❶, and scrape the sides and bottom of the bowl with a bowl scraper or rubber spatula.

Check the bottom of the bowl for any unincorporated flour. Press the dough into the bottom of the bowl to pick up any stray pieces; mix briefly to combine. If there is still unincorporated flour at the bottom of the bowl, add a small amount of water (½ teaspoon to start), and mix briefly.

Add the salt and mix on the lowest speed for 1 minute.

Stop the mixer, again pull the dough off the hook, and add the oil. Mix the dough on the lowest speed for 1 to 2 minutes, stopping the mixer from time to time to pull the dough off the hook and scrape down any dough that clings to the sides of the bowl, until all the oil is absorbed. The dough won't look completely smooth. (Your dough will be between 68°F and 72°F at this point. There's no need to take its temperature, but professionals may find this information useful.)

That's really all the mixing you need to do. A mistake I often see with beginners—and even some pros—is overmixing or overkneading pizza dough. Too much working of the dough makes it tough, and you'll end up with pizza that gives you a sore jaw from chewing. So go with the timing indications I've given here and in all my dough recipes.

4. KNEADING THE DOUGH

Use your bowl scraper to transfer the dough to an unfloured, smooth work surface (not wood). If you have a granite or marble countertop, that's ideal. Granite and marble keep your dough cool, and their smooth surface also helps keep it from sticking.

Gather the dough into a ball. Press the top of the ball firmly with heel of your dominant hand, pushing downward and slightly away from you ❷. Use your other hand to turn the dough 45 degrees, gathering it and shaping it back into a ball as you do ❸. Repeat this pushing-turning-gathering motion for 2 to 3 minutes, until the dough is smooth ❹. Cover the dough with a clean, damp, lint-free dish towel and let it rest at room temperature for about 1 hour.

5. BULK FERMENTING

Once the dough has rested, use your dough cutter to transfer it to a bowl that's big enough to allow it to rise a bit (it will increase in size by 25 to 50 percent, so don't expect it to "double in bulk" as many bread doughs do). Use your fingers to spread a few drops of water over the surface of the dough ❺, cover the bowl with plastic wrap, and put it in the refrigerator for 24 hours.

This step is called bulk fermenting because rather than forming the dough into balls, you're letting it rise as a single mass. Tomorrow at this time, you'll deflate that mass of dough (a step called degassing), ball it, and let the balls rise again for another 24 hours. You could just ball the dough right away and give the balls a 24- to 48-hour rise in the fridge, but the bulk-fermenting step results in a much better dough. When we tested this dough with and without the bulk fermenting, everyone involved agreed that the bulk-fermented dough baked up lighter, crispier,

and more flavorful, with a stronger structure (meaning the slices held their shape, rather than flopping over, when lifted).

Why would 24 hours of bulk fermenting and 24 hours of rising as balls be so much better than simply letting the balls rise for 48 hours? The difference is in the degassing. When you push the gas bubbles out of the dough, you promote yeast reproduction and further fermentation (at least up to a point) and that gives you a stronger rise and a tastier finished product.

That said, if you want to save a day, you can skip the bulk-fermenting step and proceed directly to balling your dough (see Balling the Dough, page 26). But I encourage you, at least this first time, to go for the full two-day process. Note that bulk fermenting is not necessary for doughs made with a starter.

DAY TWO

Equipment you'll need: stand mixer, bowls for mixing sauce and garlic oil, dough scraper, half sheet pan, plastic wrap

1. DEGASSING THE DOUGH

Set up your stand mixer fitted with the dough hook. Take the bowl of dough out of the fridge. Use your bowl scraper to transfer it to the mixer bowl. Turn on the mixer to the lowest speed and mix the dough for about 30 seconds. You'll hear bubbles popping and the dough will deflate to a more compact mass. Turn it out onto an unfloured work surface and gather it into a ball.

2. BALLING THE DOUGH

Turn on your scale. Use your dough cutter to cut the dough into two pieces of about the same size ❶. Weigh each piece, adjusting the quantity of each as needed to give you two 13-ounce (370-gram) pieces ❷. You may have a little extra dough, which you can discard. (Remember, when you throw away dough, always toss it in the trash or the compost bin, never in the garbage disposal, or you'll risk clogging your drain.)

Now you're going to ball the dough, a technique that stretches it to give it an even, round surface. This isn't done just because it makes neat portions of dough. It's a way to stretch a nice, tight gluten network across the surface, which will trap air and help your pizza to rise and crisp.

Pick up one of the dough balls and hold the edges between your hands with your fingers curled inward on top of the dough. Fold the left and right sides up to meet in the center. As you fold, try not to pull or tear the surface; you're just trying to stretch it so it's smooth and taut ❸.

Turn the dough 45 degrees and repeat ❹. Continue turning and folding in this way several times until the dough ball has a smooth, taut surface, then pinch the top seam together firmly to make a tight ball ❺. This sealing step is important. If you don't pinch hard enough to form a really tight seal, gas will leak out of your dough ball, it won't rise as much, and when you push out your dough in preparation for making your pizza, you may get a weak or thin spot where an air pocket formed inside your dough ball. So, remember these two key points: don't tear, and seal tightly.

3. REFRIGERATING THE DOUGH

Set the dough ball, pinched side down, on the half sheet pan ❻ and repeat with the other piece of dough, spacing the balls about 3 inches apart. (If you don't want to make two pizzas the next day, put the balls on two smaller sheet pans, so that you only have to take one out of the refrigerator and bring it to room temperature.) Wrap the pan(s) airtight with two layers of plastic wrap, sealing the wrap well under the pan(s). Put the pan(s) in a level spot in the fridge and refrigerate for 24 hours.

4. MAKING SAUCE

Since we're using an uncooked pizza sauce, I recommend that you make it a day ahead, so the flavors can meld. It's a good habit to get into: make your sauce when you ball your dough.

One of my secrets to making a really great chunky sauce with lots of flavor is to add some hand-crushed peeled tomatoes. But I don't mean just tomatoes you squish between your hands. That's okay for sauces that simmer for hours. But for a fresher sauce like this, I pull out the stems, seeds, and any tough sections; break up the flesh; and, most important, drain the tomatoes well so they don't dilute the sauce.

NEW YORK–NEW JERSEY TOMATO SAUCE

MAKES 1 CUP (245 GRAMS)

Gather and measure these ingredients:

4.5 ounces (120 grams/1/2 cup) ground tomatoes, preferably 7/11 or DiNapoli

2.2 ounces (65 grams/1/4 cup) tomato paste, preferably Contadina or SuperDolce

Pinch of dried oregano

Pinch of fine sea salt

1 teaspoon extra virgin olive oil

2 ounces (55 grams/1/4 cup) hand-crushed tomatoes (from 4 to 5 whole peeled plum or pear tomatoes, preferably Valoroso or DiNapoli; see box below)

In a bowl, combine the ground tomatoes, tomato paste, oregano, salt, and oil. Puree with an immersion blender (if you haven't yet invested in one, use a stand blender)

until smooth. Stir in the hand-crushed tomatoes. Taste the sauce and add more salt if you think it needs it (tomato products vary widely in the amount of salt they contain).

This will make a cup (245 grams) of sauce, which will be enough for two pizzas (though for this class, if you make one pizza with sauce and one without, as directed, you'll only need half of the sauce, in which case you can keep the extra in the fridge for a few days or in the freezer for up to a month).

PRO TIP

GET ON THE STICK For pureeing and blending sauces, especially in small quantities, an immersion blender is the way to go. It's more convenient than a stand blender, and it will give you a better sense of the texture you're getting as you use it.

How to Make Hand-Crushed Tomatoes

Start with the best canned plum or pear tomatoes you can find. I recommend Valoroso or DiNapoli brands. Or, if you have great fresh tomatoes, check out the roasting method in my Early Girl Tomato Sauce recipe on page 141. Whether you start with canned or cooked fresh tomatoes, you'll want to rinse your hands frequently as you work, so set up your station near the sink or have a bowl of cold water nearby. Put a strainer over a bowl. Working over a second bowl, lift a tomato, pinch off the head (stem end) and any unripe areas, and let those pieces drop into the bowl. Some tomatoes may not be deep red. I prefer not to use those,

but it's your call. Open up the tomato, remove any skins, seeds, or tough sections and add them to your discard bowl. Break the cleaned tomato into small pieces or strips and put them in the strainer. Keep in mind that these will not be blended, so if they look too coarse for your taste, run them through your fingers to make smaller pieces. Continue cleaning and crushing tomatoes until you have the amount called for in your recipe. Press gently on the tomatoes to strain as much liquid as possible. Discard the contents of the discard bowl and the bowl below the strainer. One 28-ounce can of tomatoes should yield 1 generous cup (250 grams) crushed tomatoes.

5. MAKING GARLIC OIL

Garlic oil is one of my favorite "secret ingredients" for finishing pizzas. It's quick and easy to make, but it's best made at least an hour in advance. The longer you leave it, the more the garlic flavor infuses into the oil, so I recommend making it a day ahead, at the same time you make your sauce.

GARLIC OIL

MAKES ¼ CUP (60 GRAMS)

1½ teaspoons (5 grams) minced garlic

¼ cup (55 grams) extra virgin olive oil

Combine the garlic and oil in a small bowl. Cover and store in the refrigerator for a day or two.

DAY THREE

Equipment you'll need: two pizza stones or steels, dough cutter, ruler, wooden pizza peel, large kitchen spoon, kitchen timer, cutting board, rocking pizza cutter (or pizza wheel), large round platters or boards for serving, heatproof brush and dish towel for cleaning stones or steels

Now that you've waited 48 hours, you're ready for your third day of class—the part where you get to stretch, top, bake, and, best of all, eat.

Today we're going to make two kinds of pizza: a classic pepperoni pie (or, if you prefer, a sausage or a plain cheese pizza) and a *pizza bianca* (aka "white pie," meaning one made without tomato sauce) finished with prosciutto, arugula, and shaved Parmigiano-Reggiano. We'll make them one at a time, start to finish, just to keep things simple. As you get more experienced, you can start topping your second pie once the first one has gone into the oven. But for now, it's best to top and bake your pizzas one at a time.

1. GETTING STARTED

You'll need to take the dough balls (or one of them, if you put them on separate sheet pans and only want to bake one pizza today) out of the refrigerator and set the sheet pan, still wrapped, on the counter for 1 to 2 hours (depending on how warm your kitchen is) before you want to start baking. When the dough comes out of the fridge, it will be between 35°F and 40°F, and you'll want to bring it up to 60°F to 65°F before you proceed.

After the dough has sat on the counter, still covered, for an hour, poke an instant-read thermometer directly through the plastic wrap into the center of one of the dough balls. Keep checking until your dough is between 60°F and 65°F.

While your dough is coming up to temperature, adjust your oven racks so that one is in the upper third (usually two rungs down) and one is on the bottom rung. Center a pizza stone or baking steel on each rack. Preheat the oven to 500°F for at least 1 hour. If you have a convection setting, use it. The temperature should still be 500°F but you'll need to keep a watchful eye on your pizza because it will bake more quickly.

Why two stones? Good question. This is one of my favorite discoveries for making great pizza at home. In a professional pizza oven in which the dough cooks directly on the hot brick oven floor (the deck), I always keep a pizza in a single spot for the first few minutes, rotating it occasionally to ensure it cooks evenly. To finish it, I move it to a hot spot—a place on the deck that hasn't had a pizza on it for a while, so it's extra hot and dry—to crisp and brown the bottom.

The two-stone method re-creates this technique in a home oven. You start on one stone, and when the pizza is partially cooked, you transfer it to the other stone, which acts like a hot spot, to finish the bottom. Any time you want to crisp the bottom more, move it to the other stone; whether it's the top or the bottom stone matters less than the fact that the stone you're moving the pizza to hasn't had dough on it for a while.

2. SETTING UP YOUR STATIONS

Before you start working your dough, you'll want to set out your topping and finishing ingredients, so you'll be all ready to go when the time comes. In the biz, we call the toppings station the "make line," as opposed to the "finish line" where baked pizzas get sliced and topped with any uncooked ingredients and garnishes. For your first pizza, here's what you'll need.

"MAKE LINE" INGREDIENTS FOR PEPPERONI (OR SAUSAGE) PIZZA

1/2 cup (120 grams) New York–New Jersey Tomato Sauce page 28), at room temperature

6 ounces (170 grams) whole-milk mozzarella cheese, shredded (1 1/2 cups), or 8 ounces (225 grams) if you are making a plain cheese pizza (2 cups)

4 ounces (115 grams) sliced pepperoni, or 5 ounces (140 grams) uncooked bulk fennel or Calabrese sausage, homemade (pages 54 and 55) or store-bought

"FINISH LINE"

Set out a cutting board that is larger than 13 inches and a rocking pizza cutter or pizza wheel. If you have a nice wooden board, you can serve the pizza directly from it. If not, set out a couple flat, round platters for serving. Oversized flat chargers or pizza plates work well. Set out your finishing ingredients next to the cutting board.

"FINISH LINE" INGREDIENTS FOR PEPPERONI (OR SAUSAGE) PIZZA

Garlic oil (page 29)

Grated Pecorino Romano cheese

Dried oregano

3. MAKING YOUR DUSTING MIXTURE

For shaping dough, I like to dust the work surface and peel with a mixture of whatever flour I used in the dough along with fine semolina (see page 6).

Semolina has a coarser texture than flour. It acts like mini ball bearings that keep the dough from sticking to surfaces and help it slide on and off the peel. It also adds a nice crunch and absorbs some of the moisture from the surface of your dough. But straight semolina can be too gritty, so I usually cut it with flour, varying the proportions depending on the dough and the toppings I'm using. The stickier, softer, or thinner the dough, the higher you'll want the proportion of semolina to be.

For today's pizza, combine 75 grams of the flour you used to make the dough with 75 grams of semolina in a bowl, and set it out on your countertop within easy reach.

4. TRANSFERRING THE DOUGH TO THE WORK SURFACE

Your dough balls should now be disks, about 25 percent larger in diameter than when you first made them. If you see any air bubbles, pinch them to deflate them.

Grab a generous handful of your dusting mixture and dust your countertop liberally. (You can't really err on the side of overdusting; what you don't need won't stick.)

Lift the edge of the plastic wrap and slowly peel it away from the dough disks. The more you practice this, the better you'll get at peeling away the plastic without much of the dough sticking to it. Use your fingertips to gently coax any sticky dough off the plastic.

Now you're ready to move the dough to the counter. This is an important step, and one that I really emphasize when I teach, so listen up. *The idea is to get your disk of dough onto the counter as gently as possible, keeping it as close as possible to its shape on the sheet pan.*

Remember the gluten network you stretched across the surface when you were balling the dough? You want to preserve that as much as you can. That means you don't want the edges to fold under, and you absolutely don't want to punch down the dough or squish it back into a ball. Your job is to maintain the shape, airiness, and uniform thickness of that soft, nicely risen disk as you move it to the counter for stretching. If you do that, you'll have a huge head start on stretching and shaping it into a perfect round of even thickness and circumference.

I'm emphasizing this because it can be a bit tricky to pull off as you expose the sticky interior of the dough. So here's the best method: wet your dough cutter with a few drops of water to help keep it from sticking to the dough. If you have more than one dough disk on your sheet pan and the disks are touching at all, use the dough cutter to separate them, slicing straight downward between them (and between the dough and the rim of the pan, if they're touching).

Holding the dough cutter almost parallel to the sheet pan, gently scrape under the sides of the dough in short movements toward the center to release the disk from the pan, lifting the loosened dough a bit with your other hand ❶. As you work, be careful to keep the dough in a

flat circle, and try *not* to let the edges droop under the disk as shown in ❷.

Once the dough is completely unstuck from the pan, lift the disk carefully with the dough cutter and your free hand and flip it as gently as you can onto the counter. Dust the dough with a handful of the dusting mixture ❸, then gently flip it back over so that it is right side up again, as it was when it was on the sheet pan. You will now have a nice, neat circle of dough that's easy to work with and won't stick to the counter or your hands.

5. OPENING AND STRETCHING THE DOUGH

Before you continue, dust your peel with some of the dusting mixture and set the peel aside. Working on the countertop, and starting about 3/4 inch in from the edge

of the disk, use the edges of your curved hands to press the dough all the way around. The idea is to make a slight indentation, leaving a thicker rim. This rim, which will be left untopped and will rise more, framing your pizza, is what *pizzaiolos* call the *cornicione* (cor-nee-CHO-neh), an Italian word that also means "cornice" or "molding," which says a lot about its importance in giving your pizza its structural integrity.

Press down the surface of the dough with your fingertips to flatten it slightly, being careful not to press down the rim ❶. Now, you're ready to start stretching the dough. Here's the key. You want to stretch the outside of your circle while leaving the middle alone. The middle will take care of itself as you do this. But if you stretch too much toward the center, you're likely to make it too thin and tear a hole in the dough. Holding your fingers extended, completely flat, and pointing away from you, press down gently just inside the 3/4-inch dough rim, then slide your hands away from each other 1 to 2 inches, stretching the outside edge of the dough a bit. Rotate the dough about 10 degrees and do this again. Continue rotating and stretching in this way until your dough has opened up to form a circle about 11 inches in diameter. If you see any gas bubbles around the rim that form a very thin layer of skin, you'll want to deflate them or they'll burn during baking.

Next, you'll stretch the dough using the "slapping" technique. Before you start, set your predusted peel on the work surface. Lay the dough across the open palm of one hand, and gently flip it onto the open palm of the other hand. Flip the dough a few more times from hand to hand, rotating it a bit each time ❷. As you work, remember that the more gently you handle your dough, the more tender your finished crust will be.

Now you can give the dough a little extra stretching by draping it over your two loosely clenched fists ❸, positioned so that your fingers are facing each other and the dough is hanging down vertically on the far side of your fists. Move your fists apart a little as you very gently toss the dough, causing it to turn a bit each time. You're not throwing the dough here, even though it's tempting. You're simply tossing it off of your fists just enough to

make it move around in a circle. Imagine that you're trying to keep the dough "weightless," so it's resting as lightly as possible on your fists. Remember to stay near the edge and avoid the center. As you do this, raise your hands so you can see light coming through the dough; this way, you can check to see if you're getting any thin spots. Avoid stretching these or they will turn into holes. If your dough does tear, don't panic. Do your best to pinch the tear back together and avoid stretching that area any more.

The idea is to get the dough as uniformly thin and even as possible. You'll be tentative about all this at first, and that's okay. It takes lots of practice, and, at least for beginners, it's better to understretch and have a pizza that's slightly on the thicker side than to overstretch, degas your dough too much, and develop thin spots and holes. So try just a little stretching at first, and then lay your dough out on the dusted peel ❹ and measure it with a ruler. If you've gotten to a diameter of between 12 and 13 inches—measure crosswise a few ways to be sure—and the circle looks pretty uniform, you're ready to top it. Once you've added the weight of sauce, cheese, and toppings, you can tug the rim of your pizza a bit more right on the peel, so you'll end up with a pie 13 inches in diameter, which will be just right for this amount of dough.

Throwing in the Towel

When I'm training people, I encourage them to practice both the "slapping" technique and the "fists" technique with a damp dish towel, which has a similar weight and feel to pizza dough and no risk of messing up. When I first started working in my brother's pizzeria, he made me a great practice tool. It was a beach towel, cut into two circles and sewn together to make a mock dough round that, when dampened, was the perfect weight and size for mastering my tossing skills.

6. TOPPING THE DOUGH

You've finished the hardest part. Take a deep breath and give yourself a pat on the back (but be sure to wash your hands first). Now it's time to top your dough.

To top most pizzas, we start with sauce, then add cheese and other topping ingredients, and that's what we'll be doing right now for your first pizza. You'll want to work quickly so your dough doesn't get too soft or sticky as it sits on the peel under the weight of the toppings.

Grab a large kitchen spoon and spoon the sauce onto the center of the dough ❶. Use the back of the spoon to spread the sauce outward from the center in a spiral, being careful to leave a uniform border of about 3/4 inch all the way around the edge, coming just slightly up the rim ❷. This, by the way, is what's known as your sauce line. Try to keep it nice and neat, so your pizza has a finished look without stray splashes of burned sauce around the edge. This may seem like a sparse amount of sauce, but once everything cooks, it will be just right.

Give the peel a shake to make sure the dough isn't sticking, and then pour 6 ounces (170 grams/1½ cups) shredded mozzarella onto the center of the pizza ❸. Use your fingertips to spread it out from the center so the sauce is evenly covered with cheese. Go all the way out to your sauce line but not over it. I like to push cheese out from the center this way, leaving a little less in the center, because the cheese tends to melt back into the middle as the pizza bakes.

Now arrange the pepperoni slices evenly over the cheese.

If you've decided to top your pizza with sausage rather than pepperoni, pinch flat, nickel-size pieces of the sausage and distribute them evenly over the cheese. If you'd rather make a plain cheese pie, use 8 ounces (225 grams/ 2 cups) mozzarella instead of 6 ounces (170 grams).

Use your fingertips to give the rim a few final tugs here and there as needed to maintain a nice round shape ❹.

7. MOVING THE DOUGH TO THE OVEN

Give the peel another shake to make sure the pizza isn't sticking. If you discover it is, lift the edges gently and sneak a little more dusting mixture under them.

Open the oven and pull out the top rack with the stone on it.

To transfer the pizza onto the stone, hold the peel level and parallel to the stone (not angled downward), and position the peel so the pizza is right where you will want it to be on the stone. Give the peel a gentle, quick push-and-pull motion, which should make the far end of the dough slide off onto the stone, and then immediately pull the peel sharply toward you, keeping it low and level. It's like the old trick where the magician whisks the tablecloth away, leaving all the dishes in place. You're touching a bit of dough to the stone and then whisking away the peel, and the flatter you hold it, the less you'll disrupt the dough and the ingredients on top of it. What you're *not* doing is throwing or sliding the pizza off the peel, through the air, and onto the stone. That's an important distinction because you want to keep your pizza as round and uniform as possible. So think, "Put it where you want it, and then take the peel away."

Before you slide the rack in and close the oven door, take a look at the shape of the dough. You have a few seconds to stretch it gently into the best circle it can be. I use my fingertips to pinch and pull the edge of the dough a bit. Just be careful not to touch the hot stone or the wall of the oven.

If your dough has flopped over the edge of the stone a bit, don't try to correct that now. Let it cook that way for a minute or so, and then gently pick up the edge, slide the peel under, and rotate the pizza a quarter turn. It'll flatten back out and no one will be the wiser.

8. BAKING

Set your timer for 6 minutes. This is a good moment to remember the theory of pizza relativity. Ovens vary so much that it's simply not possible to give you the exact timing for any pizza. Instead, use the times I provide as guidelines for checking the progress of your pizza. I'll always tell you what to look for, so you can adjust the timing accordingly. After a few pizzas, you'll start to learn your oven and eventually you may not need to use a timer at all because you'll develop an eye and a nose for pizza timing. When you're checking the progress of your pizza, turn on the oven light and open the door as little as necessary to keep from losing heat.

After your pizza has been in the oven for 2 to 3 minutes, take a quick peek to see if any large bubbles have formed in the dough. (This is usually the result of the dough being too cold when you pushed it out.) If there are bubbles, quickly poke a hole in them with a fork, and retop that spot with cheese. Note that it's important to do this only during the first few minutes of baking.

When the timer goes off, open the oven door. You'll see that the crust is beginning to brown nicely and that the cheese is melted and bubbly but not browned. Lift the edge of the pizza to look at the underside. It will be fairly pale. Slide the peel under the pizza and, using your fingers, quickly rotate the pizza 180 degrees on the peel and then transfer it to the center of the stone on the lower rack. This will crisp and brown the bottom of your pizza as the top continues to cook. Close the oven and set the timer for 5 minutes.

When the timer goes off, open the oven door and check out your pizza. The cheese should be bubbly and nicely browned, and the bottom should be evenly browned. Slide the peel under the pizza and transfer it to the cutting board. If you have a wooden peel, don't be tempted to slice your pizza on it. You'll scar the wood, making your peel less smooth and therefore less effective for sliding dough on and off of it.

9. SLICING AND FINISHING

Use your wheel or rocking cutter to slice the pizza into six wedges ❶. Use a pastry brush to drizzle the pizza with garlic oil ❷, then sprinkle the Pecorino Romano ❸ and oregano on top. Transfer your pizza to a platter (or leave it on the board) and call in your hungry eaters.

10. JUDGING YOUR PIZZA

Before you devour it, give your pizza a quick evaluation, using the standards judges use in competitions.

Structure: When you pick up a slice, it should support its ingredients without bending too much.

Flexibility: Bend the edge of a slice upward. You should be able to fold it easily. The dough might crack but it shouldn't break.

Top crust: The exposed crust (the *cornicione*) should be richly and uniformly browned or slightly more toasted in some spots.

Bottom crust: The bottom should also be browned with no burned or pale spots ❹.

Rise and texture: Check the cut face of a slice. The outer crust should be nicely puffed with even-size holes, like a good ciabatta, and no raw-looking dough (an undesirable phenomenon that *pizzaiolos* and judges call a "gum line" ❺.

Cheese: It should be perfectly melted and slightly brown.

11. MAKING YOUR SECOND PIZZA

You're now ready to make your second pizza, assuming that in step 1 you took both dough balls out of the fridge and let them sit at room temperature.

Before you start, slide out each oven rack and use your wide, heatproof brush and a dry dish towel to clean off any burnt semolina or other ingredients from the stones or steels. You don't want that stuff messing up your next pizza. To keep your stones or steels from cooling too much, work quickly and don't use water or even a damp towel on them.

"MAKE LINE" INGREDIENTS FOR PROSCIUTTO AND ARUGULA PIZZA

6 ounces (170 grams) whole-milk mozzarella cheese, shredded (1½ cups)

"FINISH LINE" INGREDIENTS FOR PROSCIUTTO AND ARUGULA PIZZA

6 thin slices (about 4 ounces/115 grams) prosciutto

1½ cups arugula

12 cherry tomatoes, preferably multicolor, halved (or quartered if large)

Garlic oil (page 29)

Small piece Parmigiano-Reggiano, for shaving

Follow the directions for opening and stretching the dough outlined in step 5 (pages 31 to 33). In step 6 (page 34), omit the sauce and top your dough round

with the mozzarella. Bake as directed in step 8. When your pizza comes out of the oven, transfer it to the cutting board and slice it into six wedges. Drape a slice of prosciutto over each wedge, crumpling it just a bit to give it some height, and distribute the arugula evenly over the pizza. Arrange the cherry tomatoes over the arugula, drizzle with garlic oil, then use a vegetable peeler to shave Parmigiano-Reggiano over the top.

You'll notice that for pizzas like this, which get finished with some of their topping ingredients *after* baking, it's best to slice the pizza first, then top. There are two reasons for this. If you top first, you'll end up slicing through the fresh ingredients, smashing them down and losing a lot of height and airiness. Also, by slicing first, you can distribute the toppings more evenly onto each slice, so no one gets shortchanged.

12. CLEANING YOUR STONES

Once your stones have cooled, use your dough cutter to scrape off any bits of burned cheese or sauce. Then wipe down each stone with a damp cloth. Stains are fine. You're just trying to remove any encrusted food. Don't soak your stones in water or use soap on them. If you're using baking steels, follow the manufacturer's directions for using a grill cleaning brick.

Congratulations. You've completed your Master Class. Next week, try it again, switching up the toppings. You'll be amazed how much better your pizza gets every time you make it.

My Ten Commandments of Pizza

HEY, IT'S THE PIZZA BIBLE, RIGHT? SO HERE ARE MY SACRED LAWS.

THOU SHALT USE A SCALE TO WEIGH INGREDIENTS.

THOU SHALT NOT RUSH THE RISE.

THOU SHALT USE TWO PIZZA STONES OR STEELS RATHER THAN ONE.

THOU SHALT NOT PUT COLD SAUCE ON PIZZA DOUGH.

THOU SHALT NOT PUT COLD DOUGH IN A HOT OVEN.

THOU SHALT NOT OVERTOP THY PIZZA.

THOU SHALT NOT MAKE A PIZZA LARGER THAN THY PIZZA PEEL OR STONE.

THOU SHALT RETURN THY PIZZA TO THE SAME SPOT AFTER ROTATING IT.

THOU SHALT SLICE THY PIZZA BEFORE ADDING FINISHING INGREDIENTS.

THOU SHALT BRUSH THY STONES TO CLEAN THEM AFTER EACH PIZZA.

Regional American

Pizza showed up in the United States in the late 1800s, when millions of southern Italian immigrants brought it with them. One of them, Gennaro Lombardi, is credited with opening the country's first pizzeria, when he applied for a license in 1905 to sell pizza from his grocery store in New York's Little Italy.

Thin-crust pies topped with cheese and tomatoes showed up wherever Italians settled, from New York and New Jersey to Philadelphia, Chicago, and San Francisco. But until the late 1940s, pizza was an Italian food enjoyed mostly by Italians. American GIs returning from the war changed all that. They came home craving the pizza they'd discovered in Italy, and as the economy boomed, entrepreneurs started opening pizza chains all across the country to meet the new demand. Most of them took their lead from the New York–style pizzas that started it all.

That's how, from the 1950s and on through much of the rest of the twentieth century, big, thin-crust-tomato-and-cheese pies came to dominate the American pizza menu—and how pizza was transformed from an Italian food into an American institution. It's been estimated that of the five billion pizzas sold every year worldwide, three billion are made in the United States.

What interests me more than the sameness of chain pizza are the individual styles that rose up around the country and have managed to hold onto their distinctive identities ever since. Now that we're well into the twenty-first century, it seems there's more interest than ever in what's distinctive, authentic, and original. We're getting numbed by globalization and cookie-cutterism, and we're finally seeing the value of regional and local traditions, especially when it comes to pizza. It's about time.

So here's a look at a few of America's best-known regional styles (with apologies to those, like Old Forge and New England Greek, that didn't make it into this book for space reasons). But first a quick note to the purists, passionistas, sticklers, and hecklers out there. Before you start splitting hairs about what is and isn't true New York, New Haven, Detroit, St. Louis, Chicago, or any other kind of regional pizza, let me remind you of my theory of pizza relativity. There is no absolute truth.

What you'll find in this chapter—and throughout this book—are my versions. Of course, I love and respect the regional pizzas I've eaten and studied and made all over America. But I also respect my own commitment to fine-tuning, perfecting, and making things the best they can be. My goal in this book is always to start from a point of understanding and then add refinements that make the most of today's tools, techniques, and ingredients—adapting wherever necessary for the reality of home kitchens.

I hope you'll take these recipes in that spirit, and I know there will be those of you who will let me know exactly what I've gotten right and wrong. That's why I love the pizza business. We don't just wear our heart on our sleeve. We tattoo it all over our bodies.

MASTER DOUGH WITH STARTER

MAKES ABOUT 29 OUNCES (820 GRAMS) DOUGH, ENOUGH FOR 1 PIZZA

This is what I'd call the quintessential American pizza dough, inspired by New York–style pizza: medium thin, satisfyingly chewy, and the ideal companion to mozzarella, tomato sauce, and the pizza toppings Americans love best, from pepperoni and sausage to olives, mushrooms, and other vegetables. It's the dough I teach first to new students, and the one I recommend experimenting with because it's so versatile and user-friendly.

2.2 grams (3/4 teaspoon) active dry yeast

70 grams (1/4 cup plus 1 tablespoon) warm water (80°F to 85°F)

453 grams flour (3 1/2 cups) with 13 to 14 percent protein, preferably All Trumps, Pendleton Flour Mills Power, Giusto's High Performer, King Arthur Sir Lancelot Unbleached Hi-Gluten, or Tony's California Artisan Flour

10 grams (1 tablespoon plus 1/4 teaspoon) diastatic malt

210 grams (3/4 cup plus 2 tablespoons) ice water, plus more as needed

90 grams Poolish (page 47) or Tiga (page 46)

10 grams (2 teaspoons) fine sea salt

5 grams (1 teaspoon) extra virgin olive oil

For baker's percentages, see page 302.

Put the yeast in a small bowl, add the warm water, and whisk vigorously for 30 seconds. The yeast should dissolve in the water and the mixture should foam. If it doesn't and the yeast granules float, the yeast is "dead" and should be discarded. Begin again with a fresh amount of yeast and water.

Combine the flour and malt in the bowl of a stand mixer fitted with the dough hook.

With the mixer running on the lowest speed, pour in most of the ice water, reserving about 2 tablespoons, followed by the yeast-water mixture. Pour the reserved water into the yeast bowl, swirl it around to dislodge any bits of yeast stuck to the bowl, and add to the mixer. Mix for about 15 seconds, stop the mixer, and add the poolish or tiga.

Continue to mix the dough at the lowest speed for about 1 minute, until most of the dough comes together around the hook. Stop the mixer. Use your fingers to pull away any dough clinging to the hook, and scrape the sides and bottom of the bowl with a bowl scraper or rubber spatula. Check the bottom of the bowl for any unincorporated flour. Turn the dough over and press it into the bottom of the bowl to pick up any stray pieces. If the dough isn't holding together, add small amounts of water (about 1/2 teaspoon to start) and mix until the dough is no longer dry and holds together.

Add the salt and mix on the lowest speed for 1 minute to combine.

Stop the mixer, pull the dough off the hook, and add the oil. Mix the dough for 1 to 2 minutes, stopping the mixer from time to time to pull the dough off the hook and scrape down the sides of the bowl, until all of the oil is absorbed. The dough won't look completely smooth.

Use a bowl scraper to transfer the dough to an unfloured work surface, then knead it for 2 to 3 minutes, until smooth (see Kneading the Dough, page 24). Cover the dough with a damp dish towel and let rest at room temperature for 20 minutes.

Use the dough cutter to loosen the dough and to cut it into halves or thirds (depending on the weight called for in each recipe). Weigh each piece, adjusting the quantity of dough as necessary. You may have a little extra dough.

Form the dough into balls (see Balling the Dough, page 26). Set the balls on a half sheet pan, spacing them about 3 inches apart. Or, if you will be baking the balls on different days, place each ball on a quarter sheet pan. Wrap the pan(s) airtight with a double layer of plastic wrap, sealing the wrap well under the pan(s). Put the pan(s) in a level spot in the refrigerator and refrigerate for 24 to 48 hours.

TIGA AND POOLISH STARTERS

Here are the two starters I use most frequently in this book and in my restaurants. Tiga is my slightly more hydrated version of a classic biga starter, which is usually between 50 and 60 percent water. This "Tony's biga," which I call "Tiga," has 70 percent hydration. My poolish follows the traditional proportions of equal parts water and flour, so its hydration is much higher at 100 percent. In general, unless I specify otherwise, use the same flour in your starter that you will be using in your dough. I always make starters with cold water to slow down the fermentation process for greater flavor complexity. It's helpful to use a clear glass bowl so you can see how well your starter is fermenting.

TIGA

MAKES 90 GRAMS

0.14 gram (one-third of ⅛ teaspoon) active dry yeast or 0.42 gram fresh yeast, broken into small pieces

39 grams (2 tablespoons plus 2 teaspoons) cold tap water

55 grams (¼ cup plus 3 tablespoons) flour used in dough recipe

Put the yeast in a small bowl, add the water, and whisk vigorously for 30 seconds. The mixture should bubble on top. If it doesn't and the yeast granules float, the yeast is "dead" and should be discarded. Begin again with a fresh amount of yeast and water.

Add the flour and stir well with a rubber spatula to combine. The consistency will be quite thick.

Scrape down the sides of the bowl, cover the bowl with plastic wrap, and let sit at room temperature for 18 hours. Refrigerate for 30 minutes to cool slightly before using.

If you are not using the starter right away, you can store it in the refrigerator, though I suggest keeping it for no more than 8 hours. Bring it to cool room temperature before using.

0.12 gram (one-third of ⅛ teaspoon) active dry yeast or 0.36 gram fresh yeast, broken into small pieces

47 grams (3 tablespoons plus 1 teaspoon) cold tap water

47 grams (¼ cup plus 2 tablespoons) flour used in dough recipe

PRO TIP

HANDLING STARTER A starter is generally quite sticky and thus difficult to maneuver with a rubber spatula or bowl scraper. When taking it out of the bowl to measure it or to add it to your dough, use your hands, first dampening them in ice water. The starter won't stick to your wet, cold hands.

POOLISH

MAKES 90 GRAMS

Put the yeast in a small bowl, add the water, and whisk vigorously for 30 seconds. The mixture should bubble on top. If it doesn't and the yeast granules float, the yeast is "dead" and should be discarded. Begin again with a fresh amount of yeast and water.

Add the flour and stir well with a rubber spatula to combine. The consistency will be quite thick, resembling a thick pancake batter.

Scrape down the sides of the bowl, cover the bowl with plastic wrap, and let sit at room temperature for 18 hours. Refrigerate for 30 minutes to cool slightly before using.

If you are not using the starter right away, you can store it in the refrigerator, though I suggest keeping it for no more than 8 hours. Bring to cool room temperature before using.

MASTER DOUGH WITHOUT STARTER

MAKES ABOUT 27 OUNCES (775 GRAMS) DOUGH

4.5 grams (1½ teaspoons) active dry yeast

70 grams (¼ cup plus 1 tablespoon) warm water (80°F to 85°F)

453 grams (3½ cups) flour with 13 to 14 percent protein, preferably All Trumps, Pendleton Flour Mills Power, Giusto's High Performer, King Arthur Sir Lancelot Unbleached Hi-Gluten, or Tony's California Artisan Flour

9 grams (1 tablespoon) diastatic malt

225 grams (¾ cup plus 3 tablespoons) ice water, plus more as needed

9 grams (2 teaspoons) fine sea salt

5 grams (1 teaspoon) extra virgin olive oil

For baker's percentages, see page 302.

Follow the instructions for Master Dough with Starter (page 44), omitting the addition of the Poolish or Tiga and allow the dough to rest for 1 hour rather than 20 minutes. Using a dough cutter, lift the dough into a large bowl, press it down slightly, and rub a little water over the top. Cover with a double layer of plastic wrap and refrigerate for 24 hours (see Bulk Fermenting, page 24)

Remove the dough from the refrigerator and put it in the bowl of a stand mixer fitted with the dough hook. Mix for 30 seconds on the lowest speed to degas the dough, removing any air bubbles. (See Degassing the Dough, page 26)

Move the dough to the work surface and use the dough cutter to cut the dough into halves or thirds (depending on the weight called for in each recipe). Weigh each piece, adjusting the quantity of dough as necessary. You may have a little extra dough.

Form the dough into balls (see Balling the Dough, page 26) and refrigerate for 24 hours as directed in the Master Dough recipe.

Freezing Dough

I'll start by saying that I'm not a fan of freezing pizza dough, especially in a restaurant kitchen. But I know that for some home cooks, it's more convenient to make two balls of dough and freeze one to use later. If that's you, here's what to do.

Freezing

Freezing your dough is pretty straightforward. Whether you're making a dough with starter or a yeast-only dough that you bulk-ferment, freezing should happen after you've balled your dough, wrapped it and let it sit in the refrigerator for 24 hours.

Once you've reached that point, simply place your still-wrapped sheet pan in the freezer. If you're using one of your dough balls and freezing the other one, you might want to save freezer space by gently transferring the remaining dough ball to a smaller sheet pan and rewrapping it before freezing.

Once your dough balls are completely frozen, you can remove them from the pan and store one or more balls together in a resealable plastic freezer bag for up to 2 months.

Thawing

While working on this book, I stumbled on a great water-thawing method for dough, which does two things: It speeds up the thawing process by about half an hour, and it keeps the dough moist so that it ultimately rises a bit higher and bakes a little crisper.

Fill a deep bowl with 80°F water, leaving room to add your dough balls. Unwrap the frozen dough balls and place them directly in the water (yes, the dough balls go right into the water, unwrapped). Let them sit for about 15 minutes, and then take them out of the water. They'll be thawed about one quarter of the way through and still solid in the center. Put them on a sheet pan, cover them with plastic wrap, and let them sit at room temperature for 1½ to 2 hours, until they're completely thawed. (This may take more or less time, depending on how warm your kitchen is.)

NEW YORKER

MAKES ONE 13-INCH PIZZA; 6 SLICES

I'm starting with New York because it's where pizza first landed in America. The tradition began not with slices but with whole pies cooked in coke or coal ovens. Legend has it that when Gennaro Lombardi started selling pizza at his store, he'd cut off whatever size piece you could afford, and that's how pizza by the slice got started. The pies, and the slices, eventually got larger, and that New York phenomenon continues to this day: big pizzas, sold by the slice, with the thin, pliable crust we all know—the slice you eat with your hands, folding it in half the long way and taking that first perfect bite from the point of the triangle. A great New York crust folds and cracks but never breaks.

This is my version of a classic New York tomato pie (also known as an upside-down pie because the cheese goes down first and the sauce goes on top). The New York cheese of choice is traditionally a dry (low-moisture) mozzarella sold in loaves, sometimes known as *caprese* loaves. Family-run companies in Brooklyn and throughout the New York metro area still make this cheese, which is ideal for the high heat of coal-fired ovens. It's relatively unknown on the West Coast, but I bring it in to use in my coal oven for New York– and New Haven–style pizzas. It melts shiny and white—almost plasticky looking—and it's the secret to true New York coal-fired pizza.

House-made sweet fennel sausage and pepperoni are a topping combination you'll find on the featured New York–style pizza at my restaurants. Here, I've added our Calabrese Honey Sausage (page 55) as well, an addition inspired by a recent competition.

One of my head *pizzaiolos*, Thiago Vasconcelos, decided to enter the International Pizza Challenge at the Pizza Expo in Las Vegas, and wanted to present our New York pizza in the traditional division, which allows sauce, cheese, and two toppings, making our pepperoni and sausage pie a perfect choice. But before we entered, we confirmed that "sausage" could include more than one kind, so we used both fennel and Calabrese. Thiago won first place in the division, and when you taste this blend of spicy, sweet, meaty, and creamy flavors, I think you'll see why.

continued

1 (13-ounce/370-gram) ball Master Dough, preferably with starter (page 44), made with Tiga

3 parts flour mixed with 1 part semolina, for dusting

2 ounces (55 grams/1/4 cup) whole-milk ricotta cheese, preferably New York–style Polly-O or Ricotta Cream, page 91

5 ounces (140 grams) part-skim or dry mozzarella cheese, thinly sliced (7 slices)

1 cup (245 grams) New York–New Jersey Tomato Sauce (page 53), at room temperature

1 ounce (30 grams) sliced pepperoni, preferably in natural casing

3 ounces (85 grams) Sweet Fennel Sausage (page 54)

1 (4-ounce/115-gram) link Calabrese Honey Sausage (page 55), cooked and cut on the diagonal into slices 1/4 inch thick

5 Roasted Garlic Cloves (page 209)

Oil from Roasted Garlic Cloves (page 209), for drizzling

Grated Parmesan cheese, for dusting

Dried oregano, for dusting

Remove the dough ball from the refrigerator and leave wrapped at room temperature until the dough warms to 60°F to 65°F. Meanwhile, set up the oven with two pizza stones or baking steels and preheat to 500°F for 1 hour (see Getting Started, page 29).

Put the ricotta in a pastry bag with a 1/4-inch opening or plain tip.

Dust the work surface with the dusting mixture, then move the dough to the surface and dust the top (see Transferring the Dough to the Work Surface, page 30).

Sprinkle a wooden peel with the dusting mixture. Open the dough on the work surface to a 13-inch round with a slightly raised edge (see Opening and Stretching the Dough, pages 31–33).

Move the dough to the peel. As you work, shake the peel forward and backward to ensure the dough isn't sticking.

Arrange the mozzarella slices over the top, 6 slices around the outside and 1 slice in the center, leaving a 3/4-inch border. Spoon the tomato sauce onto the center of the pizza. Then, using the back of the spoon in a circular motion and working outward from the center, spread the sauce to the rim.

Arrange the pepperoni slices over the sauce. Pinch flat, nickel-size pieces of the fennel sausage and distribute them evenly over the pepperoni. Place the slices of Calabrese sausage evenly around the pizza, then scatter the garlic cloves and drizzle some of the garlic oil over the top.

Slide the pizza onto the top stone (see Moving the Dough to the Oven, page 34). Bake for 6 minutes. Lift the pizza onto the peel, rotate it 180 degrees, and then transfer it to the bottom stone. Bake for another 6 minutes, until the bottom is browned and crisp and the top is golden brown.

Transfer the pizza to a cutting board and cut into 6 wedges. Pipe dollops of the ricotta on top and finish with a dusting of Parmesan and oregano.

NEW YORK–NEW JERSEY TOMATO SAUCE

MAKES 1 CUP (245 GRAMS), ENOUGH FOR 1 NEW YORKER OR NEW JERSEY TOMATO PIE

4.5 ounces (120 grams/$\frac{1}{2}$ cup) ground tomatoes, preferably 7/11 or DiNapoli

2.2 ounces (65 grams/$\frac{1}{4}$ cup) tomato paste, preferably SuperDolce

Pinch of dried oregano

Pinch of fine sea salt

1 teaspoon (5 grams) extra virgin olive oil

2 ounces (55 grams/$\frac{1}{4}$ cup) hand-crushed tomatoes (see page 28)

Combine the ground tomatoes, tomato paste, oregano, salt, and oil in a deep bowl or other deep container and puree with an immersion blender. Stir in the crushed tomatoes.

The sauce can be covered and refrigerated for up to 3 days before using.

SWEET FENNEL SAUSAGE

MAKES 2 POUNDS (910 GRAMS)

Along with my Calabrese Honey Sausage (page 55), this one gets used throughout my menus and all through this book. Both are flavored with a bit of honey, which adds a subtle sweetness and also helps keep the meat juicy as it cooks. Buy medium-grind pork, or even better, buy pork shoulder and ask the butcher to double grind it, first through a 1/2-inch die and then through a 3/8-inch die. If you'd like to case this sausage, follow my directions on page 56. Many people, including a lot of professionals, are surprised when I tell them that I never use cooked sausage in a pizza (unless it's a sliced cooked link). Raw sausage, when added in the quantity and piece size I call for, cooks perfectly in the time allotted.

---

1 1/2 tablespoons (9 grams) fennel seeds

1 1/2 tablespoons (9 grams) anise seeds

1 teaspoon (4.5 grams) fine sea salt

2 teaspoons (4.5 grams) freshly ground black pepper

2 1/2 tablespoons (37 grams) cold water

2 pounds (910 grams) medium-grind pork shoulder

2 tablespoons (42 grams) honey

Grind the fennel seeds lightly in a spice grinder or with a mortar and pestle, leaving some texture. Transfer them to a small bowl. Repeat with the anise seeds but grind them a bit finer, then add to the bowl. Neither spice should be ground to a powder. Add the salt and pepper and stir in the water. Adding water will help to incorporate the spices evenly into the pork.

Put the pork into a large bowl and top with the spice mixture. Using your hands, work the spices evenly into the meat. Add the honey and mix again.

Cook a small amount of the sausage in a small skillet or a microwave and taste. Adjust the seasonings to your taste. Cover the meat with plastic wrap and refrigerate for about 2 hours, until cold, or for up to 2 days before using.

For longer storage, wrap the sausage airtight and freeze for up to 2 months. Thaw in the refrigerator before using.

CALABRESE HONEY SAUSAGE

MAKES 2 POUNDS (910 GRAMS)

This sausage gets its heat three ways, but it's only medium-spicy. On the dried-spice side, I use red pepper flakes. I also add Calabrese peppers, which come in a jar, crushed and marinated with olive oil, herbs, salt, and vinegar. These magic peppers are my favorite way to add a dash of heat to pizzas (and everything else), and I love drizzling them on a fully baked pie. For fresh-chile flavor, I use serrano chiles. If you like more heat, you can increase the amount of red pepper flakes or serrano. For a milder sausage, just skip the red pepper flakes. We use this sausage in its bulk form on many of our pizzas. We also case it, cook it, and slice it for use as a pizza topping, as well as in pastas, sandwiches, appetizers and entrées.

1½ tablespoons (9 grams) fennel seeds

1½ tablespoons (9 grams) anise seeds

1 teaspoon (4.5 grams) fine sea salt

2 teaspoons (4.5 grams) freshly ground black pepper

1¼ teaspoons (2.5 grams) red pepper flakes (optional)

2½ tablespoons (37 grams) cold water

2 pounds (910 grams) medium-grind pork shoulder

2 tablespoons (42 grams) honey

1 tablespoon (15 grams) crushed Calabrese peppers

2 teaspoons (5 grams) finely chopped serrano chile with seeds

Grind the fennel seeds lightly in a spice grinder or with a mortar and pestle, leaving some texture. Transfer them to a small bowl. Repeat with the anise seeds but grind them a bit finer, then add to the bowl. Neither spice should be ground to a powder. Add the salt, pepper, and pepper flakes and stir in the water. Adding water will help to incorporate the spices evenly into the pork.

Put the pork into a large bowl and top with the spice mixture. Using your hands, work the spices evenly into the meat. Add the honey, Calabrese peppers, and serrano chile and mix again.

Cook a small amount of the sausage in a small skillet or a microwave and taste. Adjust the seasonings to your taste. Cover the meat with plastic wrap and refrigerate for about 2 hours, until cold, or for up to 2 days before using.

For longer storage, wrap the sausage airtight and freeze for up to 2 months. Thaw in the refrigerator before using.

CASING SAUSAGE

Follow these directions to case either Sweet Fennel Sausage (page 54) or Calabrese Honey Sausage (page 55). Adding a bit of water to the ground meat helps keep the sausages from bursting when you cook them. If you're planning to slice your sausages, cook them in the oven and let them cool, as directed here. You can also sauté or grill them, or simmer them in tomato sauce and treat yourself to the world's most mouthwatering sandwich or pasta.

PRO TIP

THE PINCH When you pinch small pieces of bulk sausage for distributing over pizza, the sausage tends to stick to your fingers. Try this little trick for nonstick pinching: before you start, moisten your hands with something acidic, like lemon juice or vinegar.

If possible, have a second person help you with the stuffing operation. That way, one person can push the meat through the tube while the second person guides the casing as it fills with the meat. This can be a smooth process if the meat is pushed through with a constant, steady pressure, which will help prevent air pockets from forming.

Soak the casings in cold water to cover for at least 20 minutes.

Set up the sausage stuffer according to the manufacturer's instructions. Lightly oil the stuffer tube. Slide the casing onto the tube, pushing it back and adding more casing to cover the length of the tube. Cut the casing if necessary, then tie the end securely in a knot. If you prefer, you can tie it securely with twine. Leave the remaining casing in the water.

Put the sausage in a bowl and add 2½ tablespoons of water. Squish the meat with your hands to absorb the water fully. Push enough sausage into the feeder to fill it.

Start the machine and push the plunger with constant pressure to fill the casing, leaving a few inches of casing unfilled. Once the casing is filled, slide it off the sausage stuffer and tie the open end into a knot. Twist the sausage into links approximately 5 inches long. Alternate the direction you twist with each link, twisting toward you on the first link and then away from you for the second link. Continue alternating the direction to prevent the sausages from unraveling. If you notice any air bubbles in the sausage mixture, try to massage the mixture to dissipate them. Repeat until all of the sausage is in casings.

It is best to refrigerate your filled sausages overnight before cooking. There will be less risk of the sausages bursting. Arrange the sausages on a sheet pan, cover them with plastic wrap, and refrigerate for up to 1 day before cooking, or you can freeze them for up to 2 months (if the sausage mixture has not been previously frozen).

Oil a sheet pan with olive oil and arrange the sausages on the pan. It is not necessary to cut the links apart. Let the sausage rest at room temperature for 20 minutes before cooking.

To cook the sausage, position a rack in the center of the oven and preheat the oven to 500°F. Or, if the oven is set up for pizza cooking, you can put the sheet pan holding the sausage directly on the stone on the bottom oven rack.

Cook the sausage for 4 minutes. Turn the sausage over and continue to cook for 4 to 6 minutes, until cooked through.

If you will be slicing the sausages for pizza, let them cool to room temperature, then refrigerate until cold before cutting.

Some Sausage Suggestions

To make a sausage sub (aka grinder, hero, or hoagie) or a great pasta, caramelize some onions and bell peppers in olive oil in a sauté pan, then add garlic, tomato sauce, a pinch each of salt and pepper, and a touch of cream and cook until reduced to a thick sauce. Add the cooked sausages and simmer them briefly till they're warmed through. Serve in a sub roll or over a hearty pasta like bucatini.

To make one of the most popular appetizers at Capo's, slice cooked Calabrese sausage on the diagonal and sauté the slices quickly with honey.

NEW HAVEN WITH CLAMS

MAKES ONE 14-INCH PIZZA; 6 SLICES

Early-twentieth-century pizzas were cooked in coal- or coke-fired ovens, which burn at temperatures of 1000°F or higher. Eventually gas ovens became the norm, but in New Haven, coal-fired pizzas are still a proud tradition, and at Tony's, we make this New Haven–style clam white pie in our coal oven. Here, I've adapted it with an oven-and-broiler technique that helps approximate the tasty char of a coal oven, and I recommend using baking steels rather than stones to enhance that effect.

I call for dry mozzarella cheese, which is traditional in New Haven pizzas. It's also sold as low-moisture mozzarella and, as you'd expect, it exudes less liquid during cooking than whole-milk mozzarella.

This pizza is a tribute to the famous clam pizza at Frank Pepe's pizzeria, which popularized it in the 1960s. I've added some of my own touches, like using a dough made with starter and adding bacon, which aren't traditional in New Haven, and using both canned and in-shell clams. The canned clams cook right on the pizza, and the ones in the shell are steamed with olive oil, garlic, and wine on the stove top and added to the pie after it's fully baked. This method ensures that they're perfectly cooked and helps prevent the raw or soggy spots that can result from cooking in-shell clams directly on pizza as it bakes. If you live someplace where freshly shucked clams are available and affordable, by all means use them in place of the canned ones in this recipe. Just give them a quick sauté with a little olive oil and garlic and let them cool to room temperature before you make your pizza. I like this pie on the thin side, so I push the rim out quite flat and give the edges a little extra stretch before baking.

continued

1 (13-ounce/370-gram) ball Master Dough, preferably with starter (page 44), made with Tiga but without oil

3 parts flour mixed with 1 part semolina, for dusting

2 strips (75 grams) bacon, cut crosswise into 1/2-inch pieces

1 tablespoon (14 grams) olive oil, plus more for cooking the clams

2 pounds (910 grams) littleneck clams (about 18 clams), scrubbed, rinsed, and drained

1/2 cup (113 grams) dry white wine

1 1/2 teaspoons (5 grams) minced garlic

Fine sea salt

1 (10-ounce/280-gram) can baby clams, drained

1/2 teaspoon (1 gram) chopped fresh flat-leaf parsley

Freshly ground black pepper

8 ounces (225 grams) dry mozzarella cheese, thinly sliced (about 12 slices)

Grated Pecorino Romano cheese, for dusting

Red pepper flakes, for dusting

Garlic Oil (page 29), for drizzling

Remove the dough ball from the refrigerator and leave wrapped at room temperature until the dough warms to 60°F to 65°F. Meanwhile, set up the oven with two baking steels or pizza stones and preheat to 500°F for 1 hour (see Getting Started, page 29).

Heat a small skillet over medium-high heat and add the bacon. Lower the heat to medium and cook the bacon, stirring often, for about 2 minutes, until most of the fat is rendered and the bacon is partially cooked. Set the bacon aside without draining it.

Heat a film of olive oil in a large sauté pan. When the oil is hot, add the fresh clams and cook for about 2 minutes, stirring them often. Add the wine, cover, and cook for about 1 1/2 minutes, shaking the pan from time to time, until most of the clams have opened. Add 1/2 teaspoon of the garlic and a pinch of salt, re-cover, and continue to cook for about 30 seconds to 1 minute until all of the clams have opened. Discard any clams that failed to open. Leave 12 of the nicest clams in the pan (for garnishing the pizza) and remove the remaining clams, including any that have fallen out of their shells. Pull the clam meat out of the shells, put in a bowl, and discard the shells.

Add the canned clams and toss with 1/2 teaspoon of the garlic, the parsley, the 1 tablespoon oil, a pinch of salt, and 3 grindings of pepper.

Transfer the dough to the work surface (page 30). Open the dough to a 14-inch round and push down the sides rather than creating a raised edge (see Opening and Stretching the Dough, page 33). Move the dough to a dusted wooden peel. As you work, shake the peel forward and backward to ensure the dough isn't sticking.

Arrange the mozzarella slices over the dough. Do not break up the slices; it is fine if only some of the cheese reaches the edge of the dough. Scatter the clams in the bowl, the bacon, and the remaining 1/2 teaspoon garlic over the cheese.

Slide the pizza onto the top stone (see Moving the Dough to the Oven, page 34) and bake for 5 minutes. Lift the pizza onto the peel, rotate it 180 degrees, and then transfer it to the bottom stone. Bake for another 4 to 5 minutes, until the bottom is browned and crisp and the top is golden brown. Meanwhile, reheat the clams in the sauté pan.

Turn the oven to broil and transfer the pizza to the top stone for about 1 minute for a final browning.

Transfer the pizza to a cutting board and cut into 6 wedges. Garnish with the clams in the shells and strain some of the clam cooking liquid over the top. Finish with a dusting of pecorino and pepper flakes and a drizzle of garlic oil.

NEW JERSEY TOMATO PIE

MAKES ONE 13-INCH PIZZA; 6 SLICES

At the turn of the twentieth century, pizza quickly migrated from New York to New Jersey, where, in the capital city of Trenton, a distinctive local tomato pie was born at places like Papa's and De Lorenzo's. Like New York pizza, the cheese goes down first—I prefer the evenness of sliced mozzarella—so it stays creamier and doesn't brown, and the sauce becomes more intense as it's exposed to the heat of the oven. You can add meat or other toppings (which would go between the cheese and the sauce), but I like this simple version best. And I top mine with additional hand-crushed tomatoes to make it even more of a tomato fest.

1 (13-ounce/370-gram) ball Master Dough, preferably with starter (page 44), made with Tiga

3 parts flour mixed with 1 part semolina, for dusting

6.5 ounces (185 grams) whole-milk mozzarella cheese, thinly sliced (9 slices)

1 cup (245 grams) New York–New Jersey Tomato Sauce (page 53), at room temperature

4 ounces (115 grams/1/2 cup) hand-crushed tomatoes (see page 28), at room temperature (optional)

Grated Pecorino Romano cheese, for dusting

Dried oregano, for dusting

Garlic Oil (page 29), for drizzling

Remove the dough ball from the refrigerator and leave wrapped at room temperature until the dough warms to 60°F to 65°F. Meanwhile, set up the oven with two pizza stones or baking steels and preheat to 500°F for 1 hour (see Getting Started, page 29).

Dust the work surface with the dusting mixture, then move the dough to the surface and dust the top (see Transferring the Dough to the Work Surface, page 30). Sprinkle a wooden peel with the dusting mixture. Open the dough on the work surface to a 13-inch round with a slightly raised edge (see Opening and Stretching the Dough, page 33). Move the dough to the peel. As you work, shake the peel forward and backward to ensure the dough isn't sticking.

Arrange the mozzarella slices over the top, leaving a 3/4-inch border. Spoon the tomato sauce onto the center of the pizza. Then, using the back of the spoon in a circular motion and working outward from the center, spread the sauce to the rim.

Slide the pizza onto the top stone (see Moving the Dough to the oven, page 34). Bake for 6 minutes. Lift the pizza onto the peel, rotate it 180 degrees, and then transfer it to the bottom stone. Bake for another 6 minutes, until the bottom is browned and crisp and the top is golden brown.

Transfer the pizza to a cutting board and cut into 6 wedges. Top with the crushed tomatoes, then finish with a dusting of pecorino and oregano and a drizzle of garlic oil.

DETROIT RED TOP

MAKES ONE 10 BY 14-INCH PIZZA; 4 LARGE RECTANGULAR PIECES

Detroit-style pizza was invented in the 1940s by Gus Guerra, the owner of Buddy's Rendezvous. It's rectangular, thick, and fluffy like a Sicilian pizza and is framed by a border of crispy golden brown cheese that tastes like the best part of a grilled cheese sandwich—the stuff that leaks out of the edge and gets toasted in the pan.

What makes this style unique are the two cheeses, white Cheddar and brick, which are piled extra high up the sides of the pan to encourage that charred effect; the butter used to grease the pan; and the pan itself. Legend has it that Gus came up with the idea of using heavy, square blue-steel pans originally designed to clean the oil from tools in high-pressure gas ovens in factories. How Motor City is that?

Soon other Detroit pizzerias, like Shield's and Cloverleaf, created their own versions. In 2012, Detroit pizza got a major kickstart when Shawn Randazzo, a cofounder of the Detroit Style Pizza Company, entered the International Pizza Challenge with a Detroit take on the final blind box challenge (in which contestants are given a box filled with surprise ingredients). Most people hadn't even heard of Detroit Pizza. I had tried it fifteen years before, while I was shooting a television commercial for Dolly's Pizza in Detroit, and I'd met Shawn when he attended my seminar the day before. Professionals with thirty years of experience were looking at Shawn's pizza and saying, "What the heck is that?" I said, "The guy's gonna win it." And sure enough, he took first place that year. The following year, Jeff Smokevitch, a former student of mine, won the American Pan division of the same competition with another Detroit-style pizza, and ever since, Detroit style has been the rising star of the pizza business. Fortunately, Shawn is now selling Detroit pans (see Sources, page 304), which had become increasingly difficult to find.

continued

1 (22-ounce/625-gram) ball Master Dough Without Starter (page 48)

2 tablespoons (28 grams) unsalted butter, at room temperature

2 tablespoons (28 grams) extra virgin olive oil

TOMATO SAUCE

13 ounces (360 grams/generous 1 1/2 cups) ground tomatoes, preferably Tomato Magic or DiNapoli

4.5 ounces (125 grams/1/2 cup) tomato paste, preferably Bontá or Saporito Super Heavy Pizza Sauce

1 1/2 teaspoons (7 grams) extra virgin olive oil

Pinch of fine sea salt

Pinch of dried oregano

7 ounces (200 grams) brick cheese, shredded (2 cups)

7 ounces (200 grams) white Cheddar cheese, preferably Cabot, shredded (2 cups)

Grated Pecorino Romano cheese, for dusting

Dried oregano, for dusting

Garlic Oil (page 29), for drizzling

Remove the dough ball from the refrigerator and leave wrapped at room temperature until the dough warms to 50°F to 55°F. This should take about 1 hour.

Smear the butter in a 10 by 14-inch seasoned black-steel Detroit pan. Spread the oil over the butter.

Transfer the dough to the pan and flip the dough to coat both sides with the oil. Using your fingertips, push the dough outward into an even layer. Try to reach the corners, but don't worry if the dough does not fill the pan. Put the pan in a warm spot for 30 minutes, then push the dough again to fill the corners and to degas it.

Let the dough rest for 1 to 1 1/2 hours, until it has risen (the timing depends on the temperature of the room). It will not have doubled. If the dough shrinks away from the edges of the pan, do not press on the dough again or it may not rise properly.

Meanwhile, set up the oven with two pizza stones or baking steels and preheat to 500°F for 1 hour (see Getting Started, page 29).

To make the sauce, combine all of the ingredients in a saucepan and puree with an immersion blender. Set aside.

Place the pizza pan on the top stone and bake for 6 minutes (the dough will set and be lightly colored). Remove from the oven, sprinkle the brick cheese evenly over the dough, covering to the edges. Stack 1 3/4 cups (170 grams) of the Cheddar cheese around the edges of the dough; you want it to rise slightly up the sides of the pan. Sprinkle the remaining Cheddar evenly over the top.

Return the pan to the top stone to bake for about 7 minutes. The pizza will be lightly colored and the cheese will be bubbling on the sides. Rotate the pan 180 degrees and transfer it to the bottom stone. Continue to bake for another 8 to 9 minutes, until the cheese around the edges of the pan is charred. Meanwhile, heat the tomato sauce over medium-low heat until hot.

Remove the pan from the oven. Use a long metal spatula to chisel and loosen the sides of the pizza, then remove the pizza from the pan and place it on a cutting board.

Cut the pizza into quarters. Ladle 2 vertical racing strips of tomato sauce down the length of the pizza and spread it out slightly with the bottom of the ladle. Finish with a dusting of pecorino and oregano and a drizzle of garlic oil.

ST. LOUIS

MAKES ONE 14-INCH PIZZA; 16 SMALL SQUARES

In the late 1990s I went to St. Louis for the first time in my life to perform at Camp Quality, a camp for kids with cancer. The kids spend a week having all kinds of fun experiences, including pizza throwing, cooking, eating, and generally clowning around. There were two things I knew I needed to taste while I was there: a Budweiser and a St. Louis pizza. That's how I discovered Imo's, the place that makes the definitive St. Louis–style pie. It's cracker-thin and cut into squares because it's so thin that triangular slices would collapse under the weight of the toppings (or, according to Imo family legend, because founder Ed Imo was a linoleum tile cutter and squares were what he knew). To make the crust extra thin, I start with a smaller dough ball than usual, roll it very thin and larger than the usual 13 inches diameter, dock it, and then trim it down to 13 inches and flatten the edges.

A true St. Louis pizza is made with a decidedly sweet, oregano tomato sauce and a special cheese called Provel. A creamy white blend of provolone, Swiss, and Cheddar that's virtually unknown outside St. Louis, Provel is a processed cheese that melts in that same gooey, guilty-pleasure way that Velveeta does. No wonder our kitchen staff is addicted to grilled cheese sandwiches made with it.

---

1 (8-ounce/225-gram) ball Master Dough Without Starter (page 48)

9 parts flour mixed with 1 part semolina, for dusting

Remove the dough ball from the refrigerator and leave wrapped at room temperature until the dough warms to 60°F to 65°F. Meanwhile, set up the oven with two pizza stones or baking steels and preheat to 500°F for 1 hour (see Getting Started, page 29).

To make the sauce, combine all of the ingredients in a deep bowl or other deep container and puree with an immersion blender.

Dust the work surface with the dusting mixture, then move the dough to the surface and dust the top (see Transferring the Dough to the Work Surface, page 30).

Sprinkle a wooden peel with the dusting mixture.

ST. LOUIS TOMATO SAUCE

4.2 ounces (120 grams/1/2 cup) ground tomatoes, preferably Tomato Magic or DiNapoli

4.5 ounces (125 grams/1/2 cup) tomato paste, preferably SuperDolce

3 tablespoons (55 grams) Simple Syrup (below)

Pinch of dried oregano

Pinch of fine sea salt

4 ounces (115 grams) Sweet Fennel Sausage (page 54), or 1 ounce (30 grams) sliced pepperoni, preferably in natural casing (optional)

7 ounces (200 grams) Provel cheese, shredded (2 cups)

Grated Parmesan cheese, for dusting

Dried oregano, for dusting

Garlic Oil (page 29), for drizzling

Roll out the dough into a 14-inch round, press the edges gently to flatten them, and then dock the surface of the dough (see Rolling Pizza Dough, page 103).

Move the dough to the peel. As you work, shake the peel forward and backward to ensure the dough isn't sticking.

Spoon the tomato sauce onto the center of the dough. Then, using the back of the spoon in a circular motion and working outward from the center, spread the sauce evenly over the surface, leaving a 3/4-inch border. The sauce will weigh down the dough, keeping it flat as it bakes. The dough may have contracted as it was moved, so pull the edges as necessary to restretch it into a 14-inch round. Baking the crust without the cheese will make for a crispier crust.

Slide the pizza onto the top stone (see Moving the Dough to the Oven, page 34). Bake for 4 minutes. Remove the pizza from the oven and place it on a cutting board (or work directly on the peel if there is room to set it on the work surface). If you are using sausage, pinch nickel-size pieces and scatter them evenly over the top; if you are using pepperoni, arrange the slices evenly over the sauce. Sprinkle the Provel evenly over the pizza.

Return the pizza to the top stone and bake for 3 minutes. Lift the pizza onto the peel, rotate it 180 degrees, and then transfer it to the bottom stone. Bake for another 3 to 4 minutes, until the bottom is browned and crisp and the top is golden brown.

Transfer the pizza to the cutting board. Make 3 evenly spaced cuts through the pizza in one direction (to make 4 strips of equal width), turn the pizza 90 degrees, and repeat in the other direction, to make 16 squares. Finish with a dusting of Parmesan and oregano and a drizzle of garlic oil.

SIMPLE SYRUP

MAKES 1/3 CUP (95 GRAMS)

1/4 cup (50 grams) sugar

1/4 cup (58 grams) water

Combine the sugar and water in a small saucepan and stir to mix. Place over medium-high heat and bring to a simmer, stirring until the sugar has dissolved. Remove from the heat and let cool to room temperature.

Use immediately, or transfer to a covered container and refrigerate for up to 2 weeks.

Chicago

It might surprise you to learn that Chicago-style pizza, whether we're talking about deep-dish or cracker-thin, is a relative newcomer—a mid-twentieth-century phenomenon that came on the scene in 1943 at Pizzeria Uno when the owners, Ric Riccardo and Ike Sewell, and their chef, Rudy Malnati, decided to try to invent a new

kind of pizza the world had never seen. As that restaurant became a chain and others spun off from it, deep-dish went national and ultimately worldwide. Eventually, Lou Malnati's, Giordano's, Gino's, and other restaurants in Chicago and around the country created their own versions, including cracker-thin, stuffed, and skillet baked. But what still defines most Chicago-style pizza is its crust, which typically includes two signature ingredients: cornmeal and fat, usually butter, lard, or both.

When I opened Tony's Pizza Napoletana in San Francisco, I installed seven different ovens so we could create authentic versions of all of the best-loved American and Italian pizza varieties. All but one, that is. We don't do Chicago style. That was a choice based not on preference but on necessity. Deep-dish pizzas require a much longer bake—at least 30 minutes, sometimes even longer—and that means a whole different kitchen setup and rhythm.

But I love Chicago pizza. Over the years, I've worked and judged competitions with people from some of the great pizza dynasties in the Windy City, including Lou Malnati's, Giordano's, Connie's, and others, and I was dying to bring a taste of Chicago to a hungry Bay Area crowd. So, when I found a perfect location a few blocks away, I opened another restaurant that's completely centered around Chicago-style pizzas.

I called the place Capo's, and I went full-bore Chicago. I wanted to create the vibe of a Prohibition-era speakeasy, complete with cushy leather–upholstered booths, mob-boss photos on the walls, and a long, mirrored bar. We shipped in seven tons of hundred-year-old brick, reclaimed from a building in Chicago; put in a pressed-tin ceiling; and even installed a vintage 1930s wooden phone booth. The place feels like it's been there forever.

The menu is old-school Italian-American restaurant made with new-school awesome ingredients and techniques, and the pizza is my homage to the Chicago tradition. We serve about twelve types, and you can get any of them four different ways. There's the traditional deep-dish made with a butter-and-lard cornmeal crust. We use that same dough to make stuffed pizzas with a second top crust. And we do a cast-iron-pan version, in which the same dough proofs in a cast-iron skillet before baking to create a puffier crust. We also make traditional cracker-thin Chicago pizzas using a different dough that's made with a starter and no butter or lard.

With the recipes in this chapter and the two doughs on pages 74 and 76, you can try all four styles at home. And once you get a feel for each one, you can have fun mixing and matching the fillings and toppings to suit your tastes.

Deep-Dish Tips

Crafting a great deep-dish pizza takes some time and strategy. Because this style takes so long to bake, it's assembled differently from other kinds of pizza. About half of the cheese—in my versions, sliced part-skim mozzarella—goes on the bottom and slightly up the sides, where the ingredients that go on top of it protect it from burning during its long stay in the oven. It also acts as a "liner" between the crust and the filling to keep the crust crisp. Next come the filling ingredients and, finally, more cheese. Here, I like the saltier and more intense flavor of provolone to balance the mozzarella. Toward the end of baking, I add shredded mozzarella for just a few minutes to melt it. The cheeses are "staged" in this way so that they don't overcook and exude too much fat and moisture.

Traditionally, the sauce is added to the unbaked pizza and cooks in the oven. That can make things soggy and messy. I prefer to warm the sauce briefly but not actually cook it and then add it on top, after the pie comes out of the oven. People are always surprised by that because they're used to the heavier, more concentrated flavor of a baked tomato sauce.

Splitting up the baking process with all of these staged steps means that my deep-dish pies bake more quickly than what's typical, and that gives them more strength, structure, and definition. It's all about engineering the build and the bake to cook everything just right, so the crust stays crunchy, the filling comes together as a perfect blend of flavors and textures, and the sauce adds a bright, fresh accent to balance all the richness.

- For my recipes, you'll need a round deep-dish pan 12 to 13 inches in diameter and 2 inches deep. I recommend a well-seasoned black steel pan (see Sources, page 304). Aluminum pans are too light and don't hold heat as well as steel, so your pizza doesn't brown as nicely or cook as evenly. A pan 13 inches in diameter gives you six nice-size slices. And I like "lucky thirteen" because I'm super-stitious. Some pans have a raised ridge running around the side. This is so they can be stacked for easier storage in a pizzeria. The ridge isn't necessary for a home pan.

- The pan is greased quite liberally, which, in addition to keeping the crust from sticking, also helps it bake to a rich golden brown, like a pie crust.

- If you're making a deep-dish or stuffed pizza with both cooked and raw meat (for example, pepperoni and raw sausage), layer in the cooked meat first and keep the uncooked meat toward the top of your ingredients. This way, as the uncooked meat bakes, the fat that renders out of it will flavor the ingredients below it and won't soak directly into the crust.

- *Part-skim mozzarella is what I prefer for Chicago pies because its lower fat content means it exudes less fat and thus gives you a stronger pizza.*

- *I like a buttery Chicago dough as opposed to a more cornmealy one, which tends to taste too much like corn bread. I prefer a more pie crust or pastry approach, and I like a higher-fat unsalted butter (usually labeled "European style"). It's not the country of origin that matters here, it's the butterfat content. European-style butter tends to come in at 82 to 84 percent butterfat, compared to the 80 percent of typical American butter. More fat and less water in your butter gives you lighter, flakier pastry.*

- *If you don't want to use lard, you can go with the same amount of vegetable shortening.*

- *In my restaurants, we remove our fully cooked deep-dish pizzas from the pan to slice them, and then transfer them to a clean, room-temperature pan (and here, I do use aluminum, because I like the shiny, clean look) to serve. This makes for a neater presentation and keeps the guests from having to touch a hot pan. If you have two pans at home, you can use the same method. You can also return your sliced pie to the pan you baked it in, which will help it hold its shape as it sits on the table. Or you can serve your pizza directly from the cutting board, without returning it to the pan. Whatever you do, add your final sauce, seasonings, and garnishes after the pizza is out of the pan and sliced. This will make serving much easier and neater.*

- *Use medium-grind cornmeal for dusting, not a mixture of cornmeal and flour, as I recommend when you're using semolina. Flour tends to keep cornmeal from sticking to the pizza. And straight cornmeal helps strengthen the crust and gives it a nice crunch.*

- *For deep-dish and stuffed pizzas, you roll out the dough rather than opening and stretching it as you do for most of the pizzas in this book. This is important because it gives you a perfectly consistent thickness. For rolling tips, see page 103.*

- *It's helpful to let the rolled-out dough sit in the pan for 30 minutes (with dough hanging over the edge) before filling your pizza (done for both deep-dish and stuffed). This allows the dough to relax and proof a bit and gives you better structure and flavor.*

CHICAGO DEEP-DISH DOUGH

MAKES 27 OUNCES (770 GRAMS), ENOUGH FOR 1 DEEP-DISH PIZZA

I make all of my Chicago doughs with Ceresota flour, an unbleached, unbromated all-purpose flour made from hard red winter wheat. (It is branded Ceresota in Illinois and elsewhere but is sold under the brand name Heckers in the Northeast; see Sources, page 304). It's a relatively low-gluten flour in the 12 percent range that is the traditional choice of Chicago pizzerias. It's also the flour I specify when training and certifying *pizzaiolos* in Chicago pizza at my school. If you can't find it, substitute another good-quality unbleached all-purpose flour for Chicago doughs.

Some Chicago pizzas use cooked potato or semolina in the dough and no cornmeal, but my flour-and-cornmeal dough is my favorite way to go. It's made without a starter, and, unlike most pizza doughs, its flavor and texture come more from fat than from yeast, making it a bit like a cross between a pizza dough and a pie crust. I've found that equal parts butter and lard make for the best flavor and texture. Note that this dough needs to proof for at least 24 hours; it will be even better if left for up to 48 hours.

4.5 grams (1½ teaspoons) active dry yeast

70 grams (¼ cup plus 1 tablespoon) warm water (80°F to 85°F)

430 grams (3½ cups) all-purpose flour with 12 percent protein, preferably Ceresota

23 grams (2½ tablespoons) medium-grind cornmeal

9 grams (1 tablespoon) diastatic malt

Put the yeast in a small bowl, add the warm water, and whisk vigorously for 30 seconds. The yeast should dissolve in the water and the mixture should foam. If it doesn't and the yeast granules float, the yeast is "dead" and the mixture should be discarded. Begin again with a fresh amount of yeast and water.

Combine the flour, cornmeal, and malt in the bowl of a stand mixer fitted with the dough hook. With the mixer running on the lowest speed, add the lard and butter and mix for 1 minute.

Pour in most of the ice water, reserving about 2 tablespoons, followed by the yeast-water mixture. Pour the reserved water into the yeast bowl, swirl it around to dislodge any bits of yeast stuck to the bowl, and add to the mixer.

18 grams (1 tablespoon plus
1 teaspoon) lard, cut into small pieces,
at room temperature

18 grams (1 tablespoon plus
1 teaspoon) European-style unsalted
butter, preferably 82 percent
butterfat, cut into small pieces,
at room temperature

202 grams (3/4 cup plus 2 tablespoon)
ice water, plus more as needed

9 grams (2 teaspoons) fine sea salt

For baker's percentages, see page 302.

Continue to mix the dough at the lowest speed for about 1 minute, until most of the dough comes together around the hook. Stop the mixer. Use your fingers to pull away any dough that clings to the hook, and scrape the sides and bottom of the bowl with a bowl scraper or rubber spatula.

Add the salt and mix on the lowest speed for 1 minute to combine.

Check the bottom of the bowl for any unincorporated flour. Turn the dough over and press it into the bottom of the bowl to pick up any stray pieces.

Stop the mixer, pull the dough off the hook, and scrape down the sides and bottom of the bowl. If there is still unincorporated flour at the bottom of the bowl, sprinkle with a very small amount of water and mix for 1 minute.

Use a bowl scraper to transfer the dough to an unfloured work surface, then knead it for 2 to 3 minutes, until smooth (see Kneading the Dough, page 24). Cover the dough with a damp dish towel and let it rest at room temperature for 1 hour.

Use a dough cutter to loosen the dough and move it to the scale. You will need 27 ounces (770 grams) of dough. You may have a little extra dough. Form the dough into a ball (see Balling the Dough, page 26) and set it on a half sheet pan. Wrap the pan airtight with a double layer of plastic wrap, sealing the wrap well under the pan. Put the pan in a level spot in the refrigerator and refrigerate for 24 to 48 hours.

Note on Making Vegetarian Deep-Dish Dough: You can substitute 18 grams vegetable shortening for the lard.

CHICAGO STUFFED DOUGH

MAKES 41 OUNCES (1174 GRAMS), ENOUGH FOR 1 FULLY STUFFED PIZZA

This dough is the same one I use for deep-dish pizza, but I've given you the proportions you'll need to make one and a half times as much of it, so you will have enough for both the bottom and the top crust.

6.8 grams (2¼ teaspoons) active dry yeast

92 grams (¼ cup plus 2 tablespoons) warm water (80°F to 85°F)

645 grams (5⅓ cups) all-purpose flour with 12 percent protein, preferably Ceresota

34 grams (¼ cup) medium-grind cornmeal

13.5 grams (1½ tablespoons) diastatic malt

27 grams (2 tablespoons) lard, cut into small pieces, at room temperature

27 grams (2 tablespoons) European-style unsalted butter, preferably 82 percent butterfat, cut into small pieces, at room temperature

316 grams (1⅓ cups) ice water, plus more as needed

13.5 grams (2¾ teaspoons) fine sea salt

For baker's percentages, see page 302.

Make the dough as directed for Chicago Deep-Dish Dough (page 74) up to the point where you have kneaded the dough. Then weigh out one 27-ounce (765-gram) piece of dough and one 14-ounce (400-gram) piece of dough. Cover both pieces with a damp dish towel and let rest at room temperature for 1 hour.

Form the pieces into balls (see Balling the Dough, page 26), set the balls 3 inches apart on a half sheet pan, and wrap the pan and refrigerate as directed for Chicago Deep-Dish Dough.

Note on Making Vegetarian Deep-Dish Dough: You can substitute 18 grams vegetable shortening for the lard.

DEEP-DISH TOMATO SAUCE

MAKES 2¼ CUPS (510 GRAMS)

It's best to make this uncooked sauce when you make your dough and then refrigerate it overnight so the flavors can come together.

6 ounces (170 grams/²/₃ cup) tomato paste, preferably Saporito Super Heavy Pizza Sauce

3 ounces (85 grams/¼ cup plus 2 tablespoons) ground tomatoes, preferably 7/11 or DiNapoli

³/₄ teaspoon (.5 grams) dried oregano

Pinch of fine sea salt

¹/₂ teaspoon (2.5 grams) extra virgin olive oil

9 ounces (255 grams/1¹/₃ cups) hand-crushed tomatoes (see page 28)

Combine the tomato paste, ground tomatoes, oregano, salt, and oil in a deep bowl or other deep container and puree with an immersion blender. Stir in the crushed tomatoes.

The sauce can be covered and refrigerated for up to 3 days before using.

CHICAGO DEEP DISH WITH CALABRESE AND FENNEL SAUSAGES

MAKES ONE 13-INCH DEEP ROUND PIZZA; 6 LARGE SLICES

This pie, filled with sausage and cheese, is the quintessential Chicago deep-dish pizza and a great choice for your first foray. I like a combo of spicy Calabrese and sweet fennel sausages and both mozzarella and provolone for the cheese. Some pizzerias press out a sheet of sausage that forms a solid layer over the cheese. I prefer to pinch quarter-size pieces of sausage and distribute them evenly, which makes for a less heavy pizza.

1 (27-ounce/765-gram) ball Chicago Deep-Dish Dough (page 74)

Medium-grind cornmeal, for dusting

2 teaspoons (9 grams) unsalted butter, at room temperature

9 ounces (255 grams) part-skim mozzarella cheese, thinly sliced (13 slices)

8 ounces (225 grams) Calabrese Honey Sausage (page 55)

8 ounces (225 grams) Sweet Fennel Sausage (page 54)

Grated Pecorino Romano cheese

1 teaspoon (3 grams) finely chopped garlic

9 ounces (255 grams) provolone cheese, thinly sliced (13 slices)

5 ounces (140 grams) part-skim mozzarella cheese, shredded (1¼ cups)

2 cups (455 grams) Deep-Dish Tomato Sauce (page 77), warm

Dried oregano, for dusting

Extra virgin olive oil, for drizzling

Remove the dough ball from the refrigerator and leave wrapped at room temperature until the dough warms to 55°F to 60°F. Meanwhile, set up the oven with two pizza stones or baking steels and preheat to 500°F for 1 hour (see Getting Started, page 29).

Butter the bottom and sides of a 12 by 2-inch or 13 by 2-inch round deep-dish pizza pan.

Dust the work surface with a generous amount of cornmeal, then transfer the dough to the surface (see Transferring the Dough to the Work Surface, page 30). Coat both sides of the dough with the cornmeal, and roll out the dough into a 17-inch round (see Rolling Pizza Dough, page 103).

Working quickly but carefully, lift the dough round and lower it into the center of the prepared pan. Lift the edges of the dough to ease the dough into the corners. The dough will overhang the rim of the pan ❶. Press around the edge of the dough to secure it to the pan rim ❷. Set aside to rest at room temperature for 30 minutes.

Arrange the mozzarella slices in the bottom and slightly up the sides of the pan, overlapping the slices as necessary ❸. Pinch quarter-size pieces of the sausages and distribute them evenly over the cheese.

Sprinkle with a light dusting of pecorino and the garlic. Arrange the provolone slices over the top. Run the rolling pin over the lip of the pan to cut away the excess dough. If the dough shrinks back, use your fingers to press the dough around the inside of the pan, extending it to the lip.

Place the pan on the bottom stone. Bake for 15 minutes, rotate the pan 180 degrees, and continue to bake for another 12 minutes, until the cheese is melted and the crust is a rich golden brown.

Take the pan out of the oven and sprinkle the shredded mozzarella over the top of the pizza. Place on the top stone for 2 minutes to melt the shredded cheese.

Remove from the oven and run a long metal spatula around the inside of the pan to loosen the pizza from the pan. Then, using the spatula, lift an edge and check the bottom of the crust. It should be browned and crisp. If it needs more time, return the pan to the bottom stone for 1 minute.

Using the spatula, and being careful not to pierce the bottom of the crust, lift the pizza from the pan and transfer it to a cutting board. Using a rocking cutter or a serrated knife, cut the pizza into 6 large wedges, leaving them in place. Spoon the sauce over the pizza and spread it to the edges with a small offset spatula. Finish with a dusting of pecorino and oregano and a drizzle of oil.

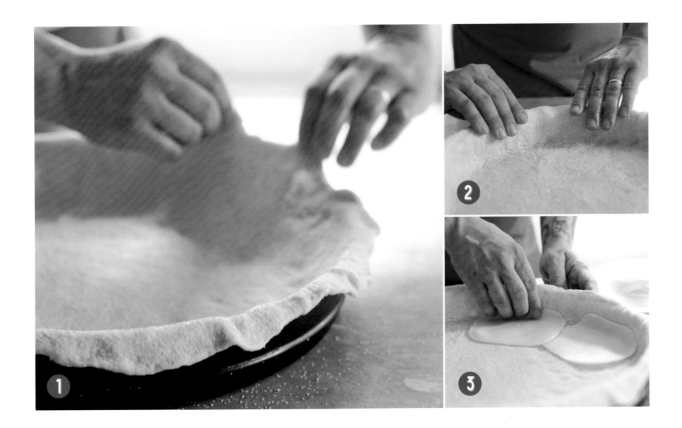

CHICAGO DEEP DISH WITH SPINACH AND RICOTTA

MAKES ONE 13-INCH DEEP ROUND PIZZA; 6 LARGE SLICES

Along with sausage, spinach and ricotta is the other classic Chicago pizza combo. You'll find some recipes—and some pizzerias—that use raw spinach. I start with raw spinach but I sauté it lightly in a little olive oil until it is just wilted and still green. Then I drain it in a colander or strainer, pressing it gently to help remove what liquid hasn't already cooked off. This approach makes a huge difference because it intensifies the spinach flavor and reduces the moisture that would result in a wet filling and a soggy crust. I like to reserve some of the spinach and ricotta to add as a garnish.

1 (27-ounce/765-gram) ball Chicago Deep-Dish Dough (page 74)

Medium-grind cornmeal, for dusting

2 teaspoons (9 grams) unsalted butter, at room temperature

9 ounces (255 grams) part-skim mozzarella cheese, thinly sliced (13 slices)

1½ cups (285 grams) well-drained Sautéed Spinach (page 83), at room temperature

Grated Pecorino Romano cheese, for dusting

1 teaspoon (3 grams) finely chopped garlic

4.5 ounces (120 grams/½ cup) whole-milk ricotta cheese, preferably New York–style Polly-O or Ricotta Cream, page 91, at room temperature

Remove the dough ball from the refrigerator and leave wrapped at room temperature until the dough warms to 55°F to 60°F. Meanwhile, set up the oven with two pizza stones or baking steels and preheat to 500°F for 1 hour (see Getting Started, page 29).

Generously butter the bottom and sides of a 12 by 2-inch or 13 by 2-inch round deep-dish pizza pan.

Dust the work surface with a generous amount of cornmeal, then transfer the dough to the surface (see Transferring the Dough to the Work Surface, page 30). Coat both sides of the dough round with the cornmeal and roll out the dough into a 17-inch round (see Rolling Pizza Dough, page 103).

Working quickly but carefully, lift the dough and lower it into the center of the prepared pan. Lift the edges of the dough to ease the dough into the corners. The dough will overhang the rim of the pan (see photo ❶, page 79). Press around the edge of the dough to secure it to the pan rim ❷. Set aside to rest at room temperature for 30 minutes.

Arrange the mozzarella slices in the bottom and slightly up the sides of the pan ❸, overlapping the slices as necessary. Reserve ½ cup (95 grams) of the spinach and scatter the remaining spinach evenly over the mozzarella.

continued

9 ounces (255 grams) provolone cheese, thinly sliced (13 slices)

5 ounces (140 grams) part-skim mozzarella cheese, shredded (1¼ cups)

2 cups (455 grams) Deep-Dish Tomato Sauce (page 77), warm

Dried oregano, for dusting

Garlic Oil (page 29), for drizzling

Sprinkle with a light dusting of pecorino and the garlic. Arrange the provolone slices over the top. Run the rolling pin over the lip of the pan to cut away the excess dough. If the dough shrinks back, use your fingers to press the dough around the inside of the pan, extending it to the lip.

Place the pan on the bottom stone. Bake for 15 minutes, rotate the pan 180 degrees, and continue to bake for another 12 minutes, until the cheese is melted and the crust is a rich golden brown.

Meanwhile, put the ricotta in a pastry bag with a ¼-inch opening or plain tip.

If the reserved spinach is cold, warm it in a pan or in the microwave.

Take the pan out of the oven and sprinkle the shredded mozzarella over the top of the pizza. Place on the top stone for 2 minutes to melt the shredded cheese.

Remove from the oven and run a long metal spatula around the inside of the pan to loosen the pizza from the pan. Then, using the spatula, lift an edge and check the bottom of the crust. It should be browned and crisp. If it needs more time, return the pan to the bottom stone for 1 minute.

Using the spatula, and being careful not to pierce the bottom of the crust, lift the pizza from the pan and transfer it to a cutting board. Using a rocking cutter or a serrated knife, cut the pizza into 6 large wedges, leaving them in place. Spoon the sauce over the top and spread it to the edges with a small offset spatula. Pipe quarter-size dollops of ricotta onto the pizza and garnish with the reserved spinach. Finish with a dusting of pecorino and of oregano and a drizzle of garlic oil.

SAUTÉED SPINACH

MAKES 1½ CUP (285 GRAMS)

Olive oil, for sautéing

1 pound (455 grams) baby spinach

Fine sea salt and freshly ground black pepper

Heat a generous film of oil in your largest skillet over medium-high heat. Shake any excess water from the spinach and add several handfuls to the skillet, leaving enough room to turn the spinach. Sprinkle with a pinch each of salt and pepper. As the spinach wilts and room is made, turn the spinach and add more to the skillet. When you have cooked about half of the spinach, transfer it to a strainer or colander.

Discard the liquid in the skillet, wipe it dry, and heat another generous film of oil over medium-high heat. Sauté the remaining spinach the same way and add to the strainer. Drain the spinach well, squeezing it gently between your hands.

The spinach can be stored in an airtight container in the refrigerator for up to 1 day.

Pizza Pans

For pizzas baked in pans, my choice is always black steel, not stainless or aluminum, which don't promote thorough, even browning. I've given more specific pan recommendations throughout the book in chapters with pan pizza recipes.

Treat any steel pan just like you would a cast-iron skillet. If it's not preseasoned, wipe it with a thin coating of vegetable oil and heat it in a 500°F oven for about 1 hour.

Clean steel pans by first lightly scraping with a plastic dough cutter and then wiping with a paper towel.

Avoid using water or soap. If a pan rusts, pour about ¼ cup of salt into it and heat it in a 500°F oven for about 30 minutes. Remove it from the oven and let it sit until it's cool enough to handle, then use paper towels to scour the pan, with the salt still in it, until there are no traces of rust.

If you find that the pizza sticks to the pan when you're baking it, reseason the pan as follows: scrape it clean and wipe a thin film of oil over the surface. Put the pan back in the still-warm oven and let it sit until the oven is cool.

MAKING STUFFED PIZZA

FULLY STUFFED

MAKES ONE 13-INCH DEEP ROUND PIZZA; 6 LARGE SLICES

To me, a great stuffed pizza has a crust that stays a bit crunchy both on top and on the bottom and never gets soggy from too much sauce or too many ingredients inside. I call this one Fully Stuffed and it is on the hearty side, but I think you'll find that the proportions of crust to fillings and sauce are just right.

1 (27-ounce/765-gram) ball and
1 (14-ounce/400-gram) ball Chicago Stuffed Dough (page 76)

Medium-grind cornmeal, for dusting

2 teaspoons (9 grams) unsalted butter, at room temperature

9 ounces (255 grams) part-skim mozzarella cheese, thinly sliced (13 slices)

8 ounces (225 grams) cooked Meatballs (page 287), crumbled

2 ounces (55 grams) sliced pepperoni, preferably in natural casing

8 ounces (225 grams) uncooked Calabrese Honey Sausage (page 55)

8 ounces (225 grams) uncooked Sweet Fennel Sausage (page 54)

1/2 cup (85 grams) Sautéed Onions (page 89)

1 cup (175 grams) Sautéed Mushrooms (page 89)

3/4 cup (110 grams) Sautéed Red Peppers (page 90)

Grated Pecorino Romano cheese, for dusting

Remove the dough balls from the refrigerator and leave wrapped at room temperature until the dough warms to 60°F to 65°F. Meanwhile, set up the oven with the pizza stone or baking steel on the bottom rack and preheat to 500°F for 1 hour (see Getting Started, page 29).

Butter the bottom and sides of a 12 by 2-inch or 13 by 2-inch round deep-dish pizza pan.

Dust the work surface with a generous amount of cornmeal, then transfer the larger dough to the surface (see Transferring the Dough to the Work Surface, page 30).

Coat both sides of the dough with the cornmeal and roll out the dough into a 17-inch round (see Rolling Pizza Dough, page 103).

Working quickly but carefully, lift the dough and lower it into the center of the prepared pan. Lift the edges of the dough to ease the dough into the corners. The dough will overhang the rim of the pan (see photo ❶, page 84). Press around the edge of the dough to secure it to the pan rim ❷. Set aside to rest at room temperature for 30 minutes.

Arrange the mozzarella slices in the bottom and slightly up the sides of the pan, overlapping the slices as necessary ❸. Distribute the meatball pieces evenly over the cheese, followed by the pepperoni. ❹ Pinch quarter-size pieces of both sausages and distribute them evenly over the pepperoni. (Adding the sausage last will keep any fat that renders during baking from softening the bottom crust.)

Scatter the onions, mushrooms, and red peppers evenly over the meats.

Sprinkle with a light dusting of pecorino and the garlic. Sprinkle with the shredded mozzarella and top with the provolone slices, covering the toppings completely and extending slightly up the sides of the pan ❺.

continued

4.5 ounces (120 grams/¹/₂ cup) whole-milk ricotta cheese, preferably New York–style Polly-O or Ricotta Cream, page 91, at room temperature

1 teaspoon (3 grams) finely chopped garlic

5 ounces (140 grams) part-skim mozzarella cheese, shredded (1¹/₄ cups)

9 ounces (255 grams) provolone cheese, thinly sliced (13 slices)

Garlic Oil (page 29)

2¹/₄ cups (510 grams) Deep-Dish Tomato Sauce (page 77), warm

Dried oregano, for dusting

PRO TIP

PASTRY BAGS Once a pastry bag is full, gather and twist the top of the bag and use a rubber band to hold it closed. I like disposable pastry bags for piping ricotta because you can just snip off the end, so you don't even need to use a metal tip.

Meanwhile, put the ricotta in a pastry bag with a ¹/₄-inch opening or plain tip.

Coat the remaining dough ball with cornmeal and roll out to a 12- or 13-inch round, depending on the size of your pan. Center the round over the pan. The dough should come right up to the edge of the pan but not overlap it ❻. If it is too wide, trim it with a paring knife.

To crimp the dough to seal it, hold your left index finger on a slight angle against the edge of the pan and use your right index finger to fold the overhanging dough over it on a diagonal ❼. Move counterclockwise around the edge of the dough, repeating the crimping to form a decorative edge.

Cut three 2-inch slits outward from the center of the crust to allow steam to escape as the pizza bakes.

Place the pan on the stone. Bake for 12 minutes, rotate the pan 180 degrees, and continue to bake for another 12 minutes. The crust should be richly browned. If it isn't, rotate the pan one more time and bake for 2 minutes.

Take the pizza out of the oven and let rest in the pan for 10 minutes.

Run a long metal spatula around the inside of the pan to loosen the pizza from the pan. Then, using the spatula, lift an edge and check the bottom of the crust. It should be browned and crisp. If it needs more time, return the pan to the stone for 1 minute.

Using the spatula, and being careful not to pierce the bottom of the crust, lift the pizza from the pan and transfer it to a cutting board. Brush the edges and outer crust with garlic oil.

Using a rocking cutter or a serrated knife, cut the pizza into 6 large wedges, leaving them in place ❽. Spoon the sauce over the pizza and spread it to the edges ❾.

Dust the top with pecorino and oregano. Pipe quarter-size dollops of ricotta over the pizza ❿, then finish with a drizzle of garlic oil.

SAUTÉED ONIONS

MAKES 1½ CUP (255 GRAMS)

1 pound (455 grams) yellow onions

Olive oil, for sautéing

Fine sea salt

Cut the onions in half through the root end. Place cut side down on the cutting board and cut off and discard the top end. Cut the onion crosswise into slices ⅛ inch thick until you reach the root end. Discard the root end.

Heat a generous film of olive oil in a skillet over medium-high heat. Add the onions and a generous pinch of salt and stir to coat the onions with the oil. Once the onions begin to sizzle, lower the heat to medium and cook, stirring often, for about 15 minutes, until the onions are tender and a rich golden brown.

The onions will keep in an airtight container in the refrigerator for up to 1 day.

SAUTÉED MUSHROOMS

MAKES 1 CUP (175 GRAMS)

8 ounces (225 grams) small to medium button mushrooms

Olive oil, for sautéing

Fine sea salt

Just before cooking, trim off the ends of the mushroom stems and quarter the mushrooms.

Heat a film of oil in a skillet over medium-high heat. Add the mushrooms and a generous pinch of salt and stir to coat the mushrooms with the oil. Spread the mushrooms into a single layer. Do not move the mushrooms for about 1½ minutes, until the bottoms are golden brown.

Shake the pan to stir the mushrooms, keeping them in a single layer. After about 30 seconds, move them again and continue to cook and stir, adjusting the heat as necessary, for about 3 minutes, until the mushrooms are evenly colored and cooked through.

The mushrooms will keep in an airtight container in the refrigerator for up to 1 day.

continued

★ ★ **89** ★ ★

SAUTÉED RED PEPPERS

MAKES ¾ CUP (110 GRAMS)

1 (8 ounce/255 gram) large
red bell pepper

Olive oil, for sautéing

Fine sea salt

Cut the sides off the red pepper. Discard the stem, ribs, and seeds. Cut the flesh lengthwise into strips ¼ inch wide.

Heat a generous film of olive oil in a skillet over medium-high heat. Add the peppers and a generous pinch of salt and stir to coat the peppers with the oil. Once the peppers begin to sizzle, cook, stirring often, for about 6 minutes, until they are tender and caramelized.

The peppers will keep in an airtight container in the refrigerator for up to 1 day.

Ricotta, Rethought

In most deep-dish pizzas, ricotta is added along with the other filling ingredients and baked. But while I was experimenting with cannoli, I got thinking about how nice that smooth, silky flavor of fresh ricotta lightened with a little mascarpone is—and how good it would be on a pizza. And after all, ricotta is already "recooked." I figured, why cook it a third time if you don't have to? So I tried piping that ricotta-mascarpone mixture onto my pizzas with a pastry bag after baking, and I'll never go back.

No, it's "not really Chicago," as people seem to love pointing out to me on an almost daily basis. But baked ricotta has a heavier, less delicate taste and texture, and cooking it also makes it weep—which makes me weep in terms of "sog factor." My method lets you taste the ricotta at its creamiest and best, and I think it looks pretty cool, too. Just be sure it's at room temperature when you pipe (or, if you prefer, spoon) it on, so the hot pizza warms it just right. If you have access to a really good brand of ricotta, like dense, slightly sweet New York–style Polly-O or Grande, you can use it straight. If you can't find those, make this creamy, rich Ricotta Cream using an artisanal ricotta rather than a typical supermarket brand.

RICOTTA CREAM

MAKES ¼ CUP (65 GRAMS)

1.5 ounces (45 grams/3 tablespoons) whole-milk ricotta cheese, at room temperature

0.5 ounce (15 grams/1 tablespoon) mascarpone cheese

1 teaspoon (5 grams) heavy cream

MAKES A GENEROUS ½ CUP (130 GRAMS)

3 ounces (90 grams/¼ cup plus 2 tablespoons) whole-milk ricotta cheese, at room temperature

1 ounce (30 grams/2 tablespoons) mascarpone cheese

2 teaspoons (10 grams) heavy cream

MAKES A GENEROUS 1 CUP (260 GRAMS)

6 ounces (180 grams/¾ cup) whole-milk ricotta cheese, at room temperature

2 ounces (60 grams/¼ cup) mascarpone cheese

1 tablespoon plus 1 teaspoon (20 grams) heavy cream

Put all of the ingredients in a small bowl. Using a handheld mixer, mix the ingredients until smooth and creamy. Let the mixture rest for 1 hour before using. The ricotta cream can be refrigerated for a few hours before using, but bring it to room temperature before using.

CAST-IRON SKILLET

MAKES ONE 12-INCH ROUND SKILLET PIZZA; 6 LARGE SLICES

Several years ago, my World Pizza Champions team got invited to do a pizza-throwing show at Wrigley Field—a major-league honor in a town that takes its pizza so seriously. It was a rainy afternoon, but we had fun anyway, and so did the crowd. That night, Jeff Stolfe, the founder of Connie's Pizza, invited me to his flagship restaurant for dinner, and that was when I first tasted Connie's signature cast-iron skillet pies. Later, I tried the city's other famous skillet pizza at Pequod's, and this version, which we serve at Capo's, is my hybrid of those two styles.

It's like a cross between a Chicago deep-dish and a Sicilian with a touch of Detroit: Chicago because it uses my deep-dish dough. Sicilian because you push the dough out in the pan (rather than rolling it), let it rise, and then bake it partway before you add any cheese or toppings, so you get a completely different texture—much lighter and puffier than deep-dish—from the same dough. And Detroit because I add a rim of crispy almost burnt cheese around the edge, Detroit-style (see page 63).

One of the nice things about this pizza is that once you parbake the crust, you can let it sit out at room temperature for up to 3 hours before you top it and finish baking. That's the technique we use at the restaurant, and it makes this pie a great choice for entertaining because you're halfway done before the guests arrive.

If you want to serve a vegetarian version, you can substitute vegetable shortening for the lard in the pan and in the dough (see Note on Making Vegetarian Deep-Dish Dough, page 75), eliminate the sausage, and add more peppers or other sautéed vegetables, like spinach, chard, kale, eggplant, or mushrooms.

In 2014, our chef at Capo's, Matt Molina, entered the International Pizza Challenge at the Pizza Expo in Las Vegas with a cast-iron skillet pizza similar to this one—The Dillinger, made with a burnt sharp-cheddar crust and a four-cheese Hangar One Vodka Smoked Alfredo sauce, topped with chicken, artichoke hearts, red onion, roasted peppers, bacon and broccolini. He not only won the American Pan division, but also went on to win World Champion Pizza Maker of the Year.

continued

1 (22-ounce/625-gram) ball Chicago Deep-Dish Dough (page 74)

Medium-grind cornmeal, for dusting

2 teaspoons (9 grams) lard or vegetable shortening, at room temperature

2 tablespoons (28 grams) extra virgin olive oil

1 ounce (30 grams) provolone cheese, sliced (1 slice)

4 ounces (115 grams) Sweet Fennel Sausage (page 54; optional)

1 teaspoon finely chopped garlic

6 ounces (170 grams) part-skim mozzarella cheese, shredded (1½ cups)

3 ounces (85 grams) white Cheddar, preferably Cabot, shredded (scant 1 cup)

2 ounces (55 grams/¼ cup) whole-milk ricotta cheese, preferably New York–style Polly-O or Ricotta Cream, page 91, at room temperature

⅓ cup (55 grams) Sautéed Red Peppers (page 90)

½ cup (115 grams) Deep-Dish Tomato Sauce (page 77), warm

Grated Pecorino Romano cheese, for dusting

Dried oregano, for dusting

Red pepper flakes, for dusting (optional)

Garlic Oil (page 29), for drizzling

Remove the dough ball from the refrigerator and leave wrapped at room temperature until the dough warms to 50°F to 55°F. This should take about 1 hour.

Smear the lard on the bottom and sides of a 12-inch cast-iron skillet (measure the skillet from side to side of the top edge). Spread the olive oil over the lard.

Dust the work surface with a generous amount of cornmeal, then transfer the dough to the surface (see Transferring the Dough to the Work surface, page 30). Coat both sides of the dough with cornmeal, and put the dough in the prepared pan. Using the fingertips of both hands, push the dough outward from the center to fill the bottom of the pan evenly. Set the uncovered pan in a warm spot for 1 to 1½ hours, until the dough has risen slightly.

Meanwhile, set up the oven with two pizza stones or baking steels and preheat to 500°F for 1 hour (see Getting Started, page 29).

Place the skillet on the bottom stone and bake for 10 minutes until golden brown.

Remove from the oven (the baked dough can rest in the pan for up to 3 hours, but remember to preheat the oven for 1 hour before continuing).

Tear the provolone into 8 pieces and arrange them on the pizza, leaving a ½-inch border. Pinch nickel-size pieces of the sausage and distribute them evenly over the cheese. Scatter the garlic over the top, and then sprinkle the mozzarella evenly over the sausage. Stack the Cheddar around the edge of the dough; you want it to rise slightly up the sides of the pan.

Place the skillet on the top stone for 7 to 10 minutes, until the top is golden brown.

Meanwhile, put the ricotta in a pastry bag with a ¼-inch opening or plain tip.

Remove the skillet from the oven and quickly scatter the red peppers over the pizza. Place the skillet on the bottom stone and bake for 3 to 6 minutes, until the cheese around the edge of the pan is charred.

Remove from the oven and run a long metal spatula around the inside of the pan to loosen the pizza from the pan. Then, using the spatula, and being careful not to pierce the bottom of the crust, lift the pizza from the pan and transfer it to a cutting board.

Using a rocking cutter or a serrated knife, cut the pizza into 6 large wedges, leaving them in place. Spoon dollops of the tomato sauce around the pizza, then pipe quarter-size dollops of ricotta on each slice. Finish with a light dusting of pecorino, oregano, and pepper flakes and a drizzle of garlic oil.

Cracker-Thin Tips

Even though they're cousins born in the same city, Chicago cracker-thin and deep-dish are pretty much total opposites. A good cracker-thin pizza is completely flat with no raised rim. It's light and delicate, and even though it's ultrathin, it's leavened and matured enough to have a nice chew rather than shatter when you bite into it. To achieve this, my cracker-thin dough has higher hydration and less yeast than deep-dish dough and is made with a starter and no lard or butter.

Cracker-thin pies are traditionally cut into squares, not slices—a style called tavern cut or party cut—which gives you pieces that are exactly right for enjoying the texture and the ratio of cheese, sauce, and toppings to crust.

- For rolling tips, see Rolling Pizza Dough, page 103.

- Roll your dough slightly larger than the desired circumference and then use a pizza wheel to trim the edge to the circumference you want. This technique cuts the lip of the dough and squares the edge. To flatten the trimmed edge further, press down on it with your fingertips. The result will be a very flat rim (as opposed to a puffed cornicione)—a hallmark of Chicago cracker-thin pizzas.

- I always dock the dough after rolling it out. This keeps it from puffing up, so it bakes evenly flat and thin. Because the edges aren't covered with sauce or ingredients that weight them down, I dock them a bit more than the center to keep them from rising.

- I bake cracker-thin pizzas with just sauce for a few minutes, which keeps the dough flat. Then I remove the pizza from the oven, add cheese and toppings, and return it to the oven to finish baking. This technique produces a crispier crust.

CRACKER-THIN DOUGH

MAKES 30 OUNCES (840 GRAMS), ENOUGH FOR 3 CRACKER-THIN PIZZAS

2.3 grams (3/4 teaspoon) active
dry yeast

70 grams (1/4 cup plus 1 tablespoon)
warm water (80°F to 85°F)

430 grams (3 1/2 cups) all-purpose
flour with 12 percent protein,
preferably Ceresota

23 grams (2 1/2 tablespoons)
medium-grind cornmeal

10 grams (1 tablespoon plus
1/4 teaspoon) diastatic malt

210 grams (3/4 cup plus 2 tablespoons)
ice water, or more as needed

90 grams Poolish (page 47)

10 grams (2 teaspoons) fine sea salt

For baker's percentages, see page 302.

Put the yeast in a small bowl, add the warm water, and whisk vigorously for 30 seconds. The yeast should dissolve in the water and the mixture should foam. If it doesn't and the yeast granules float, the yeast is "dead" and should be discarded. Begin again with a fresh amount of yeast and water.

Combine the flour, cornmeal, and malt in the bowl of a stand mixer fitted with the dough hook. With the mixer running on the lowest speed, pour in most of the ice water, reserving about 2 tablespoons, followed by the yeast-water mixture. Pour the reserved water into the yeast bowl, swirl it around to dislodge any bits of yeast stuck to the bowl, and add it to the mixer. Mix for about 15 seconds, stop the mixer, and add the poolish.

Continue to mix the dough at the lowest speed for about 1 minute, until most of the dough comes together around the hook. Stop the mixer. Use your fingers to pull away any dough that clings to the hook, and scrape the sides and bottom of the bowl with a bowl scraper or rubber spatula.

Add the salt and mix for 3 more minutes. At this point, all of the water will be absorbed but the dough may not be completely smooth.

Check the bottom of the bowl for any unincorporated flour. Turn the dough over and press it into the bottom of the bowl to pick up any stray pieces.

Use a bowl scraper to transfer the dough to an unfloured work surface, then knead it for 2 to 3 minutes, until smooth (see Kneading the Dough, page 24). Cover the dough with a damp dish towel and let rest at room temperature for 20 minutes.

Use your dough cutter to loosen the dough and to cut it into thirds. Weigh each piece, adjusting the quantity to give you three 10-ounce (280-gram) pieces. Discard any remaining dough.

Form the dough into balls (see Balling the Dough, page 26). Set the balls on a half sheet pan, spacing them about 3 inches apart. Or, if you will be baking the balls on different days, place them on separate quarter sheet pans. Wrap the pan(s) airtight with a double layer of plastic wrap, sealing the wrap well under the pan(s). Put the pan(s) in a level spot in the refrigerator and refrigerate for 24 to 48 hours.

CRACKER-THIN WITH FENNEL SAUSAGE

MAKES ONE 13-INCH PIZZA; 16 SMALL SQUARES

This is a nice, straight-ahead choice for your first crack at cracker-thin. My homemade fennel sausage makes all the difference, but of course, if you're short on time, you can use store-bought.

---

1 (10-ounce/280-gram) ball Cracker-Thin Dough (page 97)

Medium-grind cornmeal, for dusting

1/3 cup (85 grams) Cracker-Thin Tomato Sauce (page 99), at room temperature

1 teaspoon (3 grams) finely chopped garlic

1 ounce (30 grams) provolone cheese, sliced (1 slice)

6 ounces (170 grams) part-skim mozzarella cheese, shredded (1 1/2 cups)

4 ounces (115 grams) Sweet Fennel Sausage (page 54)

Grated Pecorino Romano cheese, for dusting

Dried oregano, for dusting

Red pepper flakes, for dusting (optional)

Garlic Oil (page 29), for drizzling

Remove the dough ball from the refrigerator and leave wrapped at room temperature until the dough warms to 60°F to 65°F. Meanwhile, set up the oven with two pizza stones or baking steels and preheat to 500°F for 1 hour (see Getting Started, page 29).

Dust the work surface with a generous amount of cornmeal, then transfer the dough to the surface and dust the top with cornmeal (see Transferring the Dough to the Work Surface, page 30).

Sprinkle a wooden peel with cornmeal.

Following the instructions in Rolling Pizza Dough (see page 103), roll out the dough into a thin round 13 to 15 inches in diameter. (After you make your first cracker-thin pizza, you will be able to determine how thin you like your crust.) Using a pizza wheel, trim the dough to a 13-round. Press the edges gently to flatten them, then dock the surface of the dough.

Move the dough to the peel. As you work, shake the peel forward and backward to ensure the dough isn't sticking.

Spoon the tomato sauce onto the center of the dough. Then, using the back of the spoon in a circular motion and working outward from the center, spread the sauce evenly over the surface, leaving a 1/4-inch border. The sauce will weigh down the dough, keeping it flat as it bakes. The dough may have contracted as it was moved, so pull the edges as necessary to restretch it to its original diameter. Baking the crust without the cheese will make for a crispier crust.

Slide the pizza onto the top stone (see Moving the Dough to the Oven, page 34). Bake for 3 minutes. Remove the pizza from the oven and place it on a cutting board (or work directly on the peel if there is room to set it on the work surface).

Sprinkle with the garlic. Break the provolone into several small pieces and scatter them evenly over the pizza. Mound the mozzarella in the center of the pizza and use your fingertips to spread it out evenly from the center to the edge of the sauce. Pinch nickel-size pieces of the sausage and distribute them evenly around the pizza.

Lift the pizza with the peel (if on a cutting board), rotate it 180 degrees, and transfer it to the bottom stone. Bake for 3 minutes, lift it onto the peel, rotate 180 degrees, and return it to the bottom stone. Continue to bake for 4 minutes. Move the pizza to the top stone for a final 1 minute to crisp the bottom.

Transfer the pizza to the cutting board. Make 3 evenly spaced cuts through the pizza in one direction (to make 4 strips of equal width), rotate the pizza 90 degrees, and repeat in the other direction, to make 16 squares.

Finish with a light dusting of pecorino, oregano, and pepper flakes and a drizzle of garlic oil.

CRACKER-THIN TOMATO SAUCE

MAKES A GENEROUS 1¾ CUPS (455 GRAMS)

12 ounces (340 grams/1½ cups) ground tomatoes, preferably 7/11 or DiNapoli

4 ounces (115 grams/¼ cup plus 3 tablespoons) tomato paste, preferably Saporito Super Heavy Pizza Sauce

1 teaspoon (.6 grams) dried oregano

½ teaspoon (2.5 grams) fine sea salt

1 teaspoon (5 grams) extra virgin olive oil

2 fresh basil leaves, torn

Combine the ground tomatoes, tomato paste, oregano, salt, and oil in a deep bowl or other deep container and puree with an immersion blender. Stir in the basil leaves.

The sauce can be covered and refrigerated for up to 3 days before using.

FRANK NITTI

MAKES ONE 13-INCH PIZZA; 16 SMALL SQUARES

Francesco—aka Frank "The Enforcer"—Nitti, was a notorious Chicago whiskey runner and one of Al Capone's main men. Today he lives on at Capo's as a spinach-ricotta pizza. This is the thin-crust version of the classic Chicago Deep-Dish with Spinach and Ricotta on page 80. I hope you'll try both to get a sense of how the same ingredients, prepared in two totally different styles, can create completely different pizza experiences.

1 (10-ounce/280-gram) ball
Cracker-Thin Dough (page 97)

Medium-grind cornmeal, for dusting

2 ounces (55 grams/¼ cup) whole-milk
ricotta cheese, preferably New York–
style Polly-O or Ricotta Cream, page 91,
at room temperature

⅓ cup (85 grams) Cracker-Thin Tomato
Sauce (page 99), at room temperature

1 teaspoon (3 grams) finely
chopped garlic

2 ounces (55 grams) provolone cheese,
sliced (2 slices)

5 ounces (140 grams) part-skim
mozzarella cheese, shredded (1¼ cups)

1 cup (190 grams) Sautéed Spinach
(page 83), warm

**Grated Pecorino Romano cheese,
for dusting**

Dried oregano, for dusting

**Red pepper flakes, for dusting
(optional)**

Garlic Oil (page 29), for drizzling

Remove the dough ball from the refrigerator and leave wrapped at room temperature until the dough warms to 60°F to 65°F . Meanwhile, set up the oven with two pizza stones or baking steels and preheat to 500°F for 1 hour (see Getting Started, page 29).

Put the ricotta in a pastry bag with a ¼-inch opening or plain tip.

Dust the work surface with a generous amount of cornmeal. Move the dough to the surface and dust the top with cornmeal (see Transferring the Dough to the Work Surface, page 30).

Sprinkle a wooden peel with cornmeal.

Following the instructions in Rolling Pizza Dough (see page 103), roll out the dough into a thin round 13 to 15 inches in diameter. (After you make your first cracker-thin pizza, you will be able to determine how thin you like your crust.) Using a pizza wheel, trim the dough to a 13-inch round. Press the edges gently to flatten them, then dock the surface of the dough.

Move the dough to the peel. As you work, shake the peel forward and backward to ensure the dough isn't sticking.

Spoon the tomato sauce onto the center of the dough. Then, using the back of the spoon in a circular motion and working outward from the center, spread the sauce evenly over the surface, leaving a ¼-inch border. The sauce will weigh down the dough, keeping it flat as it bakes. The dough may have contracted as it was moved, so pull the edges as necessary to restretch it to its original diameter. Baking the crust without the cheese will make for a crispier crust.

continued

PRO TIP

If you like you like your crust even thinner than a recipe calls for, just roll the dough to a bigger diameter, and then use a pizza wheel to trim it down to the final size you want, as shown in ❷, opposite. Remember that the thinner your crust is, the more quickly it will cook.

Slide the pizza onto the top stone (see Moving the Dough to the Oven, page 34). Bake for 3 minutes. Remove from the oven and place on a cutting board (or work directly on the peel if there is room to set it on the work surface).

Sprinkle with the garlic. Break the provolone into small pieces and scatter them evenly over the pizza. Mound the mozzarella in the center of the pizza and use your fingertips to spread it out evenly from the center to the edge of the sauce.

Lift the pizza with the peel (if on a cutting board), rotate it 180 degrees, and transfer it to the bottom stone. Bake for 3 minutes, lift onto the peel, rotate 180 degrees, and return it to the bottom stone. Continue to bake for 4 minutes. Move the pizza to the top stone for a final 1 minute to crisp the bottom.

Transfer the pizza to the cutting board. Make 3 evenly spaced cuts through the pizza in one direction (to make 4 strips of equal width), rotate the pizza 90 degrees, and repeat in the other direction, to make 16 squares.

Mound 1 tablespoon of the spinach on each piece. Pipe a small dollop of ricotta on top of each mound of spinach. Finish with a light dusting of pecorino, oregano, and pepper flakes and a drizzle of garlic oil.

Rolling Pizza Dough

I recommend investing in a large, heavy rolling pin with a hefty steel center rod and ball bearings in the handles. It will make a huge difference in how easily and evenly you can roll out any dough.

Sprinkle a wooden peel with cornmeal or a dusting mixture as directed.

Press the dough into a flat disk about 3/4-inch thick. Using the rolling pin, roll out the dough from side to side (rather than from the center outward) ❶. As you roll the dough, it will stick to the surface from time to time. When it begins to stick, flip it and rotate it, dusting it with additional cornmeal or dusting mixture as needed.

For some recipes in which the dough is rolled, I also direct you to trim the rolled-out dough, flatten the edge, and/or dock the dough. Here's how.

Trimming the dough: Use a pizza wheel to trim your rolled-out dough to the desired size ❷.

Flattening the edge: If you have cut the dough with a pizza wheel, the edges will be squared off by the wheel. Press the edges gently with your fingertips to flatten them ❸. This will keep them from curling as the pizza bakes.

Docking the dough: Some recipes call for docking the dough, which means poking small holes in it to inhibit rising as it bakes. Use a dough docker, a small, many-spiked roller with a handle, rolling it over the entire surface of the dough ❹. If you don't have a docker, you can use the tines of a fork.

ITALIAN STALLION

MAKES ONE 13-INCH PIZZA; 16 SMALL SQUARES

This white-pie stars succulent, juicy Italian beef, here paired with a rich, tangy horseradish cream made by whipping together horseradish and cream cheese. The name? *Italian* for the beef. And *stallion* for the horseradish, of course.

1 (10-ounce/280-gram) ball Cracker-Thin Dough (page 97)

Medium-grind cornmeal, for dusting

2 ounces (55 grams) cream cheese, at room temperature

1½ teaspoons (7.5 grams) drained prepared horseradish

2 ounces (55 grams) provolone cheese, sliced (2 slices)

5 ounces (140 grams) part-skim mozzarella cheese, shredded (1¼ cups)

4 ounces (115 grams) Sweet Fennel Sausage (page 54)

2.5 ounces (70 grams) very thinly sliced Italian Beef (page 106)

Garlic Oil (page 29), for brushing and drizzling

1 (15 grams) Peppadew pepper (see sidebar), cut into strips

1½ teaspoons (2 grams) minced fresh chives

Small piece Fontina cheese, cold, for shaving

Grated Pecorino Romano cheese, for dusting

Dried oregano, for dusting

Remove the dough ball from the refrigerator and leave wrapped at room temperature until the dough warms to 60°F to 65°F . Meanwhile, set up the oven with two pizza stones or baking steels and preheat to 500°F for 1 hour (see Getting Started, page 29).

In a small bowl, whisk the cream cheese until fluffy and smooth. Whisk in the horseradish and set aside.

Dust the work surface with a generous amount of cornmeal, then move the dough to the surface and dust the top with cornmeal (see Transferring the Dough to the Work Surface, page 30).

Sprinkle a wooden peel with cornmeal.

Following the instructions in Rolling Pizza Dough (see page 103), roll out the dough into a thin round 13 to 15 inches in diameter. (After you make your first cracker-thin pizza, you will be able to determine how thin you like your crust.) Using a pizza wheel, trim the dough to a 13-inch round. Press the edges gently to flatten them, then dock the surface of the dough.

Move the dough to the peel. As you work, shake the peel forward and backward to ensure the dough isn't sticking.

Break the provolone into several small pieces and scatter them evenly over the pizza. Mound the mozzarella in the center of the pizza and use your fingertips to spread it out evenly from the center toward the edge, leaving a ¾-inch border.

Slide the pizza onto the top stone (see Moving the Dough to the Oven, page 34). Bake for 3 minutes. Remove from the oven and place on a cutting board (or work directly on the peel if there is room to set it on the work surface). Pinch nickel-size pieces of the sausage and distribute them evenly over the pizza.

Lift the pizza with the peel (if on a cutting board), rotate it 180 degrees, and transfer it to the bottom stone. Bake for 3 minutes, lift onto the peel, rotate 180 degrees, and return it to the bottom stone. Continue to bake for 3 minutes.

Take the pizza out of the oven and arrange the beef over the top. Slide it on the top stone and bake for 1 to 2 minutes to heat the toppings and crisp the bottom.

Transfer the pizza to the cutting board. Make 3 evenly spaced cuts through the pizza in one direction (to make 4 strips of equal width), rotate the pizza 90 degrees, and repeat in the other direction, to make 16 squares. Brush the edge of the crust with a light coating of garlic oil.

Garnish the pieces with small dollops of the horseradish cream, the Peppadew peppers, and the chives. Using a vegetable peeler, shave long pieces of the Fontina over the top. Finish with a light dusting of pecorino and oregano and a drizzle of garlic oil.

Peppadew Peppers

I started using Peppadews years ago, before anyone in the pizza world had discovered them. Now, I'm happy to see their popularity is finally heating up. Peppadews are bright red, orange, or yellow and round—they look like plump cherry tomatoes—with medium heat and a natural sweetness. They're pickled in a sweet, tangy brine and sold in jars or in bulk (often at olive bars in supermarkets). What I love about them is their just-right balance of sweet, hot, tangy, and chile flavors, which makes them the perfect partner for milder cheeses like ricotta, cream cheese, and mozzarella, as well as rich, salty meats like sausage. In fact, there's almost nothing they don't go with. Get your hands on a jar and I promise you, you'll be hooked.

ITALIAN BEEF

MAKES 3½ TO 4 POUNDS (1.6 TO 1.8 KILOGRAMS)

You've probably heard of the Italian beef sandwich. Along with pizza and Chicago-style hot dogs, it's the Windy City's other leading culinary institution, offered at places like Portillo's, Al's Beef, and Mr. Beef. It's slow-cooked beef thinly shaved and drenched in an *au jus* made from the braising juices (sometimes fortified with sausage drippings), piled on a soft roll, which has also been soaked, French dip–style, in the same *au jus*, and served "hot" (with spicy *giardiniera*) or "sweet" (with sautéed red peppers).

I wanted to offer the Italian beef both in the classic sandwich and as a pizza topping, so I worked for months with our guru of deli meats, Mario Abruzzo, to perfect our recipe. Although Italian beef started out as a poor immigrant's way of stretching cheap cuts of meat, we figured that was a part of the tradition we could let go of. So ours starts with American Wagyu bottom round, which we cook in Dutch ovens at the mouth of our thousand-degree coal-fired oven. To replicate that technique, my home recipe has you first coat the top of the roast with Italian seasonings, broil it till it's nicely charred, and then cook it in liquid at 300°F—a bit hotter and faster than most braises. Trust me, it works. The meat holds its own when thinly sliced, and you get an intensely rich caramelized flavor in both the meat and the all-important *au jus*. Cook it medium-rare because it will cook more on the pizza or when you warm it in the hot *au jus*. If you own a meat slicer, this is the time to use it because the meat really needs to be shaved as thinly as possible. For the best results, shave the meat after it has been well chilled in the refrigerator. Once you've cooked the beef, you can treat yourself to one of the world's most mouthwatering sandwiches (page 109) or the Italian Stallion (page 104), or all of the above. Just be sure to start with really good bottom round with plenty of fat.

SEASONING PASTE

2 tablespoons (28 grams) fine sea salt

1 tablespoon (8 grams) freshly ground black pepper

1 tablespoon (3 grams) Italian seasoning

1 tablespoon (10 grams) granulated garlic

1 tablespoon (8 grams) onion powder

2 tablespoons (30 grams) olive oil

1 (5- to 6-pound/2.3- to 2.6-kilograms) American-Wagyu (Kobe-style) bottom round flat roast, preferably Snake River Farms

10 cloves garlic (30 grams)

Olive oil, for rubbing and drizzling

1/3 cup (75 grams) hot water

2 tablespoons (32 grams) tomato paste, preferably Saporito Super Heavy Pizza Sauce

1 tablespoon (14 grams) fine sea salt

2 yellow onions (340 grams), quartered

Position a rack in the bottom third of the oven, place a pizza stone or steel on the rack, and preheat the oven to broil.

To make the seasoning paste, in a small bowl, stir together salt, pepper, Italian seasoning, granulated garlic, and onion powder. Add the oil and stir until a dry paste forms.

Trim any silver skin from the roast. Then, trim the fat cap to form an even layer 1/2 inch thick that covers the top of the roast.

Using a paring knife, cut ten 1-inch slits in the fat-cap side of the beef, spacing them evenly over the surface. Stuff a garlic clove into each slit. Rub the top of the roast with 2 tablespoons oil, then pat the seasoning mixture in an even layer over the top and slightly down the sides of the roast.

Whisk together the water, tomato paste, and salt in a large Dutch oven, preferably made of enameled cast iron. Put the beef, seasoned side up, in the liquid. Prop up any thinner sections of beef with pieces of the onion, so the top of the roast is as level as possible. Scatter the remaining onion pieces around the beef, then add enough hot water to reach within 1 inch of the seasoning paste.

Put the uncovered pot in the oven and broil the meat for about 5 to 8 minutes, until the meat, particularly the top, is charred. Don't be concerned that it will be blackened.

Take the pot out of the oven. At this point, the oven will be over 500°F. Lower the oven temperature to 300°F and leave the oven door open for about 3 minutes to cool it down.

Drizzle the meat with a little oil and add more water as needed to maintain the original level. Cover the pot, put it back in the oven, and cook for 1 hour.

Check the temperature of the roast in the center to gauge the remaining cooking time. The finished roast should be 130°F in the thickest part of the roast for medium-rare. The total cooking time will be about 1 1/2 hours, though it will vary depending on the shape of the roast. Check the level of the water, adding more as necessary to maintain the original level.

When the roast is ready, remove the pot from the oven, uncover it, and let the meat cool in the liquid for 30 minutes.

continued

Remove the beef from the broth and let cool for about 1 hour, until cooled to room temperature. Wrap the beef in a few layers of plastic wrap and refrigerate for at least 6 hours or up to 2 days.

Meanwhile, strain the broth through a fine-mesh strainer into a saucepan. You want it to have an intense flavor as it will be the *au jus* sauce. Bring it to a simmer and cook until reduced to 7 to 8 cups. Strain into a storage container (it will be stored separately from the beef), let cool to room temperature, cover, and refrigerate for up to 2 days. Before using the broth, remove and discard any fat that has risen and solidified on the surface.

Before using the meat on a pizza or in a sandwich, trim and discard the fat. The meat should be sliced very thinly, actually shaved. As noted earlier, a meat slicer is the best way to accomplish this. If that isn't an option, use a sharp knife to slice it as thinly as possible.

ITALIAN BEEF SANDWICH

MAKES 2 SANDWICHES

Broth from Italian Beef (page 106)

2 (6-inch) Italian sandwich rolls, unsliced

1 pound (455 grams) shaved Italian Beef (page 106)

4 to 6 tablespoons (55 to 80 grams) "hot" (spicy) coarsely chopped giardiniera, or 2/3 cup (100 grams) Sautéed Red Peppers (page 90), warm

Preheat the oven to 400°F.

Put 1 cup of the broth in a skillet and set aside.

Put the remaining broth in a 3-quart saucepan that is slightly wider than the length of a sandwich roll and set aside.

Cut off both ends of each roll so the rolls will absorb more broth, then cut the rolls in half horizontally, stopping just short of one long side so the halves are attached. Gently nudge the rolls open so they remain hinged. Set them, cut side up, on a sheet pan and place in the oven to toast for 4 to 5 minutes, until slightly dry but not browned.

Meanwhile, bring the broth to a simmer, add the meat to the skillet, stirring often with a pair of tongs, until the broth is simmering and the beef is heated through.

Working quickly, and using the tongs, pick up the toasted roll and dip the roll into the saucepan of simmering broth, until the entire roll is moistened but not soggy. Transfer the roll to a cutting board.

To serve with the *giardiniera*, spoon the *giardiniera* on the bottom of the each roll, then lift the beef with the tongs and arrange it over the vegetables.

To serve with the red peppers, lift the beef with the tongs and arrange it on the bottom of each roll, then scatter the peppers over the beef.

Close each sandwich and cut in half. If the cut side of the bun looks dry, dip the ends in the broth.

CHICAGO-INSPIRED COCKTAILS

Hey, while that Chicago pizza's baking, why not get things rolling with one of these Capo's signatures—four tributes to old Chicago created with the help of our master mixologist, Elmer Mejicanos.

AGED SPIRITS

3 parts Cyrus Noble bourbon

2 parts Carpano Antica Formula vermouth

1½ parts Rémy Martin unaged Cognac

1 part Bénédictine

FINISHED COCKTAIL

2½ ounces aged spirits or aged Cognac or brandy

3 dashes of Angostura bitters

3 dashes of Peychaud's bitters

1 king ice cube

1 strip orange zest, cut with a vegetable peeler, about 1 inch wide and 2 inches long, any pith scraped off with a paring knife

THE MADE MAN

MAKES 1 COCKTAIL

Our best-selling Capo's cocktail. As a nod to the whole Prohibition theme of the place, we age Cyrus Noble San Francisco bourbon with Carpano Antica Formula vermouth (which, by the way, makes a great Negroni), Bénédictine, and unaged Rémy Martin in oak casks, stacked on a ledge over the front door. After several weeks, when the mixture has taken on a mellow, smoky-oaky flavor, we decant it into bottles to serve as the base for this drink. Think of it as a Chicago speakeasy twist on the New Orleans Vieux Carré, which is also made with bourbon and Angostura and Peychaud's bitters. We serve it over a single king cube, which not only looks cool but also melts more slowly than smaller cubes, so the drink doesn't get diluted. If you want to skip the barrel-aging step, just use an aged Cognac or brandy.

Decide how much of the aged spirits you would like to make and mix together all of the ingredients in the proportions given. Pour the mixture into a mini barrel and let it sit at room temperature to age for 4 weeks. Taste it, and if you feel it needs further aging, let it sit for 1 more week in the barrel. Transfer the spirits to a bottle(s).

To make the cocktail, pour the aged spirits into a mixing glass and add both bitters. Stir for 6 to 8 seconds. Put a king ice cube in a rocks glass and strain the drink into the glass.

Hold the strip of zest centered about 4 inches above the glass and twist it to release its oils into the drink. Then rub the zest around the outside of the glass, about 1½ inches down from the rim of the glass. (This way, when you sip, you will smell the aroma of the zest but your lips will rest above the bitterness of the oils.) Drop the zest into the drink.

THE WISE GUY

MAKES 1 COCKTAIL

2 fluid ounces rye whiskey, preferably Wild Turkey

3/4 fluid ounce agave nectar

3/4 fluid ounce freshly squeezed lemon juice

1 teaspoon (7 grams) orange marmalade

Pinch of freshly ground black pepper

Ice cubes, for the shaker, plus 1 king cube, for serving

1 branch (or a pinch) dried oregano

Our second-most popular Capo's cocktail, this one was named Cocktail of the Week by *SF Weekly* shortly after we opened. It's super refreshing on a hot day—lemony, sweet, and easy to make. And the oregano and pinch of pepper make it a perfect match to our food. A dried oregano sprig is a very cool garnish. You can buy a bunch of dried oregano branches, or put fresh oregano sprigs in the microwave on a paper towel and zap them for 30-second intervals until they're dry.

Put the rye, agave, lemon juice, marmalade, and pepper in a cocktail shaker. Add ice cubes, cover, and shake several times to mix and chill the drink.

Put a king ice cube in a rocks glass. Hold a cocktail strainer over the shaker with one hand and hold a fine-mesh strainer over the glass with the other. Pour from the shaker into the glass, double straining the cocktail.

If you have a dried oregano branch, sprinkle a few of the leaves over the cube, then break off a small, delicate piece and place it on the cube. If not, it tastes just as good topped with a pinch of dried oregano.

THE CAPONE

MAKES 1 COCKTAIL

1 Amarena cherry

1/2 orange slice

1/2 teaspoon (2.5 grams) maple syrup

3 dashes of aromatic bitters, preferably Fee Brothers Old Fashion

2 dashes of orange bitters, preferably Fee Brothers West Indian

2 fluid ounces rye whiskey, preferably Templeton

Ice cubes, for serving

1 fluid ounce seltzer water

This is our new-fashioned version of an old-fashioned, using Templeton rye whiskey, which was Al's favorite, and bottled sweet-tart Italian Amarena cherries instead of old-school maraschinos.

Put the cherry, orange slice, maple syrup, and both bitters in a rocks glass. Using a muddler, muddle the ingredients. Stir in the whiskey, add ice, and top with the seltzer water.

CHICAGO COCKTAIL

MAKES 1 COCKTAIL

Light brown sugar, for dipping the glass rim

1/2 orange slice

1 1/2 fluid ounces Courvoisier

3/4 fluid ounce Cointreau

1/4 fluid ounce freshly squeezed lemon juice

2 dashes of Angostura bitters

Ice cubes, for the shaker

1 fluid ounce Prosecco, preferably Col de' Salici Prosecco Superiore, chilled

This blend of Courvoisier, Cointreau, bitters, and lemon gets shaken and double strained (through both the shaker's strainer and a mesh strainer, to catch any ice chips that would dilute the drink), then finished with a float of Prosecco. I like a more floral, not-too-dry Prosecco here.

Put brown sugar on a small, flat rimmed dish just larger in diameter than the rim of a martini glass. Shake the dish to spread the sugar in an even layer 1/4 inch thick. Run the orange slice around the rim of the glass to moisten it, then dip the rim in the sugar to coat evenly.

Pour the Courvoisier, Cointreau, lemon juice, and bitters in a cocktail shaker. Add ice cubes, cover, and shake several times to mix and chill the drink. Hold a cocktail strainer over the shaker with one hand and hold a fine-mesh strainer over the sugar-rimmed glass with the other. Pour from the shaker into the glass, double straining the cocktail.

Top off with the Prosecco.

Sicilian

As New York–style pizza, with its round shape and relatively thin crust, spread across the United States in the twentieth century, another kind of pizza, baked in a well-oiled sheet pan, started to show up, first on Long Island and then in New York, Boston, New Jersey, Connecticut, and other places where lots of southern

⟫⟶

Italian immigrants settled. People called it Sicilian, though it's not necessarily an exact replica of pizza served in Sicily. It does resemble *sfincione*, a traditional Sicilian focaccia-like pan pizza with toppings. But it also has its roots in *pizza in teglia*, the pan pizza popular in Puglia and throughout southern Italy.

I use the term *Sicilian* in the American sense: a fluffy, rectangular pan pizza similar to focaccia (so similar, in fact, that I make my focaccia using the same dough, page 120). And my definition of the perfect Sicilian is thick but light and fluffy, with a bottom crust that's crisp and golden brown. My Sicilians are large, and they look like a lot of food when they come to the table, but they're not as filling as their appearance might lead you to believe, and they're very digestible, thanks to the long rise we give the dough. That means that they don't leave you feeling like a blimp, even after a few slices.

The secrets to getting this style right include the pan (iron or steel rather than aluminum), the generous amount of olive oil you use to grease it (so that the bottom of the crust essentially fries), and, of course, the dough itself. My dough has a very high hydration level of 70 percent (and as you get more expert at working with it, you can take that level even higher), which gives the finished pizza the perfect combination of ultralight, puffy interior and crispy exterior.

I've given you dough recipes with and without the addition of a starter. As you can probably guess, I prefer the starter version because it has more flavor and a nice, tender texture. But if you don't have the advance time to make a starter, the version with no starter is also excellent.

The large amount of water in this dough makes it soft, sticky, and a little trickier to handle than most pizza doughs. That's why instead of kneading, which simply isn't possible with a dough this wet, I use the stretch-and-fold method shown on page 121.

The key to making a great Sicilian is the second rise that happens in the pan. You push the dough out in the pan, let it sit for half an hour until the gluten network has relaxed enough that you can push the dough all the way to the corners of the pan, and then you let it rise for another 1 1/2 to 2 hours. This entire pan-rising process is a step that can't be skipped or rushed.

I always bake my Sicilians using a two-step method. First, the dough is baked blind, that is, with no toppings. Then I let it rest for at least 30 minutes before topping it and giving it a second bake. This resting period helps seal the crust so the top and bottom stay crisp during the second bake, when the sauce, cheese, and toppings are cooking.

The parbaked crust can sit for up to 10 hours before the second bake, which makes Sicilians great for parties, entertaining, and potlucks because there's not much to do at the last minute. If you opt to go directly into the second bake after 30 minutes, leave the oven on while the pizza is resting. If you parbake your crust further ahead of time, be sure to preheat the oven for at least an hour before the second bake.

Sicilian Tips

- You'll need a 12 by 18-inch steel Sicilian pan (see page 305).

- For the pan-rising step, which needs a warm environment, I suggest setting the pan on top of the range as your oven preheats.

- Make sure your pan is well seasoned (see page 83). If you sense that your dough is sticking during the first bake, drizzle some olive oil around the edge of the pan when it comes out of the oven.

- Use pure olive oil to oil the pan before parbaking, rather than extra virgin olive oil. Extra virgin oil has a lower smoke point and can't withstand the prolonged high heat of the baking process.

- Don't be tempted to skimp on the quantity of oil used in the pan. The quantity called for in my recipes might seem like a lot, but it's critical to keep the dough from sticking and to help it brown and crisp on the bottom.

- Always remove a Sicilian pizza from the pan to slice it. You'll get much neater results than if you slice it in the pan. I cut Sicilians into a dozen slices, and I like to return them to the pan and bring it right to the table to serve. It's a great way to go when you've got a large group. If you've got a pizza stand (see page 5), that's even better.

SICILIAN

SICILIAN DOUGH WITH STARTER

MAKES 39 OUNCES (1.1 KILOGRAMS), ENOUGH FOR 1 BROOKLYN, PEPPERONI AND SAUSAGE, BURRATINA DI MARGHERITA, PURPLE POTATO AND PANCETTA, OR LA REGINA PIZZA, OR 2 LOAVES CIABATTA

3 grams (1 teaspoon) active dry yeast

90 grams (¼ cup plus 2 tablespoons) warm water (80°F to 85°F)

578 grams (4½ cups) flour with 13 to 14 percent protein, preferably All Trumps, or Pendleton Flour Mills Power

13 grams (1½ tablespoons) diastatic malt

296 grams (1¼ cups) ice water

116 grams Poolish (page 47)

13 grams (2¾ teaspoons) fine sea salt

7 grams (½ tablespoon) extra virgin olive oil

Olive oil, for coating the pan

For baker's percentages, see page 302.

Put the yeast in a small bowl, add the warm water, and whisk vigorously for 30 seconds. The yeast should dissolve in the water and the mixture should foam. If it doesn't and the yeast granules float, the yeast is "dead" and should be discarded. Begin again with a fresh amount of yeast and water.

Combine the flour and malt in the bowl of a stand mixer fitted with the dough hook.

With the mixer running on the lowest speed, pour in most of the ice water, reserving about 2 tablespoons, followed by the yeast-water mixture. Pour the reserved water into the yeast bowl, swirl it around to dislodge any bits of yeast stuck to the bowl, and add to the mixer. Mix for about 15 seconds, stop the mixer, and add the poolish.

Continue to mix the dough at the lowest speed for about 1 minute, until most of the dough comes together around the hook. Stop the mixer. Use your fingers to pull away any dough clinging to the hook, and scrape the sides and bottom of the bowl with a bowl scraper or rubber spatula.

Add the salt and mix on the lowest speed for 1 minute to combine.

Stop the mixer, pull the dough off the hook, and add the extra virgin oil. Mix the dough for 1 to 2 minutes, stopping the mixer from time to time to pull the dough off the hook and scrape down the sides of the bowl, until all of the oil is absorbed. The dough won't look completely smooth.

Coat a half sheet pan with a film of olive oil. Using the bowl scraper, scrape the dough onto the prepared pan. The dough will be extremely sticky—too sticky to knead .

Working with wet hands, stretch and fold the dough (see Stretch-and-Fold Method, page 121).

Cover the pan with a damp dish towel or plastic wrap and let the dough rest at room temperature for 20 minutes.

Use a dough cutter to loosen the dough and move it to the scale. Weigh the dough, adjusting the quantity of dough as necessary for the recipe. You will need 35 ounces (990 grams) for making any of the pizzas. If making 2 loaves Ciabatta, you will need to weigh out 19 to 20 ounces (about 550 grams) for each loaf. You may have a little extra dough.

Form the dough into a ball or balls and return the ball(s) to the oiled sheet pan (spacing them 3 inches apart if you have made 2 balls). Wrap the pan airtight with a double layer of plastic wrap, sealing the wrap well under the pan. Put the pan in a level spot in the refrigerator and refrigerate for 24 to 48 hours.

SICILIAN DOUGH WITHOUT STARTER

LARGE BATCH MAKES 35 OUNCES (990 GRAMS) DOUGH, ENOUGH FOR 1 BROOKLYN, PEPPERONI AND SAUSAGE, BURRATINA DI MARGHERITA, PURPLE POTATO AND PANCETTA, OR LA REGINA PIZZA, OR 1 FOCACCIA

SMALL BATCH MAKES 28 OUNCES (795 GRAMS), ENOUGH FOR 1 GRANDMA OR 2 QUATTRO FORNI PIZZAS

LARGE BATCH

6 grams (2 teaspoons) active dry yeast

100 grams (¼ cup plus 3 tablespoons) warm water (80°F to 85°F)

578 grams (4½ cups) flour with 13 to 14 percent protein, preferably All Trump's or Pendleton Flour Mills Power

12 grams (1 tablespoon plus 1 teaspoon) diastatic malt

305 grams (1⅓ cups) ice water

12 grams (2¼ teaspoons) fine sea salt

6 grams (½ tablespoon) extra virgin olive oil

Olive oil, for coating the pan

SMALL BATCH

5 grams (1¾ teaspoons) active dry yeast

83 grams (⅓ cup) warm water (80°F to 85°F)

462 grams (3½ cups) flour with 13 to 14 percent protein, preferably All Trump's or Pendleton Flour Mills Power

9 grams (1 tablespoon) diastatic malt

240 grams (1 cup) ice water

9 grams (2 teaspoons) fine sea salt

5 grams (1 teaspoon) extra virgin olive oil

Olive oil, for coating the pan

For baker's percentages, see page 302.

Follow the instructions for Sicilian Pizza Dough with Starter (page 118), omitting the poolish and allowing the dough to rest for 1 hour rather than 20 minutes. Using a dough cutter, lift the dough into a large bowl, press it down slightly, and rub a little water over the top. Cover with a double layer of plastic wrap and put in the refrigerator for 24 hours.

Remove the dough from the refrigerator and put it in the bowl of a stand mixer fitted with the dough hook. Mix the dough for 30 seconds on the lowest speed to degas the dough, removing any air bubbles.

Lightly oil a half sheet pan. Move the dough to the scale, weigh the dough, and adjust the quantity of dough as necessary for the recipe. You may have a little extra dough.

Form the dough into a ball or balls and refrigerate for 24 hours as directed in Sicilian Dough with Starter. If you are making Quattro Forni pizzas (page 143), store each ball on a separate quarter sheet pan, as you must invert the pan to move the dough before using.

Stretch-and-Fold Method

To stretch and fold the dough, first put it on an oiled half sheet pan or work surface.

Stretch it out slightly to form a rustic square measuring roughly 10 to 12 inches on a side. Visualizing the numbers on a clock, fold in 9:00 and 3:00 to meet in the center, pressing down on the seam to lightly to seal the dough ❶.

Repeat the folding, this time folding in 12:00 and 6:00 to meet in the center ❷.

Fold in each of the four corners to meet in the center and press the center to seal ❸.

Turn the dough over and repeat the process, folding in 2:00 and 8:00, sealing the seam, and then repeating the folding, this time folding in 10:00 and 4:00 ❹.

Fold in each of the four corners and turn the dough over. Tuck under all four sides and use the palms of your hands to shape and round the sides of the dough ❺.

PARBAKING SICILIAN DOUGH

1 (35-ounce/990-gram) ball Sicilian Dough (page 118 and 120)

¼ cup (60 grams) olive oil, plus more for drizzling

Remove the dough ball from the refrigerator and leave wrapped at room temperature until the dough warms to 50°F to 55°F. This should take 1 to 2 hours.

Pour the oil into the center of a well-seasoned 12 by 18-inch steel Sicilian pan.

The dough is very sticky, so the easiest way to remove it from the sheet pan is to hold the sheet pan upside down over the Sicilian pan and use a bowl scraper to release the dough, letting it fall into the pan. Using the bowl scraper, flip the dough over to coat both sides with the oil.

Using flat, fully extended fingers of both hands, press the dough outward in all directions, extending it toward the corners to make an even layer ❶. The dough may be stretched toward the corners. If you work gently, the dough should stretch without tearing ❷. Don't worry if the dough doesn't reach the corners. Set, uncovered, in a warm spot and let rest for 30 minutes.

After resting, the dough is ready to push outward a second time. It will not be degassed, so use a light touch to push the dough, rather than pulling it ❸, repositioning it in the pan as needed to achieve an even thickness and to reach to the corners.

Let the dough rest again (still uncovered) for 1½ to 2 hours, until it has risen almost to the rim of the pan. The timing will depend on the temperature of the room. At this point, do not touch or press on the dough again, even if it has pulled away from the edges, or it may not rise properly.

Meanwhile, set up the oven with two pizza stones or baking steels and preheat to 450°F for 1 hour (see Getting Started, page 29).

While the dough is rising, prepare the toppings for the pizza as directed in each recipe.

Keeping the pan level, gently set it on the top stone and bake for 7 minutes. Rotate the pan 180 degrees and transfer it to the bottom stone. Bake for another 7 minutes, until the top of the crust is a rich golden brown ❹.

continued

Remove the pan from the oven and use a wide metal spatula to lift a side of the crust to see if it is sticking to the pan. If it is, drizzle a little oil around the sides of the pan to help loosen it. Now run the spatula around the edges and under the entire crust to be sure it isn't sticking and has completely released from the pan.

Take the crust out of the pan and let rest on a cooling rack for at least 30 minutes or up to 2 hours (for longer storage, see note).

It is not necessary to wash the pan or add more oil to it. But if any bits of dough are stuck to the pan, remove them.

When ready to finish the pizza, if you have turned off the oven, preheat it to 450°F for 1 hour. Return the parbaked crust to the pan before topping and baking.

Note on Longer Storage of Parbaked Sicilian Dough: The parbaked crust can be held for up to 10 hours. To keep it moist, wrap it in a large plastic bag and tie securely. Clean and reoil the pan before baking.

THE BROOKLYN

MAKES ONE 12 BY 18-INCH PIZZA; 12 SQUARES

This simple, satisfying Sicilian is modeled on the style served for more than seventy years at L&B Spumoni Gardens in Bensonhurst, Brooklyn. It's topped "inverted-style," with sliced whole-milk mozzarella added first and tomato sauce on top like a traditional tomato pie, so you get that intense reduced-tomato flavor. If you want to add other toppings, like Sautéed Mushrooms (page 89) or pepperoni, keep the quantity light; you can scatter the toppings right over the sauce before baking, Bensonhurst-style.

1 parbaked Sicilian Dough (page 122)

12 ounces (340 grams) whole-milk mozzarella cheese, sliced (12 slices)

1 1/2 cups (370 grams) Sicilian Tomato Sauce (page 126), at room temperature

Olive oil, for drizzling if needed

Grated Pecorino Romano cheese, for dusting

Dried oregano, for dusting

Garlic Oil (page 29), for drizzling

If you have turned off the oven after parbaking the dough, reheat it to 450°F for at least 1 hour.

Arrange the mozzarella slices evenly over the top of the dough, leaving a 3/4-inch border on all sides. Spoon the tomato sauce onto the center of the pizza, then, using the back of the spoon in a circular motion and working outward from the center, spread the sauce evenly over the cheese.

Place the pan on the top stone and bake for 7 minutes. Rotate the pan 180 degrees, transfer it to the bottom stone, and bake for 6 minutes, until the top is a rich golden brown. Using a wide metal spatula, lift a corner of the pizza and peek at the bottom. If you want it darker and crunchier, transfer the pan to the top stone to bake for 1 to 2 minutes. Keep a watchful eye so the cheese does not overcook.

Run the spatula around the edges of the pizza to make sure it has not stuck in any area. If you suspect a problem, drizzle a bit of olive oil down the side of the pan and work slowly to loosen in that area.

Lift the pizza onto the spatula and transfer it to a cutting board. Make 2 evenly spaced cuts the length of the pizza (to make 3 strips of equal width), then make 3 evenly spaced cuts across the width of the pizza (to make 4 strips of equal width), to make 12 squares.

Finish with a dusting of pecorino and oregano and a drizzle of garlic oil.

SICILIAN TOMATO SAUCE

MAKES 3³/₄ CUPS (930 GRAMS)

Make this sauce a day ahead, or at least a few hours in advance, so the flavors come together. I like Greek oregano for what I think of as a classic East Coast flavor.

---

17 ounces (480 grams/2 cups) ground tomatoes, preferably 7/11 or DiNapoli

8 ounces (225 grams/³/₄ cup plus 3 tablespoons) tomato paste, preferably SuperDolce

1¹/₂ teaspoons (1 gram) dried oregano

1 teaspoon (3 grams) finely chopped garlic

1 teaspoon (5 grams) fine sea salt

8 ounces (225 grams/1 cup) hand-crushed tomatoes (see page 28)

1 large fresh basil leaf, torn

Combine the ground tomatoes, tomato paste, oregano, garlic, and salt in a deep bowl or other deep container and puree with an immersion blender. Stir in the crushed tomatoes and basil.

The sauce can be covered and refrigerated for up to 3 days before using.

PEPPERONI AND SAUSAGE

MAKES ONE 12 BY 18-INCH PIZZA; 12 SQUARES

When you're using only a few ingredients, they've got to be good. That's why I recommend making your own sausage and getting your hands on natural-casing pepperoni (see Sources, page 304) for this classic Sicilian. If you'd like to go more full bore, try the version known on my menus as the Fratellanza (Italian for "brotherhood," and named for the Italian social club in Emeryville that I grew up going to). It's topped, in this order, with Molinari dry salami (the traditional raffle prize at all Fratellanza Club dinners), sautéed mushrooms, pepperoni and fennel sausage and gets a sprinkling of oregano after baking.

1 parbaked Sicilian Dough (page 118 and 120)

1¼ cups (310 grams) Sicilian Tomato Sauce (page 126), at room temperature

10 ounces (285 grams) whole-milk mozzarella cheese, shredded (2½ cups)

3 ounces (85 grams) sliced pepperoni, preferably in natural casing

7 ounces (200 grams) Sweet Fennel Sausage (page 54)

Grated Pecorino Romano cheese, for dusting

Dried oregano, for dusting

Red pepper flakes, for dusting

Garlic Oil (page 29), for drizzling

If you have turned off the oven after baking the dough, reheat it to 450°F for at least 1 hour.

Spoon the tomato sauce onto the center of the dough, then, working in a circular motion outward from the center, spread the sauce evenly over the top, leaving a ³⁄4-inch border on all sides. Mound the mozzarella in the center of the pizza and use your fingertips to spread it out evenly from the center to the edge of the sauce. Arrange the pepperoni over the cheese. Pinch dime-size pieces of the sausage and distribute them evenly over the pepperoni.

Place the pan on the top stone and bake for 7 minutes. Rotate the pan 180 degrees, transfer it to the bottom stone, and bake for 6 minutes, until the top is a rich golden brown. Using a wide metal spatula, lift a corner of the pizza and peek at the bottom. If you want it darker and crunchier, transfer the pan to the top stone to bake for 1 to 2 minutes. Keep a watchful eye so the cheese does not overcook.

Run the spatula around the edges of the pizza to be certain it has not stuck in any area. If you suspect a problem, drizzle a bit of olive oil around the sides of the pan and work slowly to loosen in that area. Lift the pizza onto the spatula and transfer it to a cutting board. Make 2 evenly spaced cuts down the length of the pizza (to make 3 strips of equal width), then make 3 evenly spaced cuts across the width of the pizza (to make 4 strips of equal width), to make 12 squares.

Finish with a dusting of pecorino, oregano, and pepper flakes and a drizzle of garlic oil.

BURRATINA DI MARGHERITA

MAKES ONE 12 BY 18-INCH PIZZA; 12 SQUARES

When I entered the International Tournament of Champions in Lecce, Italy, along with Joe Carlucci, my World Pizza Champions team colleague, we got off to a rough start. We arrived in Lecce, which is way down near the tip of Puglia, the heel of the Italian boot, at 3:00 a.m. after thirty-six hours of flying, spent the rest of the night making our dough in the hotel room, and then went shopping for ingredients, dead tired, at sunrise.

Since Lecce is the epicenter of *burrata* cheese, I thought I'd work that into my Sicilian entry. *Burrata* is mozzarella that's formed into a pouch, filled with more mozzarella and cream, and then wrapped in leaves. As it sits, it comes together as a fresh, moist "super mozzarella" that's insanely rich. In Lecce, they make huge burrata balls, and they treat them like sacred works of art.

I found some beautiful ones, double wrapped in straw, in a market and brought them with me to the competition. I had planned to add it to my fully cooked pizza just before serving, but when I opened one up, it was milkier and softer than I had expected, so I wasn't sure what to do with it. You can imagine the look on the judges' faces when I plopped it into a bowl, stuck my immersion blender into it, and pulverized it into a smooth emulsion. It must have been like watching someone taking a razor blade to a Da Vinci.

But when I drizzled it over my pizza and baked it, it really worked, and I think in the end those judges were actually pretty psyched to see an American guy taking their pride and joy to a place they'd never imagined. They might also be happy to know that in the United States I don't emulsify the *burrata*. Instead, I dot it onto the pizza with a spoon, as directed here. Look for *burrata* that's not sitting in too much liquid in its package. The texture will be less runny and better for spooning. Serve this pizza right away, because the *burrata* will run a bit as it warms up.

By the way, if our big day in the Lecce sun started out rough, it ended unbelievably well. This pizza won the pan division, and we also won the classic division with a zucchini, Pugliese olive, and sun-dried tomato pie. And at one point during the day, a mysterious

continued

old man, whom I never saw again, told me I should enter the acrobatics competition, too. After years of pizza throwing, I was moving from acrobatics to pizza making and wasn't eager to go back, but the guy kept insisting. I thought it was because he figured we weren't going to win anything with our pizzas and felt sorry for us. But it turned out he sensed that I'd have a chance at sweeping three divisions. Despite my exhaustion, I let him talk me into it, and I ended up winning the first and only Triple Crown in the history of the competition.

---

1 parbaked Sicilian Dough
(page 118 and 120)

1¼ cups (310 grams) Sicilian Tomato Sauce (page 126), at room temperature

9 ounces (255 grams) whole-milk mozzarella cheese, shredded
(2¼ cups)

Olive oil, for sautéing and drizzling

12 (115 grams) cherry tomatoes, halved

Fine sea salt and freshly ground black pepper

Pinch of superfine sugar (optional)

1 (8-ounce/225-gram) ball burrata cheese, well drained, at room temperature

5 Cerignola or Pugliese olives, pitted and slivered

5 fresh basil leaves, rolled up lengthwise and cut crosswise into fine julienne

Balsamic Glaze (page 131), in a small squeeze bottle

If you have turned off the oven after parbaking the dough, reheat to 450°F for at least 1 hour.

Spoon the tomato sauce onto the center of the dough, then, using the back of the spoon in a circular motion and working outward from the center, spread the sauce evenly over the top, leaving a ¾-inch border on all sides. Spread the mozzarella out evenly over the sauce.

Place the pan on the top stone and bake for 7 minutes. Rotate the pan 180 degrees, transfer it to the bottom stone, and bake for 6 minutes, until the top is a rich golden brown. Using a wide metal spatula, lift a corner of the pizza and peek at the bottom. If you want it darker and crunchier, transfer the pan to the top stone to bake for 1 to 2 minutes. Keep a watchful eye so the cheese does not overcook.

While the pizza cooks, heat a film of oil in a small skillet over medium-high heat. Add the cherry tomatoes and a pinch each of salt and pepper and the sugar, if the tomatoes are not sweet enough. Sauté the tomatoes, tossing them constantly, for about 30 seconds, just until they have softened slightly.

Run the spatula around the edges of the pizza to make sure it has not stuck in any area. If you suspect a problem, drizzle a bit of oil down the side of the pan and work slowly to loosen in that area.

Lift the pizza onto the spatula and transfer it to a cutting board. Make 2 evenly spaced cuts the length of the pizza (to make 3 strips of equal width) and make 3 evenly spaced cuts across the width (to make 4 strips of equal width), to make 12 squares.

Distribute spoonfuls of the burrata around the pizza and top with the cherry tomatoes and olives. Sprinkle with the basil and grind some pepper on top. To finish, squeeze a zigzag of the glaze across the pizza.

BALSAMIC GLAZE

MAKES ¼ CUP (95 GRAMS)

1 cup (255 grams) balsamic vinegar

Put the vinegar in a small, heavy saucepan over medium heat. Once steam is rising from the surface, reduce the heat to the lowest setting to keep the vinegar below a simmer. No bubbles should break through the surface. If the lowest setting is still too hot, place the pan over a diffuser.

Once the vinegar has reduced by three-fourths, remove it from the heat.

The glaze can be stored in a covered container at room temperature for several months.

PURPLE POTATO AND PANCETTA

MAKES ONE 12 BY 18-INCH PIZZA; 12 SQUARES

This nontraditional Sicilian is my own creation, and it's a big seller at my takeout Slice House. The purple potatoes need to soak for a full hour to remove some of their starch, so start them soaking when you preheat the oven. They'll get a bit paler as they cook, but they still add a cool splash of color. For this pizza, I like smoked pancetta, a northern Italian specialty also known as *pancetta affumicata*. It's a bit harder to find than regular pancetta, which is cured but not smoked. Smoked pancetta is fully cooked and has a mild, sweet-smoky flavor. It doesn't crisp when it bakes on top of the pizza. Buy it sliced, like bacon, and freeze the slices for about 20 minutes to make cutting it easier. If you can't find it, substitute a good thick-cut smoked bacon.

1 parbaked Sicilian Dough
(page 118 and 120)

4 ounces (115 grams) small purple potatoes (about 3), about 1¹⁄₂ inches in diameter

3 ounces (85 grams) sliced smoked pancetta

10 ounces (285 grams) whole-milk mozzarella cheese, shredded
(2¹⁄₂ cups)

1 tablespoon (9 grams) minced garlic

Olive oil, for drizzling if needed

2-ounce (55-gram) piece feta cheese, preferably water-packed Greek

1 teaspoon (2 grams) finely chopped fresh rosemary

³⁄₄ cup (120 grams) Basil Pesto
(page 134), at room temperature

If you have turned off the oven after parbaking the dough, reheat it to 450°F for at least 1 hour.

While the oven heats, using a mandoline, cut the potatoes into paper-thin slices and drop them into a bowl of very cold salted water. Let soak for 30 minutes, drain, and repeat with a new batch of salted water. Drain again and dry on paper towels.

Meanwhile, cut the pancetta into lardons (matchsticks) about 1 inch long and ¹⁄₈ inch wide and thick. Don't worry about cutting them perfectly; a bit of irregularity is more appealing. Heat a small skillet over medium-high heat. Add the pancetta, lower the heat to medium, and cook, stirring often, for about 2 minutes, until most of the fat is rendered and the pancetta is partially cooked. Set aside without draining.

Mound the mozzarella in the center of the dough and use your fingertips to spread it evenly over the top, leaving a ³⁄₄-inch border on all sides. Scatter the garlic over the cheese. Arrange the potatoes in a single layer across the top, and distribute the pancetta over the potatoes.

Place the pan on the top stone and bake for 8 minutes. Rotate the pan 180 degrees, transfer it to the bottom stone, and bake for 5 minutes. Taste a potato slice. If it isn't tender, return the pizza to the top stone to bake for 1 minute, until the potatoes are tender. Using a wide metal spatula,

continued

lift a corner of the pizza and peek at the bottom. If you want it darker and crunchier, transfer the pan to the top stone to bake for 1 to 2 minutes.

Run the spatula around the edges of the pizza to make sure it has not stuck in any area. If you suspect a problem, drizzle a bit of olive oil down the side of the pan and work slowly to loosen in that area.

Lift the pizza onto the spatula and transfer it to a cutting board. Make 2 evenly spaced cuts the length of the pizza (to make 3 strips of equal width) and make 3 evenly spaced cuts across the width of the pizza (to make 4 strips of equal width), to make 12 squares.

Hold the piece of feta over the pizza and crumble it evenly over the top. Finish with a sprinkling of the rosemary and serve with the pesto in a bowl on the side.

BASIL PESTO

MAKES 2¼ CUPS (355 GRAMS)

8 cups (140 grams) lightly packed fresh basil leaves

6 cloves (18 grams) garlic

¼ cup (30 grams) pine nuts, lightly toasted and cooled

1¼ cups (280 grams) olive oil, plus more if needed

1 cup (80 grams) grated Parmesan cheese

2 teaspoons (14 grams) agave syrup

2 teaspoons (10 grams) freshly squeezed lemon juice

¼ teaspoon (1.5 grams) fine sea salt

¼ teaspoon (.5 grams) freshly ground black pepper

Put half of the basil in a blender. Add the garlic, pine nuts, and oil and blend to combine. Scrape down the sides of the jug. Add the remaining basil along with the cheese, agave syrup, lemon juice, salt, and pepper and blend until smooth, stopping and scraping down the sides as necessary.

Pour the pesto into a bowl. If you would like a thinner pesto, mix in additional oil.

Use the pesto immediately, or cover and refrigerate for up to 2 days.

LA REGINA

MAKES ONE 12 BY 18-INCH PIZZA; 12 SQUARES

One of my head *pizzaiolos*, Laura Meyer, has lived and studied in Italy and speaks Italian fluently. So when the world championships in Parma, Italy, rolled around, she was excited to give it a shot. We flew over together and planned her entry in the *pizza in teglia* ("pan pizza," or what we would call Sicilian) division. I advised her not to go too off the wall—Italians don't love that, especially from Americans—but to add a little twist that would be just creative enough.

Laura settled on a classic pizza alla diavola, which is made with whole-milk mozzarella, tomato sauce, and slices of the spicy oblong salami known as *soppressata piccante*. Her clever addition was a scattering of arugula on top of the finished pizza. Tasting the mildness of the Italian mozzarella, she decided to blend in a bit of *provola* for extra flavor. And because we were in Parma, she finished her creation with shavings of Parmigiano-Reggiano, and some Piave for good measure.

I was so proud watching her compete entirely in Italian, her image splashed up on a giant screen. When they announced the final results, Laura heard the word *vincitrice*— the feminine form of "winner," and, being the only woman in the finals, she knew she'd won before she even heard her name. In addition to a title she will hold all her life, she won a pizza oven, a magnum of Prosecco, and a five-kilo block of Parmesan cheese, which she hand-carried all the way back home. We added the pizza to our menu, and I asked Laura to give it a name. "Now that I've been crowned," she said, without missing a beat, "how about *La Regina*, Italian for 'queen'?"

In 2014, Laura won a second world championship at Pizza Expo in Las Vegas with her rosemary-infused "La Bella Rosa" pizza.

continued

1 parbaked Sicilian Dough
(page 118 and 120)

1¹/4 cups (310 grams) Sicilian Tomato
Sauce (page 126), at room temperature

6 ounces (170 grams) whole-milk
mozzarella cheese, shredded
(1¹/2 cups)

4 ounces (115 grams) provolone
cheese, shredded (1 cup)

12 large slices (2 ounces/55 grams)
soppressata piccante

Olive oil, for drizzling if needed

Large handful of arugula leaves

12 thin slices (6 ounces/170 grams)
prosciutto

Small piece Piave cheese, cold,
for shaving

Small piece Parmigiano-Reggiano
cheese, cold, for shaving

Extra virgin olive oil, for drizzling

If you have turned off the oven after parbaking the dough, reheat to 450°F for at least 1 hour.

Spoon the tomato sauce onto the center of the dough, then, using the back of the spoon in a circular motion and working outward from the center, spread the sauce evenly over the top, leaving a ³/4-inch border on all sides. Mound the mozzarella and provolone in the center of the pizza and use your fingertips to spread them out evenly over the sauce. Arrange the soppressata over the cheese, placing 4 slices lengthwise and 3 slices across, so that once the pizza is cut, each piece will have a slice.

Place the pan on the top stone and bake for 7 minutes. Rotate the pan 180 degrees, transfer it to the bottom stone, and bake for 6 minutes, until the top of the crust is a rich golden brown. Using a wide metal spatula, lift a corner of the pizza and peek at the bottom. If you want it darker and crunchier, transfer the pan to the top stone to bake for 1 to 2 minutes. Keep a watchful eye so the cheese does not overcook.

Run the spatula around the edges of the pizza to make sure it has not stuck in any area. If you suspect a problem, drizzle a bit of olive oil down the side of the pan and work slowly to loosen in that area.

Lift the pizza on the spatula and transfer it to a cutting board. Make 2 evenly spaced cuts the length of the pizza (to make 3 strips of equal width), then make 3 evenly spaced cuts across the width of the pizza (to make 4 strips of equal width), to make 12 squares.

Scatter the arugula over the top and drape a slice of prosciutto over each piece. Garnish with shavings of Piave and Parmigiano-Reggiano and finish with a drizzle of extra virgin olive oil.

SICILIAN

GRANDMA

MAKES ONE 12 BY 18-INCH PIZZA; 12 SQUARES

SICILIAN

Unlike all of the other pizzas in this chapter, this simple home-style Sicilian doesn't include the parbaking step. Like those other pizzas, you let the dough rise in the pan, but then you just top it and bake it. It also calls for a smaller amount of dough—28 ounces versus 35 ounces—made without a starter. The result is a thinner, crispier crust—and a homey pizza that's light on the toppings and tastes like something your grandma would make, if your grandma was Italian and lived on Long Island. That's where pizzerias like Prince Umberto's and Gigante's started putting this style on the menu under the name Grandma.

Tradition calls for topping this pizza simply, with mozzarella, crushed tomatoes, and a little garlic and oregano. You can use either fresh mozzarella (*fior di latte*) or, even better, Homemade Mozzarella (page 190), which tends to exude less liquid during baking. Or just use shredded whole-milk mozzarella.

I've provided directions on how to make a 28-ounce Sicilian dough ball. But if you want a little extra treat, make a standard 35-ounce ball without starter and trim off 7 ounces to make some Garlic Knots (page 283), or Bacon Twists (page 284). That's what Grandma would want you to do.

---

1 (28-ounce/795-gram) ball Sicilian Dough without Starter (page 120)

¼ cup (60 grams) olive oil

1¼ cups (285 grams) hand-crushed tomatoes (see page 28) or Early Girl Tomato Sauce (page 141)

1 teaspoon (3 grams) finely chopped garlic

Dried oregano, for seasoning and sprinkling

Remove the dough ball from the refrigerator and leave wrapped at room temperature until the dough warms to 60°F to 65°F. Meanwhile, set up the oven with two pizza stones or baking steels and preheat to 500°F for 1 hour (see Getting Started, page 129).

Pour the olive oil in the center of a 12 by 18-inch well-seasoned steel Sicilian pan.

The dough is very sticky, so the easiest way to remove it from the sheet pan is to hold the sheet pan upside down over the Sicilian pan and use a bowl scraper to release the dough, letting it fall into the prepared pan. Using the bowl scraper, flip the dough over to coat both sides with the oil.

Refer to the photographs (on page 123) for pushing out the dough, keeping in mind that this is less dough than what's used in the photographs.

continued

Fine sea salt and freshly ground black pepper

8 ounces (225 grams) fresh whole-milk mozzarella cheese, homemade (page 190) or store-bought fior di latte, or 10 ounces (285 grams) whole-milk mozzarella cheese, shredded (2½ cups)

Extra virgin olive oil, for drizzling

Grated Pecorino Romano cheese, for dusting

Garlic Oil (page 29), for drizzling

Using flat, fully extended fingers of both hands, press the dough outward in all directions, extending it toward the corners to make an even layer ❶. The dough may be stretched toward the corners. If you work gently, the dough should stretch without tearing ❷. Don't worry if the dough does not reach the corners. Set, uncovered, in a warm spot and let rest for 30 minutes.

After resting, the dough is ready to push outward a second time. It will not be degassed, so use a light touch to push the dough, rather than pulling it ❸, repositioning it in the pan as needed to achieve an even thickness and to reach the corners.

Let the dough rest again (still uncovered) for about 1 hour, until the dough has risen but has not quite doubled. The timing will depend on the temperature of the room. At this point, do not touch or press on the dough again, even if it has pulled away from the edges, or it may not rise properly.

In a bowl, toss the crushed tomatoes with the garlic and a pinch each of oregano, salt, and pepper.

If you're using fresh mozzarella, tear it into 16 irregular chunks and arrange them on the pizza. Sprinkle the cheese lightly with salt. If you're using shredded mozzarella, mound it in the center of the dough and use your fingertips to spread it out evenly over the surface, leaving a ¾-inch border.

Spoon the tomatoes evenly on top of the cheese (you will not cover the entire surface) and drizzle with extra virgin oil.

Place the pan on the top stone and bake for 8 minutes. Rotate the pan 180 degrees, transfer it to the bottom stone, and bake for 7 minutes, until the cheese has melted and the bottom is richly browned and crisp (use a wide metal spatula and lift a corner to check). If liquid has leached from the fresh cheese, transfer the pizza to the top stone for 1 minute to evaporate some of the moisture.

Run the spatula around the edges of the pizza to make sure it has not stuck in any area. If you suspect a problem, drizzle a bit of olive oil down the side of the pan and work slowly to loosen in that area.

Lift the pizza onto the spatula and transfer it to a cutting board. Make 2 evenly spaced cuts the length of the pizza (to make 3 strips of equal width), then make 3 evenly spaced cuts across the width of the pizza (to make 4 strips of equal width), to make 12 squares.

Finish with a dusting of Pecorino and oregano and a drizzle of garlic oil.

EARLY GIRL TOMATO SAUCE

MAKES 1½ TO 2½ CUPS (340 TO 570 GRAMS)

When Early Girls are in season in the late summer and fall, hunt them down and make this sweet, rich sauce. If you drain most of the liquid, you can use it in place of crushed tomatoes to top pizzas like the Grandma (page 139). If you want a looser sauce for pasta and other dishes, don't drain it.

4 pounds (1.8 kilograms) ripe Early Girl tomatoes, stems removed

¼ cup (60 grams) extra virgin olive oil

Pinch of fine sea salt

Pinch of superfine sugar, plus more as needed

2 sprigs rosemary

5 cloves garlic

Position a rack in the top third of the oven and preheat the oven to 500°F. Line a half sheet pan with parchment paper.

Put the tomatoes in a large metal bowl. Drizzle with the oil, then toss to coat the tomatoes evenly. Spread the tomatoes in a single layer on the prepared sheet pan and place in the oven. Set the bowl aside, unwashed.

Roast the tomatoes for about 30 minutes, until the skins are cracked, slightly charred, and pulling away from the flesh.

Return the tomatoes to the bowl and sprinkle with the salt and sugar to taste. Nestle the rosemary sprigs and garlic in the tomatoes and cover the bowl tightly with plastic wrap. Let the tomatoes rest at room temperature for 30 minutes to cool down and infuse the flavors.

Remove the plastic wrap and discard the garlic and rosemary. Set a strainer over another bowl. Working over a third bowl, lift a tomato, pull away the skin, and discard the skin in the bowl. Open the tomato and drop any seeds or tough sections into the bowl. Crush the cleaned tomato in your hands, dropping the pieces into the strainer. Repeat with the rest of the tomatoes.

With your hand or a spoon, lightly stir the tomatoes in a circular motion to remove as much liquid as you like. If you will be using the tomatoes on the Grandma pizza (page 139), drain most of the liquid to give you about 1¼ cups (285 grams) crushed tomatoes. If you will be using it as a sauce for pizza, leave more liquid, but be sure the sauce has enough body to be spooned onto a pizza without the liquid running. It can be kept even looser if it will be tossed with pasta.

The sauce can be refrigerated in an airtight container for up to 3 days before using.

QUATTRO FORNI

MAKES ONE 8-INCH SQUARE PIZZA; 4 SQUARES

Once you've mastered Sicilian pizza, I suggest you give this one a try. It's essentially a Sicilian with an added step. If you love that crunchy, buttery quality of a Sicilian crust, just imagine what deep-frying could add to the equation.

Quattro forni means "four ovens" in Italian, and the idea of a *tre forni* pizza, baked in three different ovens, has been floating around Italy for a while. But I'm pretty sure no one else has upped the ante to four yet.

I got serious about the idea of cooking a pizza in more than one oven when I entered the International Pizza Challenge in Las Vegas in 2012. The final round of the Best of the Best competition was a blind box challenge, in which you got a box of surprise ingredients. I wanted to have an ace in the hole—something that would set my pizza apart regardless of what the ingredients in the box turned out to be. So I decided to cook my pizza in three of the ovens they had made available to us: gas to start, then electric to crisp the crust, and finally wood fired to add that distinctive smoke-char flavor. The judges totally got it, and I ended up nosing out Italy, Canada, and Australia to win first place.

When I opened Capo's, I wanted to work this idea in, to take full advantage of our multiple ovens, and I experimented with adding a fourth step in the cooking process: deep-frying. Okay, it's not technically an oven, but I called the pizza Quattro Forni, and it acquired cult status almost overnight—partly because, owing to the complexity of the process, we only make twenty a day, so snagging one is kind of an insider thing.

This recipe re-creates the Capo's Quattro Forni for a home kitchen. Ideally, you need two ovens: one gas or electric and one wood fired. You'll also need to set up a pot of oil on the stove top with a deep-frying thermometer. If you don't have a wood-fired oven, don't let that stop you. Just skip the final charring step and call your pizza a Tre Forni. You won't get the full effect, but either way, you'll have a mile-high, sensationally crispy-soft pizza with that mysteriously awesome doughnutty flavor that only fried dough can give you.

continued

I like the simple finish of prosciutto in this recipe. But I also encourage you to try other toppings. Some favorites at Capo's—added after the pizza is fully cooked and sliced—include arugula, *soppressata piccante*, Calabrese peppers, shaved Parmigiano-Reggiano, and Hot Pepper Oil (page 223).

1 (14-ounce/400-gram) ball Sicilian Dough Without Starter (page 120)

2 tablespoons (30 grams) olive oil

Canola oil, for deep-frying

4 ounces (115 grams) whole-milk mozzarella cheese, sliced (4 slices)

Generous 1/2 cup (140 grams) Sicilian Tomato Sauce (page 126)

1/2 teaspoon (11/2 grams) finely chopped garlic

Grated Pecorino Romano cheese, for dusting

Dried oregano, for dusting

Garlic Oil (page 29), for drizzling

4 thin slices (2 ounces/55 grams) prosciutto (optional)

Prepare your fire in the wood oven (see Building a Fire, page 195).

Remove the dough ball from the refrigerator and leave wrapped at room temperature until the dough warms to 60°F to 65°F. Meanwhile, set up the oven with two pizza stones or baking steels and preheat to 500°F for 1 hour (see Getting Started, page 29).

Pour the olive oil in the center of an 8-inch square steel pan.

The dough is very sticky, so the easiest way to remove it from the sheet pan is to hold the sheet pan upside down over the prepared steel pan and use a bowl scraper to release the dough, letting it fall into the pan. Using the bowl scraper, flip the dough over to coat both sides with the oil.

Refer to the photographs (on page 123) for pushing out the dough, keeping in mind that this is less dough than what's used in the photographs.

Using flat, fully extended fingers of both hands, press the dough outward in all directions, extending it toward the corners to make an even layer ❶. The dough may be stretched toward the corners. If you work gently, the dough should stretch without tearing ❷. Don't worry if the dough does not reach the corners. Set, uncovered, in a warm spot and let rest for 30 minutes.

After resting, the dough is ready to push outward a second time. It will not be degassed, so use a light touch to push the dough, rather than pulling it ❸, repositioning it in the pan as needed to achieve an even thickness and to reach to the corners.

Let the dough rest again (still uncovered) for about 1 hour, until the dough has risen almost to the rim of the pan. The timing will depend on the temperature of the room. At this point, do not touch or press on the dough again, even if it has pulled away from the edges, or it may not rise properly.

When you are ready to bake the pizza, pour canola oil to a depth of 2 inches into a wide, deep pot (at least 10 inches wide and 6 inches deep) and heat to 350°F, regulating the heat as needed to maintain the temperature. Set a cooling rack over a half sheet pan and put the pan next to the stove.

Place the pan with the dough on the bottom stone and bake for 7 minutes. The top should be golden brown and the bottom a richer brown (to check the bottom, lift a corner with a metal spatula). Remove the pan from the oven, turn the pizza over (still in the pan), and let rest for 2 minutes to flatten the top.

Carefully transfer the crust, top side down, to the hot oil and fry for 2½ to 3 minutes, until browned on the underside. Using a pair of tongs, turn the pizza over and fry for about 2½ minutes longer, until browned on the second side. Using the tongs, transfer the pizza to the cooling rack.

Arrange the mozzarella slices evenly over the top of the pizza, leaving a ½-inch border on all sides. Spoon the tomato sauce onto the center of the pizza, then, using the back of the spoon in a circular motion and working outward from the center, spread the sauce evenly over the cheese. Sprinkle with the garlic.

Using a peel, set the pizza on the top stone for about 2 minutes, to melt the cheese.

Lift the pizza with a long-handled metal peel and bring to the wood-burning oven. Hold the peel toward the fire, starting about 10 inches from the flame to crisp one edge of the pizza; how far away you hold your peel will depend on the intensity of the fire, then rotate the pizza on the peel to crisp all the edges, about 30 seconds total (see photo ❸ Doming the Pizza, page 199).

Transfer the pizza to a cutting board. Cut into 4 squares.

Finish with a dusting of pecorino and oregano and a drizzle of garlic oil. Drape a slice of prosciutto over each square.

California Style

As a lifelong food guy, I feel like I was born in the right place at the right time: a farm in Northern California in the 1970s. In my life, and my career, I've seen the whole American food revolution unfold—from fruit stands to farmers' markets and from locally sourced ingredients to the "discovery" of Mediterranean, Latin, and Asian flavors. And I'm proud to be a native son of the state where it all began.

In that spirit, I love creating completely original pizzas, with fresh ingredients, unconventional techniques, organic and ancient-grain flours, and surprising flavor combinations. When it came time to group them together on my menu, I realized there's no name for this pizza category. So I settled on two simple words that seem to sum up the whole confident, inventive spirit of the West: California Style.

CAL-ITALIA

MAKES ONE 13-INCH PIZZA; 6 SLICES

In 2006, I packed up my gear and traveled to the Mall of America for the Food Network Pizza Champions Challenge. Over the course of a very grueling day, we competed for three Guinness World Records in front of a big audience and a panel of famous judges. I won two of the world-record rounds: Biggest Pizza Continuously Spinning for Two Minutes, and Most Consecutive Rolls Across the Shoulders in 30 Seconds.

By comparison, round three, the cooking challenge, felt as easy as pie. Four of us gathered at our stations to get our marching orders: create a gourmet pizza in ten minutes using none of the top ten toppings—no pepperoni, no sausage, you get the idea. So, my instinct was to combine two of my favorite pizza worlds, California and Italy. I grabbed five totally traditional Italian ingredients: prosciutto, fig jam, Gorgonzola, Asiago, and balsamic vinegar. They're classic, but the thing is, you'd never find them on a pizza in Italy, at least not all together. But to us "why not?" Californians, the combination makes perfect sense as a pizza topping, and it made sense to the judges, too.

1 (13-ounce/370-gram) ball Master Dough, preferably with starter (page 44), made with Poolish

3 parts flour mixed with 1 part semolina, for dusting

2-ounce (55-gram) piece Asiago cheese, cold, for shaving

6 ounces (170 grams) whole-milk mozzarella cheese, shredded (1½ cups)

1½ ounces (45 grams) Gorgonzola cheese, broken into small pieces

Remove the dough ball from the refrigerator and leave wrapped at room temperature until the dough warms to 60°F to 65°F. Meanwhile, set up the oven with two pizza stones or baking steels and preheat to 500°F for 1 hour (see Getting Started, page 29).

Dust the work surface with the dusting mixture, then move the dough to the surface and dust the top (see Transferring the Dough to the Work Surface, page 30).

Sprinkle a wooden peel with the dusting mixture.

Open the dough on the work surface to a 13-inch round with a slightly raised edge (see Opening and Stretching the Dough pages 31–33).

Move the dough to the peel. As you work, shake the peel forward and backward to ensure the dough isn't sticking.

continued

CALIFORNIA STYLE

2 to 3 tablespoons (40-60 grams) fig jam, preferably Dalmatia brand

3 ounces (85 grams) thinly sliced prosciutto (about 6 slices)

Balsamic Glaze (page 131), in a small squeeze bottle

Using a vegetable peeler, shave the Asiago over the surface of the dough, leaving a 3/4-inch border. Mound the mozzarella in the center of the pizza and use your fingertips to spread it out evenly over the Asiago.

Slide the pizza onto the top stone (see Moving the Dough to the Oven, page 34).

Bake for 7 minutes. Lift the pizza onto the peel and distribute the Gorgonzola pieces evenly over the top. Rotate the pizza 180 degrees, transfer it to the bottom stone, and bake for 3 to 4 minutes, until the bottom is browned and crisp and the top is golden brown.

Transfer the pizza to a cutting board and cut into 6 wedges. Spoon small dollops of fig jam (about 1/4 teaspoon each) around the pizza. Tear the prosciutto slices lengthwise into 2 or 3 strips and drape the pieces over the pizza slices. To finish, squeeze a thin spiral of balsamic glaze onto the pizza.

Stone-Ground: What's Old is New Again

Like cold-pressed olive oil, stone-ground flour is an ancient tradition that's making a comeback as a high-quality "slow food" alternative. Grinding grains between stones, as opposed to the steel rollers used in most high-volume mills, is a gentler process that generates less heat, preserving more of the grain's nutrients, flavor, and natural sweetness. And because it's less finely milled, stone-ground flour has a lower simple-sugar content and a lower glycemic index than conventionally milled flour. A stone-ground renaissance is already going strong in Italy, where chefs like Simone Padoan are turning out fantastic pizzas and breads using their own stone-ground flours and blends. It's a trend we're going to be seeing more of in the U.S., and I encourage you to check out the stone-ground flours that are now sold at specialty grocery stores. I like Mulino Marino (see page 15) brand; their 0 flour is great for starters, which can be blended into doughs made with their 00 flour. For professionals, I recommend using the autolyse method (page 9) with high hydration for these and other stone-ground flours.

MULTIGRAIN DOUGH

MAKES 28 OUNCES (795 GRAMS) DOUGH

This dough is made with white flour, whole wheat flour, and a hint of rye in the poolish starter. That combination gives it a slightly nutty flavor that works particularly well with sweet-savory topping combos.

2.5 grams (1 teaspoon) active dry yeast

75 grams (1/4 cup plus 1 tablespoon) warm water (80°F to 85°F)

408 grams (3 cups) flour with 12 to 13 percent protein, preferably Harvest King or Central Milling Organic High Mountain Hi-Protein

45 grams (1/4 cup plus 1 tablespoon) whole wheat flour, preferably Central Milling Organic Whole Wheat Medium

9 grams (1 tablespoon) diastatic malt

23 grams Rye Poolish (page 152)

225 grams (3/4 cup plus 3 tablespoons) ice water

14 grams (1 tablespoon) fine sea salt

5 grams (1 teaspoon) extra virgin olive oil

For baker's percentages, see page 302.

Put the yeast in a small bowl, add the warm water, and whisk vigorously for 30 seconds. The yeast should dissolve in the water and the mixture should foam. If it doesn't and the yeast granules float, the yeast is "dead" and should be discarded. Begin again with a fresh amount of yeast and water.

Combine both flours and the malt in the bowl of a stand mixer fitted with the dough hook. With the mixer running on the lowest speed, pour in most of the ice water, reserving about 2 tablespoons, followed by the yeast-water mixture. Pour the reserved water into the yeast bowl, swirl it around to dislodge any bits of yeast stuck to the bowl, and add it to the mixer. Mix for about 15 seconds, stop the mixer, and add the poolish.

Continue to mix the dough at the lowest speed for about 1 minute, until most of the dough comes together around the hook. Stop the mixer. Use your fingers to pull away any dough clinging to the hook, and scrape the sides and bottom of the bowl with a bowl scraper or rubber spatula.

Add the salt and mix on the lowest speed for 1 minute to combine. Check the bottom of the bowl for any unincorporated flour. Turn the dough over and press it into the bottom of the bowl to pick up any stray pieces. If there is still unincorporated flour, add a small amount of water (about 1/2 teaspoon to start) and mix until the dough is no longer dry and holds together.

Stop the mixer, pull the dough off the hook, and add the oil. Mix the dough for 1 to 2 minutes, stopping the mixer from time to time to pull the dough off the hook and scrape down the sides of the bowl, until all the oil is absorbed. The dough won't look completely smooth.

continued

Use the bowl scraper to transfer the dough to an unfloured work surface. The dough is sticky, so dust with just enough flour to allow you to knead it, then knead for 2 to 3 minutes, until smooth (see Kneading the Dough, page 24). Cover the dough with a damp dish towel and let rest at room temperature for 20 minutes.

Use a dough cutter to loosen the dough and to cut it into halves or thirds (depending on the weight called for in each recipe). Weigh each piece, adjusting the quantity of dough as necessary. You may have a little extra dough.

Form the dough into balls (see Balling the Dough, page 26). Set the balls on a half sheet pan, spacing them about 3 inches apart. Or, if you will be baking the balls on different days, place each ball on a quarter sheet pan. Wrap the pan(s) airtight with a double layer of plastic wrap, sealing the wrap well under the sheet pan(s). Put the pan(s) in a level spot in the refrigerator and refrigerate for 24 to 48 hours.

RYE POOLISH

MAKES 90 GRAMS

0.12 gram (one-third of 1/8 teaspoon) active dry yeast

47 grams (3 tablespoons plus 1 teaspoon) cold water

47 grams (about 1/3 cup) dark rye flour, preferably Central Milling Organic Dark Rye

Put the yeast in a small bowl, add the water, and whisk vigorously for 30 seconds. The mixture should bubble on top. If it doesn't and the yeast granules float, the yeast is "dead" and should be discarded. Begin again with a fresh amount of yeast and water.

Add the flour and stir well with a rubber spatula to combine. The consistency should resemble a thick pancake batter.

Scrape down the sides of the bowl, cover the bowl with plastic wrap, and let sit at room temperature for 18 hours. Refrigerate for 30 minutes to cool slightly.

If you are not using the starter right away, you can store it in the refrigerator, though I suggest keeping it for not more than 8 hours. Bring to cool room temperature before using.

HONEY PIE

MAKES ONE 13-INCH PIZZA; 6 SLICES

Up on the roof of Tony's Pizza Napoletana, we have two beehives, which we harvest three times a year. The honey is light gold and perfect for drizzling on food as a garnish, so I came up with this pizza to showcase it. It's a simple multigrain "white pie" that's all about the finishes: crispy beer-battered caramelized onions, Calabrese peppers, shaved provolone, fresh chiles, chives, and, of course, a generous drizzle of honey. Honey on pizza might sound a bit strange to you, but over the years, I've really come to appreciate the balance of sweet, savory, hot, sour, and bitter, and I use honey all the time to bring out other flavors, especially spicy ones.

1 (13-ounce/370-gram) ball
Multigrain Dough (page 151)

3 parts flour mixed with 1 part
semolina, for dusting

1 large white onion

Olive oil, for caramelizing the onion

Fine sea salt

Canola oil, for deep–frying

1/4 cup beer, plus more if needed

4 1/2 tablespoons (35 grams)
all-purpose flour, plus more if needed

Freshly ground black pepper

7 ounces (200 grams) whole-milk
mozzarella cheese, shredded
(1 3/4 cups)

1 teaspoon (5 grams) crushed
Calabrese peppers

2 tablespoons (42 grams) honey,
or to taste

Remove the dough ball from the refrigerator and leave wrapped at room temperature until the dough warms to 60°F to 65°F. Meanwhile, set up the oven with two pizza stones or baking steels and preheat to 500°F for 1 hour (see Getting Started, page 29).

Cut the onion in half through the root end. Put the onion halves cut side down on a cutting board and cut off and discard both ends on each half. Take a look at the vertical lines on the outside of an onion half. Hold a sharp knife (at an angle) to match the first line and cut through it. Continue to cut the onion along the lines, changing the angle of the knife about every 1/2 inch to match the location of the next line. You will have crescent-shaped slivers of onion. Cutting the onion this way allows it to soften more evenly than when cut crosswise. Repeat with the remaining onion half.

Heat a film of olive oil in a skillet over medium-high heat. Add the onion, season with salt, and cook, stirring often, for about 4 minutes, until softened. Lower the heat to medium and continue to cook and caramelize the onion for 3 to 4 minutes, until a rich golden brown. Transfer the onion to a strainer to drain, then drain briefly on paper towels.

About 30 minutes before you are ready to bake the pizza, pour canola oil to a depth of 2 inches into a wide, deep pot (at least 10 inches wide and 6 inches deep) and heat to 350°F. Set a cooling rack over a quarter sheet pan and put the pan next to the stove in a warm spot.

continued

2 tablespoons (14 grams) thinly sliced serrano chiles (with seeds)

Small piece provolone cheese, cold, for shaving

1 tablespoon (4 grams) minced fresh chives

In a bowl, whisk together the beer and flour until well combined. It should have the consistency of a thin pancake batter.

Fry a few pieces of onion to check the coating. If the coating is too thick, whisk in more beer. If it is too thin, whisk in more flour. Add some of the onion pieces (do not overcrowd the pot) to the hot oil and fry, stirring them from time to time and adjusting the heat as necessary to maintain the temperature, for about 3 minutes, until crisp and evenly browned. Using a wire skimmer, transfer the onion pieces to the rack to drain and season immediately with salt and pepper. Repeat with the remaining onion pieces.

Dust the work surface with the dusting mixture, then move the dough to the surface and dust the top (see Transferring the Dough to the Work Surface, page 30).

Sprinkle a wooden peel with the dusting mixture. Open the dough on the work surface to a 13-inch round with a slightly raised edge (see Opening and Stretching the Dough, page 33).

Move the dough to the peel. As you work, shake the peel forward and backward to ensure the dough isn't sticking.

Mound the mozzarella in the center of the dough and use your fingertips to spread it out evenly from the center, leaving a 3/4-inch border.

Slide the pizza onto the top stone (see Moving the Dough to the Oven, page 34). Bake for 6 minutes. Lift the pizza onto the peel, rotate it 180 degrees, and then transfer it to the bottom stone. Bake for 4 to 5 minutes, until the bottom is browned and crisp and the top is golden brown.

Transfer the pizza to a cutting board and cut into 6 wedges. Divide the Calabrese peppers evenly among the slices and spread them with the back of a spoon. Drizzle about 1 tablespoon of the honey evenly over the pizza, then sprinkle with half of the serrano chiles. Scatter the fried onions evenly over the top, then, using a vegetable peeler, garnish with shavings of provolone. Drizzle the remaining 1 tablespoon honey (or more, if you like) over the pizza and sprinkle with the remaining serrano chiles and with the chives.

EDDIE MUENSTER

MAKES ONE 13-INCH PIZZA; 6 SLICES

I've always liked the mild flavor and creamy melt of Muenster, which seldom turns up on pizzeria menus, so I decided to feature it on its own pizza. To offset the soft cheese, I came up with an unusual baking technique: the dough is baked blind, in the style of flatbread, then it is flipped, pressed down, baked bottom side up, and finally topped and baked again. What this method gives you is a thin-crust pizza that is more pliable than most. And that result, which I really like, inspired me to add back a bit of crunch in another way: by topping the finished pizza with homemade kale chips. I rounded out the flavors with bacon, a drizzle of our rooftop honey, spicy Calabrese peppers, and a squeeze of fresh lemon juice. Then all it needed was a name. The Muenster took care of that.

CALIFORNIA STYLE

1 (13-ounce/370-gram) ball Master Dough, preferably with starter (page 44), made with Poolish

3 parts flour mixed with 1 part semolina, for dusting

1½ strips (2 ounces/55 grams) bacon, cut crosswise into ½-inch pieces

3 large leaves (50 grams) Tuscan kale (cavolo nero)

Canola oil, for deep-frying

Fine sea salt

6 ounces (170 grams) Muenster cheese, thinly sliced (9 slices)

1½ teaspoons (7 grams) crushed Calabrese peppers, or to taste

1 teaspoon (7 grams) honey, or to taste

1 lemon wedge

Remove the dough ball from the refrigerator and leave wrapped at room temperature until the dough warms to 60°F to 65°F. Meanwhile, set up the oven with two pizza stones or baking steels and preheat to 500°F for 1 hour (see Getting Started, page 29).

Heat a small skillet over medium-high heat and add the bacon. Lower the heat to medium and cook the bacon, stirring often, for about 1½ minutes, until most of the fat is rendered and the bacon is partially cooked. Set the bacon aside without draining it.

Cut the large ribs from the kale leaves and discard them. Rinse the kale and dry thoroughly. Cut the kale into 1-inch pieces. You'll need 1 cup (35 grams) for the pizza.

About 30 minutes before you are ready to bake the pizza, pour canola oil to a depth of 2 inches into a wide, deep pot (at least 10 inches wide and 6 inches deep) and heat to 350°F. Set a cooling rack over a quarter sheet pan and put the pan next to the stove in a warm spot.

No matter how well you have dried the kale, the oil will splatter as the kale fries, so have a splatter screen or lid in one hand as you drop the kale into the hot oil with the other. Cover the pot immediately. Adjust the heat as necessary to maintain the temperature. When the major popping

continued

sounds subside, remove the screen and continue frying for 2 to 3 minutes, until the oil has stopped bubbling. (That will let you know the moisture has evaporated and the kale is crisp.) Using a wire skimmer, transfer the kale to the rack to drain and season immediately with salt.

Dust the work surface with the dusting mixture, then move the dough to the surface and dust the top (see Transferring the Dough to the Work Surface, page 30).

Sprinkle a wooden peel with the dusting mixture.

Following the instructions in Rolling Pizza Dough (see page 103), roll out the dough into a round 15 inches in diameter. Using a pizza wheel, trim the dough to a 13-inch round, flatten the dough, then dock the surface of the dough.

Move the dough to the peel. As you work, shake the peel forward and backward to ensure the dough isn't sticking.

Slide the pizza onto the top stone (see Moving the Dough to the Oven, page 34). Bake for 2 minutes. Lift the pizza onto the peel (it will be set but not colored), turn it over, and, using a large, wide metal spatula, press it down to flatten any bubbles. Rotate the round 180 degrees, and then transfer to the bottom stone. Bake for 1 minute.

Remove the pizza round from the oven and place on a cutting board (or work directly on the peel if there is room to set it on the work surface). Arrange the cheese slices over the top, leaving a 3/4-inch border, then scatter the bacon over the cheese.

Lift the pizza with the peel (if on a cutting board), slide it onto the top stone, and bake for 2 minutes. Lift the pizza back onto the peel, rotate it 180 degrees, and then transfer to the bottom stone. Bake for 2 minutes, until the bottom is browned and crisp and the top is golden brown.

Transfer the pizza to a cutting board and cut into 6 wedges. Divide the Calabrese peppers evenly among the slices and spread them with the back of a spoon. Scatter the kale over the top and finish with a drizzle of honey.

Serve the pizza, squeezing the juice from the lemon wedge over the slices just before eating.

GUANCIALE AND QUAIL EGG

MAKES ONE 13-INCH PIZZA; 6 SLICES

This pizza takes bacon and eggs to a whole new place—California, where the bacon becomes rich, flavorful *guanciale* (bacon made from hog cheeks or jowls) and the eggs come from our state bird. Throw in some potatoes, and you've got a whole brunch on a pizza!

1 (13-ounce/370-gram) ball Multigrain Dough (page 151)

1 part flour mixed with 1 part semolina, for dusting

¹/₂ teaspoon (0.5 grams) ground dried lavender

2 tablespoons (28 grams) fine sea salt

1 (3-ounce/85-gram) white potato, 2 inches in diameter

7 ounces (200 grams) whole-milk mozzarella cheese, shredded (1³/₄ cups)

0.6 ounce (18 grams) thinly sliced guanciale

1 ounce (30 grams) thinly sliced cured chorizo, preferably Fra' Mani

3 quail eggs

¹/₄ cup (55 grams) fromage blanc

1 teaspoon (5 grams) crushed Calabrese peppers

Fresh rosemary, minced, for sprinkling

Remove the dough ball from the refrigerator and leave wrapped at room temperature until the dough warms to 60°F to 65°F. Meanwhile, set up the oven with two pizza stones or baking steels and preheat to 500°F for 1 hour (see Getting Started, page 29).

To make the lavender salt, stir together the lavender and salt. If you have a mortar and pestle, crush them together for a finer grind. Set aside.

Using a mandoline, cut the potatoes into paper-thin slices and drop them into a bowl of very cold salted water. Let soak for 30 minutes, drain, and repeat with a new batch of salted water. Drain again and dry on paper towels.

Dust the work surface with the dusting mixture, then move the dough to the surface and dust the top (see Transferring the Dough to the Work Surface, page 30).

Sprinkle a wooden peel with the dusting mixture. Open the dough on the work surface to a 13-inch round with a slightly raised edge (see Opening and Stretching the Dough, page 33).

Move the dough to the peel. As you work, shake the peel forward and backward to ensure the dough isn't sticking.

Mound the mozzarella in the center of the dough and use your fingertips to spread it out evenly over the surface, leaving a ³/₄-inch border. Arrange the potato slices over the cheese.

Slide the pizza onto the top stone (see Moving the Dough to the Oven, page 24). Bake for 7 minutes.

continued

Remove the pizza from the oven and place on a cutting board (or work directly on the peel if there is room to set it on the work surface). Arrange the guanciale and chorizo slices evenly over the top. Crack the quail eggs onto the pizza, spacing them evenly. Lift the pizza with the peel (if on a cutting board), rotate it 180 degrees, and transfer it to the bottom stone. Bake for 3 minutes, until the bottom is browned and crisp and the top is golden brown. If the eggs need a little more time, keep the pizza in the oven until they are just set.

Transfer the pizza to a cutting board and cut into 6 wedges, leaving the eggs uncut. Garnish with small spoonfuls of fromage blanc and bits of Calabrese peppers. Finish with a sprinkle of rosemary and a light dusting of the lavender salt.

CAMPARI

MAKES ONE 13-INCH PIZZA; 6 SLICES

I'm a huge fan of the bittersweet, herby flavor of Campari, and I'd always wanted to figure out how to work it into a pizza. Then it hit me: a ruby-red Campari reduction drizzled over the hot pizza as a finishing touch, so that Campari is the first thing you taste when you bite into a slice. After all, it's an aperitif, right? So that first taste makes you hungry, and your hunger is immediately satisfied by pizza with pancetta, escarole, and creamy goat cheese. It's like cocktails and antipasto all in one.

I took this pizza to the World Pizza Championships in Salsomaggiore, Italy, and got Campari to sponsor me. That meant, among other things, that when I brought my pizza into the hall, I was escorted by Miss Campari—six feet two in stilettos, not counting her Campari-red hat. Every judge in the room stopped chewing and froze as we walked in. The pizza placed eighth out of four hundred entrants from around the world and made quite an impression as the competition's first pizza ever to feature an aperitif—or a supermodel.

One 13-ounce (370-gram) ball Master Dough, preferably with starter (page 44), made with Poolish

4 parts flour mixed with 1 part semolina, for dusting

CAMPARI SYRUP

1/3 cup (75 grams) Campari

1/4 cup (65 grams) blood orange syrup, such as Torani

Few drops of Angostura bitters

To make the Campari syrup, pour the Campari into a small, heavy saucepan and bring to a boil over high heat. Boil for 1½ minutes, add the blood orange syrup, return to a boil, and boil for another 2 minutes. Add the bitters and continue to boil for 1 minute longer. Remove the pan from the heat. To check the consistency, lift some of the syrup on a spoon and drizzle it over a plate. It should have the consistency of maple syrup. If it is too thin, return it to the heat and continue to boil it, checking it frequently. You should have about 3 tablespoons syrup. Transfer the syrup to a small squeeze bottle. It can be stored at room temperature for up to 3 days.

Remove the dough ball from the refrigerator and leave wrapped at room temperature until the dough warms to 60°F to 65°F. Meanwhile, set up the oven with two pizza stones or baking steels and preheat to 500°F for 1 hour (see Getting Started, page 29).

continued

1 ounce (30 grams) sliced pancetta

7 ounces (200 grams) whole-milk mozzarella cheese, shredded (1¾ cups)

Red pepper flakes, for sprinkling

1.5 ounces (45 grams) fresh goat cheese, preferably Laura Chenel

2 ounces (55 grams) escarole, thick stems removed, cut into ¾-inch (2-centimeter) pieces

2 ounces (30 grams) Peppadew peppers, cut into strips

Extra virgin olive oil, for drizzling

Meanwhile, cut the pancetta into lardons (matchsticks) about 1½ inches long and ¼ inch wide and thick. Don't worry about cutting them perfectly; a bit of irregularity is more appealing. Heat a small skillet over medium-high heat. Add the pancetta, lower the heat to medium, and cook, stirring often, for about 2 minutes, until most of the fat is rendered and the pancetta is partially cooked. Set aside without draining.

Dust the work surface with the dusting mixture, then move the dough to the surface and dust the top (see Transferring the Dough to the Work Surface, page 30).

Sprinkle a wooden peel with the dusting mixture. Open the dough on the work surface to a 13-inch round with a slightly raised edge (see Opening and Stretching the Dough, page 33).

Move the dough to the peel. As you work, shake the peel forward and backward to ensure the dough isn't sticking.

Mound the mozzarella in the center of the dough and use your fingertips to spread it out evenly over the surface, leaving a ¾-inch border. Scatter the pancetta evenly over the cheese.

Slide the pizza onto the top stone (see Moving the Dough to the Oven, page 34). Bake for 7 minutes. Lift the pizza onto the peel, rotate it 180 degrees, and then transfer it to the bottom stone. Bake for 4 to 5 minutes, until the bottom is browned and crisp and the top is golden brown.

Transfer the pizza to a cutting board and cut into 6 wedges. Top with a few pinches of pepper flakes and crumble the goat cheese evenly over the surface. Scatter the escarole and Peppadew peppers evenly over the pizza and finish with a drizzle of the Campari syrup and the oil.

ORGANIC THREE CHEESE

MAKES ONE 12-INCH PIZZA; 6 SLICES

This pizza is all organic all the time, from the crust to the toppings. It's a tribute to two of my favorite organic California cheeses: Cowgirl Creamery's Mt. Tam, a buttery triple-cream, and Nicasio Valley Cheese Company's Nicasio Reserve, a light, Swiss-Italian–style cheese. To cut through their richness, I like the bitter edge of dandelion greens. If you'd rather go for something a bit milder, try broccoli rabe, chard, kale, romanesco, or whatever flavorful greens are in season.

CALIFORNIA STYLE

1 (9-ounce/255 gram) ball Organic Dough (page 173)

Flour, for dusting

2 ounces (55 grams) dandelion greens

Olive oil, for cooking the greens

Fine sea salt

5 ounces (140 grams) organic sharp white Cheddar cheese, preferably Sierra Nevada, shredded (1¼ cups)

½ teaspoon (1.5 grams) minced garlic

2 ounces (55 grams) Cowgirl Creamery Organic Mt. Tam cheese

1-ounce (30-gram) piece Nicasio Valley Cheese Company's Organic Nicasio Reserve cheese, cold, for shaving

Red pepper flakes, for sprinkling

Remove the dough ball from the refrigerator and leave wrapped at room temperature until the dough warms to 60°F to 65°F. Meanwhile, set up the oven with two baking steels or pizza stones and preheat to 500°F for 1 hour (see Getting Started, page 29).

Cut out the ribs from the dandelion greens and discard them. Cut each green in half lengthwise. Rinse under cold water and shake to remove the excess water.

Heat a film of olive oil in a skillet over medium heat. Add the dandelion greens and a sprinkle of salt and stir constantly for about 1½ minutes, until the leaves have wilted. Transfer to a plate and set aside.

When you are ready to open the dough, turn on the broiler. (If your oven has multiple broiler settings, set it on highest setting the first time you try this pizza. If you find that the top of your pizza is getting too dark before the crust is fully baked, switch to the medium setting.)

Dust the work surface with flour, then move the dough to the surface and dust the top (see Transferring the Dough to the Work Surface, page 30).

Sprinkle a wooden peel with flour. Open the dough on the work surface to a 12-inch round with a slightly raised edge (see Opening and Stretching the Dough, page 33).

Move the dough to the peel. As you work, shake the peel forward and backward to ensure the dough isn't sticking.

continued

Mound the Cheddar in the center of the dough and use your fingertips to spread it out evenly over the dough, leaving a 3/4-inch border.

Because broilers have different strengths, keep a watchful eye on the pizza, as it can burn quickly. Slide the pizza onto the top steel (see Moving the Dough to the Oven, page 34). Broil for about 1 minute. Lift the pizza onto the peel, rotate it 180 degrees, and return it to the top steel to continue broiling for another minute, until the edges of the dough are a rich golden brown with some black speckles.

Remove the pizza from the oven and sprinkle the garlic over the top.

Transfer the pizza to the bottom steel. Leaving the oven on broil, bake for 1 minute, rotate 180 degrees, and return to the bottom steel for another minute, until the bottom is a rich brown.

Transfer the pizza to a cutting board and cut into 6 wedges. Arrange the dandelion greens evenly over the pizza. Pinch pieces of the Mt. Tam and place them on the pizza. Using a vegetable peeler, shave pieces of the Nicasio Reserve over the top, then finish with a pinch of pepper flakes.

CALIFORNIA STYLE

EGGPLANT AND OLIVE

MAKES ONE 13-INCH PIZZA; 6 SLICES

Eggplant is an awesome pizza topping, and the best way to handle it is to cook it completely and then add it to the fully baked pizza. The fried capers add little salty-crunchy explosions of flavor. The trick to getting them right is to fry them very slowly, so you cook the moisture out of them gradually, making them crisp but still a bit soft in the center.

One 13-ounce (370-gram) ball Khorasan Dough (page 176)

Flour, for dusting

1 small (12 ounces/340 grams) globe eggplant, cut crosswise into slices 1/4 inch thick

Olive oil, for brushing

Canola oil, for deep-frying

1 1/2 tablespoons (18 grams) capers, rinsed and dried on paper towels

1/2 teaspoon (1.5 grams) finely chopped garlic

Fine sea salt

8 ounces (225 grams) whole-milk mozzarella cheese, shredded (2 cups)

Remove the dough ball from the refrigerator and leave wrapped at room temperature until the dough warms to 60°F to 65°F. Meanwhile, set up the oven with two pizza stones or baking steels and preheat to 500°F for 1 hour (see Getting Started, page 29).

Meanwhile, place the eggplant slices in a single layer on a sheet pan. Generously brush both sides of each slice with olive oil. When the oven is ready, put the pan on the top stone and bake for about 10 minutes. Turn the slices over and continue to bake for another 10 minutes, until the slices are soft and a rich golden brown. Transfer the eggplant to a bowl and cover with plastic wrap for about 15 minutes, to loosen the skin.

Meanwhile, pour canola oil to a depth of 1/2 inch into a small, heavy saucepan and heat to 275°F. Add the capers to the hot oil. As the capers fry, check the oil to make sure it remains between 260°F and 275°F. If it gets too hot, lift the pan off the heat until it cools to the correct temperature. Fry the capers, moving them in the oil from time to time, for about 5 minutes, until the bubbles have subsided and the capers are crisp. Using a fine mesh wire skimmer, transfer the capers to paper towels to drain.

**5 oil-cured black olives,
pitted and halved lengthwise**

**5 Mediterranean mixed olives,
pitted and halved lengthwise**

**5 Castelvetrano olives,
pitted and halved lengthwise**

1 lemon wedge

**Small piece organic sharp white
Cheddar cheese, preferably Cabot,
cold, for shaving**

Red peppers flakes, for sprinkling

Peel off and discard the skin from the eggplant slices, then dice the warm eggplant. Add the garlic and toss to mix well, then season lightly with salt, keeping in mind that the olives and capers are salty. You will need 1/2 cup (85 grams) cooked eggplant for this recipe. Set aside. Reserve the remaining eggplant for another use.

Dust the work surface with the flour, then move the dough to the surface and dust the top (see Transferring the Dough to the Work Surface, page 30).

Sprinkle a wooden peel with flour. Open the dough on the work surface to a 13-inch round with a slightly raised edge (see Opening and Stretching the Dough, page 33).

Move the dough to the peel. As you work, shake the peel forward and backward to ensure the dough isn't sticking.

Mound the mozzarella in the center of the dough and use your fingertips to spread it out evenly over the dough, leaving a 3/4-inch border.

Slide the pizza onto the top stone (see Moving the Dough to the Oven, page 34). Bake for 6 minutes. Lift the pizza onto the peel, rotate it 180 degrees, and then transfer it to the bottom stone. Bake for 4 to 5 minutes, until the bottom is browned and crisp and the top is golden brown.

Transfer the pizza to a cutting board and cut into 6 wedges. Top the slices evenly with the eggplant, olives, and capers and squeeze lemon juice over the top. Using a vegetable peeler, shave the Cheddar over the top, then finish with a pinch of pepper flakes.

FIG, ALMOND, AND MONTEREY JACK

MAKES ONE 13-INCH PIZZA; 6 SLICES

Mission figs, almonds, and Monterey Jack are three of California's proudest food products. No wonder they taste so good together. I like adding ripe figs to pizzas during the last few minutes of baking. They don't really cook; they just get warm enough to bring out their sweet caramel flavor. The nutty taste of the einkorn wheat in the dough is just right with this combo of fruit, nuts, and cheese.

1 (13-ounce/370-gram) ball Einkorn Dough (page 178)

Flour, for dusting

8 ounces (225 grams) watercress (2 to 3 bunches)

Olive oil, for sautéing

Fine sea salt

6 ounces (170 grams) Monterey Jack cheese, shredded (1½ cups)

2 large figs, preferably Mission figs, cut into slices ¼ inch thick

1½ ounces (45 grams) fresh goat cheese, preferably Laura Chenel

12 salted roasted almonds, slivered

1 orange

Remove the dough ball from the refrigerator and leave wrapped at room temperature until the dough warms to 55°F to 57°F. Meanwhile, set up the oven with two baking steels or pizza stones and preheat to 500°F for 1 hour (see Getting Started, page 29).

Meanwhile, pull the leaves from the watercress and discard the stems. You should have about 3 cups (90 grams) lightly packed leaves.

Heat a film of olive oil in a skillet over medium heat. Add the watercress leaves and a sprinkle of salt and stir constantly for about 45 seconds, until the leaves have wilted. Transfer to a plate and set aside.

When you are ready to open the dough, turn on the broiler. (If your oven has multiple broiler settings, set it on the highest setting the first time you try this pizza. If you find that the top of your pizza is getting too dark before the crust is fully baked, switch to the medium setting.)

Sprinkle a wooden peel with flour, then move the dough to the peel and dust the top. Open the dough on the peel to a 13-inch round with a slightly raised edge (see Opening and Stretching the Dough, page 33). As you work, shake the peel forward and backward to ensure the dough isn't sticking. As noted in its recipe, this dough is less elastic than other doughs in the book and pushes out easily, so you may want to push it out, rather than stretch it, to avoid tearing.

Mound the Monterey Jack in the center of the dough and use your fingertips to spread it out evenly over the surface, leaving a ¾-inch border.

continued

Because broilers have different strengths, keep a watchful eye on the pizza, as it can burn quickly. Slide the pizza onto the top steel (see Moving the Dough to the Oven, page 34). Broil for 1 to 1½ minutes. Lift the pizza onto the peel, rotate it 180 degrees, and return it to the top steel to continue broiling for another 30 seconds to 1 minute, until the edges of the dough are a rich golden brown with some black speckles.

Remove the pizza from the oven and arrange the figs evenly over the top.

Transfer the pizza to the bottom steel. Leaving the oven on broil, bake 1 minute, rotate it 180 degrees, and bake for another minute, until the bottom is a rich brown.

Transfer the pizza to a cutting board and cut into 6 wedges. Arrange small bits of the goat cheese around the pizza and sprinkle with the almonds. Using a Microplane grater, grate the zest of half of the orange over the top. Scatter the watercress over the pizza and finish with a sprinkling with salt.

To round out your library of crust options, here are four doughs made with today's increasingly popular organic, ancient, and sprouted grains.

ORGANIC DOUGH

MAKES 27 OUNCES (765 GRAMS) DOUGH

This dough produces a nutty, slightly earthy crust. You can use it in any recipe that calls for Master Dough, and it's particularly good when made with the broiler method (as in Organic Three Cheese, page 165), on the grill, or in a wood-fired oven.

The bran starter takes a few extra days to make, but that's the secret of the flavor complexity it adds. You start by fermenting wheat bran in water for a couple of days to make bran water, which you then combine with flour and ferment with successive feedings of flour. Don't worry: although the bran water and the starter have a funky, almost spoiled smell, once the starter is added to the dough, that funkiness becomes yeasty, wheaty, sweet, and aromatic in the best way. The recipe makes three 12-inch pizzas with a slightly thinner crust than Master Dough.

1 gram (¼ teaspoon plus ⅛ teaspoon) active dry yeast

70 grams (¼ cup plus 1 tablespoon) warm water (80°F to 85°F)

Put the yeast in a small bowl, add the warm water, and whisk vigorously for 30 seconds. The yeast should dissolve in the water and the mixture should foam. If it doesn't and the yeast granules float, the yeast is "dead" and should be discarded. Begin again with a fresh amount of yeast and water.

continued

430 grams (3½ cups) organic flour with 12 to 13 percent protein, preferably Central Milling Organic Type 70 Malted

23 grams (3 tablespoons) organic whole wheat flour, preferably Central Milling Organic Whole Wheat Medium

202 grams (¾ cup plus 1 tablespoon) ice water

140 grams Bran Starter (page 175)

10 grams (2 teaspoons) fine sea salt

For baker's percentages, see page 302.

Combine both flours in the bowl of a stand mixer fitted with the dough hook. With the mixer running on the lowest speed, pour in most of the ice water, reserving about 2 tablespoons, followed by the yeast-water mixture. Pour the reserved water into the yeast bowl, swirl it around to dislodge any bits of yeast stuck to the bowl, and add to the mixer. Mix for about 15 seconds, stop the mixer, and add the starter.

Continue to mix the dough at the lowest speed for about 1 minute, until most of the dough comes together around the hook. Stop the mixer. Use your fingers to pull away any dough clinging to the hook, and scrape the sides and bottom of the bowl with a bowl scraper or rubber spatula.

Add the salt and mix on the lowest speed for 1 minute to combine. Check the bottom of the bowl for any unincorporated flour. Turn the dough over and press it into the bottom of the bowl to pick up any stray pieces. If there is any unincorporated flour, add a ½ teaspoon of water and mix again.

Stop the mixer, pull the dough off the dough hook, and scrape down the sides and bottom of the bowl. Mix for another 1 minute. The dough won't look completely smooth.

Use the bowl scraper to transfer the dough to an unfloured work surface, then knead it for 2 to 3 minutes, until smooth (see Kneading the Dough, page 24). Cover the dough with a damp kitchen towel and let rest at room temperature for 20 minutes.

Use a dough cutter to loosen the dough and to cut the dough into thirds. Weigh each piece, adjusting the quantity of dough as necessary to give you three 9-ounce (255-gram) balls. You may have a little extra dough.

Form the dough into balls (see Balling the Dough, page 26). Set the balls on a half sheet pan, spacing them about 3 inches apart. Or, if you will be baking the balls on different days, place each ball on a quarter sheet pan. Wrap the pan(s) airtight with a double layer of plastic wrap, sealing the wrap well under the pans. Put the pan(s) in a level spot in the refrigerator and refrigerate for 24 to 48 hours.

BRAN WATER

20 grams (1/3 cup) organic bran

200 grams (3/4 cup plus 2 tablespoons) cold water

About 250 grams (1 2/3 cup) organic whole wheat flour, preferably Central Milling Organic Whole Wheat Medium

BRAN STARTER

MAKES 140 GRAMS

To make the bran water, stir together the bran and water in a bowl. Cover with plastic wrap and leave at room temperature for 2 to 3 days, until it smells very strongly fermented. Strain through a fine-mesh strainer, reserving the water and discarding the bran.

To make the starter, stir together 50 grams (3 1/2 tablespoons) of the bran water (discard any remaining bran water) and 50 grams (1/3 cup) of the flour in a glass bowl. Cover with plastic wrap and leave at room temperature for 24 hours.

To feed the starter, put 40 grams of the starter in a clean bowl and discard the remainder. Add 50 grams (1/3 cup) of the flour and 50 grams (3 1/2 tablespoons) cold water to the bowl and stir to combine. Scrape down the sides of the bowl, cover with plastic wrap, and leave at room temperature for 12 hours.

Continue to feed the starter the same way every 12 hours. It will be ready to use after three feedings but will develop even more flavor after another two feedings.

KHORASAN DOUGH

29 OUNCES (820 GRAMS) DOUGH

The growing concern about gluten intolerance has generated an interest in returning to so-called ancient grains that have been less hybridized and modified than most modern wheat. One of these is Khorasan, a type of wheat most widely available under the brand name Kamut. It is believed to date back to ancient Egypt, and although it does contain gluten, many people with gluten sensitivity say they find it more digestible than other wheat varieties. I'll let you be the judge, but I will say that I like its nutty, slightly sweet flavor and soft texture in a pizza crust. When you're making dough with Khorasan, you'll find that it is a very thirsty grain—one that drinks up more water than most types of wheat—but, it's quite workable and easy to handle. Because the protein level of Khorasan is usually on the low side, I've added a little extra salt to help strengthen the dough.

2.5 grams (1 teaspoon) active dry yeast

70 grams (¼ cup plus 1 tablespoon) warm water (80°F to 85°F)

453 grams (3½ cups) Khorasan flour, preferably Central Milling Organic White Khorasan

210 grams (¾ cup plus 2 tablespoons) ice water

90 grams Poolish (page 47)

15 grams (1 tablespoon) fine sea salt

Olive oil

For baker's percentages, see page 302

Put the yeast in a small bowl, add the warm water, and whisk vigorously for 30 seconds. The yeast should dissolve in the water and the mixture should foam. If it doesn't and the yeast granules float, the yeast is "dead" and should be discarded. Begin again with a fresh amount of yeast and water.

Place the flour in the bowl of a stand mixer fitted with the dough hook. With the mixer running on the lowest speed, pour in most of the ice water, reserving about 2 tablespoons, followed by the yeast-water mixture. Pour the reserved water into the yeast bowl, swirl it around to dislodge any bits of yeast stuck to the bowl, and add to the mixer. Mix for about 15 seconds, stop the mixer, and add the poolish.

Continue to mix the dough at the lowest speed for about 1 minute, until most of the dough comes together around the hook. Stop the mixer. Use your fingers to pull away any dough clinging to the hook, and scrape the sides and bottom of the bowl with a bowl scraper or rubber spatula. Check the bottom of the bowl for any unincorporated flour. Turn the dough over and press it into the bottom of the bowl to pick up any stray pieces.

Add the salt and mix on the lowest speed for 1 minute to combine.

Stop the mixer, pull the dough off the dough hook, and scrape down the sides and bottom of the bowl. Mix for another 1 minute. The dough won't look completely smooth.

Use the bowl scraper to transfer the dough to an unfloured work surface, then knead it for 2 to 3 minutes, until smooth (see Kneading the Dough, page 24). Cover the dough with a damp dish towel and let rest at room temperature for 20 minutes.

Use your dough cutter to loosen the dough and to cut the dough in half. Weigh each piece, adjusting the quantity to give you two 13-ounce (370-gram) balls. Discard any extra dough.

Form the dough into balls. (See Balling Dough, page 26) Set the balls on a half sheet pan, spacing them about 3 inches apart. Or, if you will be baking the balls on different days, place each ball on an oiled quarter sheet pan. Wrap the pan(s) airtight with a double layer of plastic wrap, sealing the wrap well under the pan(s). Put the pan(s) in a level spot in the refrigerator and refrigerate for 24 to 48 hours.

Keen on Quinoa

Of all the "new" ancient grains, quinoa is one of my favorites, especially the red variety, so I wanted to figure out how to use it in pizzas. I've found that it's best as a finishing accent. Cook it in boiling salted water (check the package directions for times and quantities), and then sprinkle it (warm or at room temperature) on a fully baked pizza after it comes out of the oven. You'll find that it adds a surprising amount of nutty flavor, crunchy "pop," and visual interest (not to mention all that great quinoa nutrition).

EINKORN DOUGH

MAKES ABOUT 26 OUNCES (740 GRAMS) DOUGH

Einkorn dates back to the Stone Age and is believed to be the first form of wheat cultivated by man. Its name means "one grain" in German, which describes how it grows: single, small grains on each side of the shaft, unlike modern wheat, which has larger grains clustered in a spiral around the shaft. Because it's small and low yield, einkorn has been largely overlooked by wheat growers but now it's making a serious comeback, partly because, like Khorasan, it's believed by many people with gluten issues to be more digestible. This dough is less elastic than the other doughs in this book, so be careful not to tear it as you work with it. You can push it out quite easily, so you may want to skip the step of stretching it in your hands.

2.3 grams (³/4 teaspoon) active dry yeast

70 grams (¹/4 cup plus 1 tablespoon) warm water (80°F to 85°F)

453 grams (3³/4 cups) einkorn flour, preferably Jovial

202 grams (³/4 cup plus 1 tablespoon) ice water

14 grams (1 tablespoon) fine sea salt

For baker's percentages, see page 302

Put the yeast in a small bowl, add the warm water, and whisk vigorously for 30 seconds. The yeast should dissolve in the water and the mixture should foam. If it doesn't and the yeast granules float, the yeast is "dead" and should be discarded. Begin again with a fresh amount of yeast and water.

Put the flour in the bowl of a stand mixer fitted with the dough hook. With the mixer running on the lowest speed, pour in most of the ice water, reserving about 2 tablespoons, followed by the yeast-water mixture. Pour the reserved water into the yeast bowl, swirl it around to dislodge any bits of yeast stuck to the bowl, and add to the mixer.

Continue to mix the dough at the lowest speed for about 1¹/2 minutes, until most of the dough comes together around the hook. Stop the mixer. Use your fingers to pull away any dough clinging to the hook, and scrape the sides and bottom of the bowl with a bowl scraper or rubber spatula.

Add the salt and mix on the lowest speed for 1 minute to combine. Check the bottom of the bowl for any unincorporated flour. Turn the dough over and press it into the bottom of the bowl to pick up any stray pieces.

Stop the mixer, pull the dough off the dough hook, and scrape down the sides and bottom of the bowl. Mix for another minute.

Use the bowl scraper to transfer the dough to an unfloured work surface. The dough will be sticky, so dust with only enough flour to allow you to knead it, then knead it for 2 to 3 minutes, until smooth (see Kneading the Dough, page 24). Cover the dough with a damp dish towel and let rest at room temperature for 1 hour.

Dust you hands with some of the flour. Use a dough cutter to loosen the dough and to cut the dough in half. Weigh each piece, adjusting the quantity of dough as necessary to give you two 13-ounce (370-gram) balls. You may have a little extra dough.

Form the dough into balls (see Balling the Dough, page 26). Set the balls on a half sheet pan, spacing them about 3 inches apart. Or, if you will be baking the balls on different days, place each ball on a quarter sheet pan. Wrap the pan(s) airtight with a double layer of plastic wrap, sealing the wrap well under the pan(s). Put the pan in a level spot in the refrigerator and refrigerate for 24 hours.

A Word About Gluten-Free Dough

I thought long and hard about including a gluten-free dough recipe in this book, but I ultimately opted not to, because to make a decent one involves buying large quantities of several varieties of flour, as well as gums and starches, which just isn't practical for home cooks. Instead, I sampled several commercially available mixes, and I recommend you try Cup4Cup Pizza Crust Mix. The addition of egg and olive oil to this mix helps create a particularly nice crust with a pleasant, chewy texture.

SPROUTED WHEAT DOUGH

MAKES 29 OUNCES (822 GRAMS) DOUGH

If you've been hearing about the increasing popularity and enhanced nutritional benefits of sprouted grains, and you'd like to give them a try, here's a dough to get you started. When a grain is soaked in water and allowed to sprout before it's ground, the sprouting process increases the proportion of nutrients to starch in the grain and makes it more digestible. Some grain mills dry the sprouted grain and grind it into a flour. Others, like Central Milling, grind still-moist sprouted grain into a mash with the texture of a heavy dough (see photo, opposite), and sell it frozen. This process preserves more of the nutrients in the grain than drying and grinding, and I like the earthy flavor and chewy texture that a sprouted grain mash adds, so that's what I call for here. The mash is quite stiff, and your dough won't come together as quickly as others in this book, but with a little extra kneading, it will soften and become workable. The bottom of your crust may tend to brown more quickly than it does with other doughs, so keep an eye on it the first few times you bake it to get a feel for the right timing for your oven.

1.2 grams (½ teaspoon) active dry yeast

60 grams (¼ cup) warm water (80°F to 85°F)

340 grams (2¼ cups) organic flour with 12 to 13 percent protein, preferably Central Milling Organic High Mountain Hi-Protein Flour

100 grams (¼ cup plus 3 tablespoons) ice water

227 grams Poolish (page 47)

113 grams sprouted wheat, preferably from Central Milling, broken into 1-inch sections

Put the yeast in a small bowl, add the warm water, and whisk vigorously for 30 seconds. The yeast should dissolve in the water and the mixture should foam. If it doesn't and the yeast granules float, the yeast is "dead" and should be discarded. Begin again with a fresh amount of yeast and water.

Put the flour in the bowl of a stand mixer fitted with the dough hook. With the mixer running on the lowest speed, pour in most of the ice water, reserving about 2 tablespoons, followed by the yeast-water mixture. Pour the reserved water into the yeast bowl, swirl it around to dislodge any bits of yeast stuck to the bowl, and add to the mixer. Mix for about 15 seconds, stop the mixer, and add the poolish. Mix for another 30 seconds, stop the mixer and add the sprouted wheat.

It will be more difficult to combine these ingredients because of the weight and texture of the sprouted wheat. Be patient and scrape down the bowl often during the process.

14 grams (2 teaspoons) honey

9 grams (2 teaspoons) fine sea salt

23 grams (1 1/2 tablespoons) olive oil

For baker's percentages, see page 302

Turn the mixer to the lowest speed for about 1 minute, scraping the bowl as necessary. Add the honey and continue to mix for 1 more minute. Most of the dough should come together around the hook and the ingredients should be close to being fully incorporated. Stop the mixer. Use your fingers to pull away any dough clinging to the hook, and scrape the sides and bottom of the bowl with a bowl scraper or rubber spatula.

Add the salt and mix on the lowest speed for 1 minute to combine.

Stop the mixer, pull the dough off the dough hook, and scrape down the sides and bottom of the bowl. Add the oil and mix for another 1 minute. The dough won't look completely smooth.

Use the bowl scraper to transfer the dough to an unfloured work surface, then knead it for 3 to 4 minutes, until smooth (see Kneading the Dough, page 24). Cover the dough with a damp kitchen towel and let rest at room temperature for 20 minutes.

Use a dough cutter to loosen the dough and to cut the dough in half. Weigh each piece, adjusting the quantity of dough as necessary to give you two 13-ounce (370-gram) balls. You may have a little extra dough.

Form the dough into balls (see Balling the Dough, page 26). Set the balls on the half sheet pan, spacing them about 3 inches apart. Or, if you will be baking the balls on different days, place each ball on a quarter sheet pan. Wrap the pan(s) airtight with a double layer of plastic wrap, sealing the wrap well under the pan(s). Put the pan in a level spot in the refrigerator and refrigerate for 24 to 48 hours.

Napoletana

True Neapolitan pizza is made in a wood-fired oven, which burns at around 900°F. For those lucky people who have access to a wood oven, I've given a dough recipe and directions for making these pizzas that way. For everyone else, I've included a slightly different dough and an oven-and-broiler baking technique that will get you remarkably close.

All of these pizzas can be sliced into wedges for sharing, American style, or served whole with a fork and knife, Italian style, as a meal for one.

UNDER THE VOLCANO

Naples is a crazy place. It's sprawling, loud, messy, hot, and irresistibly romantic all at the same time. After all, it's right at the foot of Mount Vesuvius, the still-smoldering volcano that took out Pompeii and that's long overdue for an eruption of equal magnitude. And the thing that Naples is probably the most crazy about is pizza.

Let's just say it falls somewhere between tradition and religion.

Now, whether you're a fan of thin-crust, lightly charred Neapolitan pizza or not, you have to realize that in Italy, the pizza of Naples is the gold standard that defines the category—the way Champagne does for sparkling wine—and, just like Champagne, it's given national-treasure status. The Associazione Verace Pizza Napoletana (AVPN) was founded in 1984 to give DOC (Denomination of Controlled Origin) status to Neapolitan pizza, strictly regulating everything from the ingredients and the size to the cooking methods. The two most famous types of Neapolitan pizza are marinara, with tomato sauce, garlic, oregano, and olive oil, and margherita, with tomato sauce, fresh mozzarella, basil, and olive oil. Da Michele, one of the city's oldest and best-known pizzerias has served only these two varieties since 1870, referring in their promotional materials to all other pizza toppings as *papocchie*—Neapolitan slang for "phony tricks."

As a *pizzaiolo*, achieving certification from the AVPN is the ultimate stamp of approval. Well, almost. The ultimate would be winning the World Pizza Cup in Naples.

Once a year, pizza makers come from all over the planet to do battle on hallowed pizza ground. I went in 2007 and competed in several categories, the most intimidating of which, by far, is the STG (Specialità Tradizionale Garantita, or "Guaranteed Traditional Specialty") Napoletana. It's the holy grail. You can choose margherita, margherita extra, or marinara. I went with the classic margherita. The dough is salt, water, flour, and yeast or starter. The topping is San Marzano tomatoes, sea salt, fresh mozzarella, and basil. Period. When something is that simple and that sacred, and you're going to make it for a panel of Neapolitan *pizzaiolos*, you're looking at a challenge of Vesuvian proportions, even under the best of conditions. No wonder an American had never won.

On June 13, the day of the competition, it was over 100°F degrees outside and muggy. But inside the tightly sealed tented arena, it was even worse, with six wood-burning ovens blazing at 900 degrees. When my number for the Neapolitan category was called, I grabbed my wooden kit box with my dough and my tools and walked over to meet the judges.

A young contestant from Naples rolled his eyes at my kit and mumbled something that sounded snide. I looked at the translator, who said, "He makes fun of you. He says, you know, you can get those in metal now." As I was wondering whether or not to reply, my judge, an elderly third-generation Neapolitan *pizzaiolo* came to my defense. "Before there was metal, there was wood," he said. "Maybe he's old-fashioned. Maybe he likes tradition." I took a deep breath and smiled. I do like tradition, and especially at a time like this.

When I was making my dough the day before, I tasted the tap water. Not good. Campania is a volcanic region, and the municipal water tastes and smells like sulfur. All the international competitors had chosen to use bottled water. But I went with the smelly stuff from the tap. I figured the judges were from here, and this was the water they worked with every day.

For good luck, I used a bit of dough I'd brought with me from California as an "old-dough" starter. I let my dough balls rise in a wooden box, another nod to tradition. The dough looked and felt perfect, and I swear it had a faint aroma that I can only describe as "authentic."

But that was yesterday. In the sweltering heat of the tent, the dough I'd prepared so carefully was almost "blown"—the dreaded condition of overrising, after which it starts to soften and deflate. Another few minutes could mean disaster.

Drenched in sweat and barely breathing between the humidity and the stress, I opened my first dough ball and pushed it out.

You're assigned a single judge, who follows you to the prep station and the oven to watch every move you make, scribbling notes on a clipboard. Mine was from Naples, and I could feel his squinting skepticism as I reached for my spoon and laid out a neat spiral of sauce, starting at the center, exactly as dictated in the official competition rules. Unlike most of the competitors, I had seeded my tomatoes for a more concentrated flavor, the one break from tradition that I thought might actually improve on it. Then I added the basil, salt, and mozzarella, which I had drained briefly in cheesecloth to remove some of the water.

Once your dough is shaped, you have to slide your pizza onto the peel without ever picking it up, and you need to center it just right so the edges don't hang over. You've got one shot, and in the sweltering rain-forest heat of the tent, the dough was unusually soft and moist. Professional *pizzaiolos* had been screwing up all day, making football-shaped pizzas and worse.

I shaped my dough to a 9½-inch round—much smaller than the regulations require—topped it, and told my judge I was ready for my peel. More looks of skepticism. But when I slid my pizza onto the peel, I stretched it to a perfect 13 inches—a risky technique that worked just right this time. I slid it onto the oven floor and breathed a sigh of relief, which turned into a gasp as a glowing ember broke off from an overhanging piece of wood and just missed hitting my pizza.

I counted, "one alligator, two alligators," turning my pizza every 15 "alligators," and pulled it out at what turned out to be exactly 89.5 seconds. Any more than 90 seconds and I would have been disqualified on the spot.

I plated my pizza and slid it over to the judge, who aggressively lifted one side high off the plate and held it up for what should have been a second or two to see if it would bulge or break. He held it up for five seconds, then ten, then twenty. It didn't break. "*Molto bene*," he said, but his tone sounded more angry than approving. He dropped the pizza back onto the plate, poked it to test its texture, and then grudgingly waved me on to the judge's table.

There, a tan, impeccably dressed, leather-faced Neapolitan woman interviewed me about every detail of my pizza in the hopes of tripping up the "Americano."

"Your cheese?"

"*Fior di latte.*"

"Not *mozzarella di bufala?*"

I knew it was a trick question. Only the margherita "extra" is made with buffalo mozzarella. "No, signora."

She looked at me, stone-faced. "How much sugar?"

Another trick question. "None, signora"

"How much oil in your dough?

"None in the dough, signora, only drizzled on the top before I baked it."

"And your tomatoes."

"San Marzano, signora. Seeded."

She raised an eyebrow and smirked.

Then the judges took a taste and showed absolutely no reaction. But I knew my pizza was just what I wanted it to be, and I walked away knowing that even though I was going to lose, I had done my best.

My team—Tony Palombino, Glenn Cybulski, Billy Manzo, Nacy Puglisi, and my wife, Julie—were gathering around me to try a bit of what was left, when an assistant came over to me and swooped it out from under our noses, saying that the judges wanted to taste my pizza one more time. This was a good sign. Those judges taste sixty slices a day. They take one bite and throw the rest in the trash, and they never taste anything twice.

That afternoon, I had lunch with a bunch of Neapolitans, and I knocked over my glass of wine. I was starting to clean it up, when they all stopped me, and said, "No! Rub it on your forehead! It's good luck." I have never

rubbed anything on my forehead so fast. Then I rubbed some more all over my body just for good measure. "I need all the luck I can get!" I said, and we all had a good laugh.

"You know, there's another reason it's your lucky day, Tony," one guy said. "It's your saint's day." I hadn't realized that June 13 is the feast day of Saint Anthony of Padua.

That night, with thousands of people packed into the arena, my team and I sat at a table together, waiting to hear the results. They announced third place, and then second place, and then there was a long pause. I'll never forget the words I heard next.

"The first prize in the Neapolitan category goes to . . . from Castro Valley, California, United States . . . Tony Gemignani."

There was a split second of heavy silence. And then Vesuvius erupted.

Amid the screaming and pandemonium, a dozen cops surrounded our table, told us to stay calm, stand up, and follow them quickly to the front to claim the trophy. "Don't show any excitement," they told me. All I wanted to do was whoop and scream and dance on the table. But I figured I should respect their instructions. They seriously wanted to make sure we didn't get stabbed or shot.

It was one of the greatest, weirdest moments of my life. And I keep it alive at my restaurant every day. In honor of 6/13, I came up with a little crazy Neapolitan numerology of my own. I added the 6 and 1 to make 7, then added the 3 on the end to make 73. And ever since, I've made 73 STG, AVPN-certified margherita pizzas every night. Not one more or one less. Like I said, I love traditions.

NAPOLETANA DOUGH

MAKES 28 OUNCES (795 GRAMS) DOUGH, ENOUGH FOR THREE 9 TO 10-OUNCE BALLS

An authentic Napoletana pizza has to be made with Italian *doppio zero* (double zero) flour. Double zero is a designation that indicates the fineness of the grind, with the scale going from 2, the coarsest, to 00, the finest. Double-zero flour is milled from soft wheat, which has less elastic gluten than hard wheat. The result is a tender dough that requires a light touch and a gentle hand when you're working with it. Caputo and San Felice are the two revered double-zero brands for Neapolitan pizza. I always tell my students they're like the Coke and Pepsi of Naples, and I recommend both. Caputo is easier to find in American supermarkets. I prefer to use fresh yeast in this dough, because it's the traditional Neapolitan way.

The only difference between my wood-fired and my home-oven Napoletana dough is that I add a bit of malt to the home-oven version to help with browning. With the intense heat of a wood-fired oven, there's no need for malt.

7 grams fresh yeast, broken into small pieces or 2.3 grams (¾ teaspoon) active dry yeast

70 grams (¼ cup plus 1 tablespoon) warm water (80°F to 85°F)

453 grams (3¾ cups) 00 flour, preferably Caputo or San Felice, plus more for kneading as needed

10 grams (1 tablespoon plus ¼ teaspoon) diastatic malt if baking in a home oven

210 grams (¾ cup plus 2 tablespoons) ice water

90 grams Poolish (page 47)

10 grams (2 teaspoons) fine sea salt

For baker's percentages, see page 302.

Put the yeast in a small bowl, add the warm water, and whisk vigorously for 30 seconds. The yeast should dissolve in the water and the mixture should foam. If it doesn't and the yeast granules float, the yeast is "dead" and should be discarded. Begin again with a fresh amount of yeast and water.

Combine the flour and malt (if using) in the bowl of a stand mixer fitted with the dough hook. With the mixer running on the lowest speed, pour in most of the ice water, reserving about 2 tablespoons, followed by the yeast-water mixture. Pour the reserved water into the yeast bowl, swirl it around to dislodge any bits of yeast stuck to the bowl, and add to the mixer. Mix for about 15 seconds, stop the mixer, and add the poolish.

Continue to mix the dough at the lowest speed for about 1 minute, until most of the dough comes together around the hook. Stop the mixer. Use your fingers to pull away any dough clinging to the hook, and scrape the sides and bottom of the bowl with a bowl scraper or rubber spatula.

continued

PRO TIP

A NOTE FOR PROFESSIONALS

The Associazione Verace Pizza Napoletana guidelines require a dough ball weighing between 180 and 250 grams. For home cooks, the recipe I've given here has been rounded slightly, so that it makes enough for 3 9-ounce/225-gram dough balls.

Add the salt and mix on the lowest speed for 1 minute to combine. Stop the mixer, pull the dough off the hook, and continue to mix the dough on the lowest speed for about 1 minute. The dough won't look completely smooth, but if you rub some between your fingers, you should not feel any undissolved salt. If you do, continue to mix for another minute.

Using the bowl scraper, transfer the dough to an unfloured work surface, then knead it for 2 to 3 minutes, until smooth (see Kneading the Dough, page 24). If the dough is too sticky to knead, sprinkle it with just enough flour to allow you to work with it. Cover the dough with a damp dish towel and let it rest at room temperature for about 20 minutes.

Use your dough cutter to loosen the dough and to cut it into thirds. Weigh each piece, adjusting the quantity of dough as necessary to give you equal weights of 9 ounces (255 grams) each. You may have a little extra dough.

Form the dough into balls (see Balling the Dough, page 26). Set the balls on a half sheet pan, spacing them about 3 inches apart. Or, if you will be baking the balls on different days, place one on a quarter sheet pan and the other two on a second quarter sheet pan, spacing them 3 inches apart. Wrap the pan(s) airtight with a double layer of plastic wrap, sealing the wrap well under pan(s). Put the pan(s) in a level spot in the refrigerator and refrigerate for 36 to 48 hours. If the dough will be baked in a home oven, it is best to refrigerate it for the full 48 hours.

NAPOLETANA TOMATO SAUCE

MAKES ABOUT 1⅓ CUPS (340 GRAMS), ENOUGH FOR 3 NAPOLETANA PIZZAS

Yes, it's really just tomatoes and salt, so it's important to use great San Marzano tomatoes. My students are often surprised by the thin consistency of this sauce, but that's how it's supposed to be. If you like a slightly sweeter, more intense sauce, you can add a small amount of high-quality ground tomatoes (see page 17) before you pass the sauce through the food mill. You'll be breaking the official AVPN rules, which specify San Marzanos only, but I won't tell if you don't.

2 (28-ounce/795-gram) cans
San Marzano tomatoes, preferably
Strianese

Fine sea salt

Follow the instructions for hand-crushed tomatoes on page 28, but leave the cleaned tomatoes in large pieces and save the strained tomato juice in the bowl under the strainer.

Set up a food mill with a fine screen and place over a clean bowl. Work the tomatoes through the food mill, scraping the bottom of the screen with a rubber spatula when you are done. You should have about 1⅓ cups (340 grams) tomato sauce. Check the thickness. It should be on the thin side, so that when it is spread over the dough, you can actually see the dough through parts of it. If it seems too thick, stir in a bit of the reserved juice. Season the sauce with a little salt.

The sauce can be stored in an airtight container in the refrigerator for up to 2 days.

PRO TIP

SALT BEFORE YOU BAKE Just before I bake any Napoletana pizza, I season the fully assembled pie with a pinch of sea salt. It really makes the flavors of the sauce and the other ingredients pop.

HANDMADE MOZZARELLA

MAKES 1 POUND (455 GRAMS) FRESH MOZZARELLA

Sure, you can buy fresh mozzarella in most supermarkets, and most of the time, that's probably what you'll want to do. But it's not always great, and there is a better halfway-homemade alternative. It's the method we use to make fresh mozzarella in all my restaurants. I say halfway because making mozzarella completely from scratch with fresh milk is a bit tricky, but starting with fresh mozzarella *curd* takes half of the work out of the equation and gives you some fantastic cheese.

These days, it's getting easier to find blocks of mozzarella curd online. Turning it into homemade mozzarella is fast and fun, and I promise you that when you taste your first bite, you'll appreciate the delicate texture and flavor. The process is also very cool to watch, so once you get the hang of it, it makes a great party activity.

Hand-pulled mozzarella tends to be a bit drier and more compact than the fresh mozzarella you buy in the store, which makes it excellent for topping a pizza. You can use it in any recipe that calls for fresh mozzarella (which is also known as *fior di latte* when made with cow's milk, as opposed to *mozzarella di bufala* when made with the milk of water buffalos).

The process involves shaving the curd and softening it in hot water until it's stretchy, then kneading and shaping it and putting it in a cold saltwater brine. Taste the curd before you start working with it, and you'll discover that it contains no salt. It's the brining process that gives mozzarella its mildly salty flavor.

It's easiest to shave the curd when it's cold, so do that step first and then let the shaved curd come to room temperature before proceeding. Use a stainless-steel bowl to soften the shavings, because it will help retain the heat of the water. When shaping the hot curd, make sure your hands are very clean or, even better, wear disposable surgical gloves both for sanitation and to protect your hands.

3 cups (680 grams) water,
plus 8 quarts (7.25 kilograms)

1 cup (140 grams) kosher salt

25 ounces (710 grams) ice

1 pound (455 grams) mozzarella
curd, cold

To make the brine, pour the 3 cups water into a saucepan and stir in the salt. Place over high heat and heat, stirring from time to time, until all of the salt has dissolved. Pour the salted water into a deep container, add the ice, and stir to melt. The water should be cold; if it isn't, put it the refrigerator to chill. It must be cold when the mozzarella is added.

Pour the 8 quarts water into a large pot, place over medium-high heat, and heat to 175°F to 180°F. Adjust the heat as needed to maintain the temperature.

Using a very sharp knife, cut the curd into thin shavings (see photo ❶, page 192). Put the curd in a wide stainless-steel bowl and let it come to room temperature. Ladle the hot water over the curd just to cover and let sit undisturbed for 1 minute ❷.

With the rounded handle of a wooden spoon, gently move the curds to check if they have softened. As you move them, bring them together into a single mass. If the curds have not softened enough to come together, quickly drain off about half of the water and add new hot water to the bowl.

It is important to act quickly (if the cheese is overworked, it will become rubbery). When all the curd has softened, slip the handle of the spoon under the mass of cheese and lift up. The cheese will stretch down on either side of the handle ❸. Fold the cheese over, drop it back into the water, and repeat the lifting, folding, and returning to the water once or twice more. When the cheese is beginning to tighten, it's time to make the balls.

Quickly fold the long stretch of cheese over once or twice and hold it in the palm of one hand. Holding your hand vertically, and using your other hand to help you guide the cheese, squeeze your hand so that the cheese emerges from the top in a dome shape. The size of the ball will depend on how wide you make the opening of your hand ❹ ❺.

When the ball is the size you would like, squeeze and twist the bottom of the ball to release it ❻ ❼. Place it in the cold brine ❽.

Repeat to make additional balls. If the hot water covering the mozzarella cools down too much and the cheese begins to stiffen, pour some of the water out and add more hot water to soften the curd.

Let the mozzarella balls sit in the brine for at least 30 minutes or up to 1 hour if you prefer a saltier flavor. Remove the balls from the brine, place them in a container, and add cold water to cover. Cap tightly and refrigerate for up to 5 days.

continued

MAKING MOZZARELLA

Fresh Mozzarella Tips

- When you're taking store-bought or homemade mozzarella out of its brining liquid and you're not planning to use it all, always use a clean spoon, not your fingers. This will help to keep the mozzarella remaining in the container from spoiling.

- If you're storing store-bought fresh mozzarella for more than a day or two, pour out the liquid and replace it with fresh water with a pinch of salt dissolved in it.

- When using mozzarella on a pizza, give it a gentle squeeze before you tear or slice it to remove some of the liquid. If it looks very wet, you can also blot it on paper towels.

- Ovoline ("egg-size"), 4-ounce balls of fresh mozzarella, are the perfect size for making individual Neapolitan pizzas.

- When topping a pizza with fresh mozzarella, I like to tear it by hand, rather than slice it, because I find it exudes less moisture that way.

- Once you've mastered shaping mozzarella curd, you can do all kinds of cool things. To make a mozzarella roll, cover a work surface with plastic wrap and spread out 1 pound softened curd into a rectangle about ¼ inch thick. Top it with an even layer of prosciutto and arugula, chopped tomatoes and basil, slivered serrano chiles, or whatever other ingredients you like. Roll up the curd tightly like a jelly roll, wrap it in plastic wrap, and chill it briefly, then slice and serve. Or make tomato-stuffed bocconcini (small balls) by forming balls of softened curd around cherry tomatoes. I like gold tomatoes, which make the bocconcini look like soft-boiled eggs when you slice them in half.

WOOD-FIRED PIZZA BASICS

There's no getting around the fact that wood-fired pizza takes some practice. When your oven is cranking at its peak 900°F temperature, a pizza should only take about 90 seconds to bake. This means you'll need 100 percent focus and attention, and you'll also need to master your peel-handling technique before you can produce nice round, perfectly cooked pies.

It's all a question of maneuvering the pizza in the oven. You'll build your pizza on a long-handled wooden peel and transfer it from that peel directly onto the oven floor. Then you'll rotate it as it cooks using a second peel—we call it a *palino*—with a long handle and a small circular palette made of thin metal. Rotating the dough is the tricky part, and it will take some practice, but as long as you don't let your pizza sit too long in one position, you'll be fine.

Readiness is everything with wood-fired pizza. Before you start, make sure all of your tools, including cutting boards and serving plates, are lined up at a table near the oven. And most important, make sure everyone's standing by ready to eat. Wood-fired pizza waits for no one.

EQUIPMENT AND MATERIALS

- For the firewood, I like oak, split into small logs, because it burns hot and clean; almond or other high-quality hardwood is also good

- Brown-paper bags or newspaper, for building your fire

- Nontoxic fire-starter cubes (optional)

- Kindling

- Long-handled ash scraper

- Optional though handy, an infrared thermometer that registers up to at least 900°F

- Long-handled ovenproof brush and damp towel

- Wood shavings or chips

- Long-handled wooden peel to build and transfer the pizza (or, for more advanced *pizzaiolos*, a perforated metal peel, see page 305)

- *Palino*, a small, circular metal peel with a long handle, for rotating the pizza

- Cutting board for slicing pizzas

- Serving plates or boards

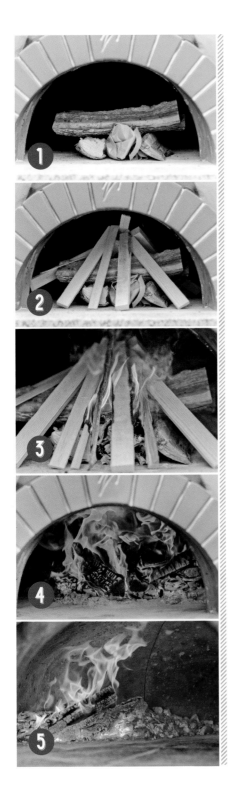

BUILDING YOUR FIRE

You'll need to build your fire about 2½ hours (depending on the weather, your oven, and your wood) before you're ready to make your first pizza.

1. Start by placing two logs parallel, aligned front to back, in the area between the mouth and the center of the oven. Make sure the logs are a few inches back from the mouth, or the flames may shoot out and blacken the front of the oven. Space the logs far enough apart so that you can put a crumpled brown-paper bag or a few twisted sheets of newspaper between them. Put three fire-starter cubes (if using) on the bag. Add two more logs, placing them log cabin–style (perpendicular) to the first two logs ❶. Lean eight to ten pieces of kindling, teepee-style, around your woodpile ❷. Light the bag and leave the oven door off ❸.

2. Assuming your wood and kindling are well seasoned and dry, you will have a robust fire within a few minutes. As the logs burn, you'll need to add more wood, just like you would with a home fireplace. Every 10 to 15 minutes or so, add two to four logs at a time, depending on the size of your oven.

3. After 45 minutes to 1 hour, the part of the oven dome directly above the fire will go from dark black to white-gray, and you will have a large pile of flaming embers. Use your ash scraper to push the embers to the area between the center and back of the oven ❹, and check your fire every 15 minutes, tossing in more logs as necessary to keep a strong fire going, for 45 minutes to 1 hour.

4. As the oven heats, the entire dome will slowly go from black to white-gray. Once this happens, use your ash scraper to rake the embers to the left side of the oven ❺. I always rake them to the left side because that gives me a good angle for cooking and maneuvering the pizza on the right side. Allow the fire to burn, adding wood occasionally, for 45 minutes longer. If you have an infrared thermometer, aim it at the center of the oven floor; the temperature should be about 800°F; the dome will be at least 1000°F. These temperatures will indicate that your overall oven temperature is about 900°F. The first pizza you cook will also help you judge the intensity of the heat, and you can adjust the fire accordingly.

continued

5. Brush the floor of the oven with your long-handled oven brush, pushing any ashes into the fire. Then, wrap a damp cloth around the brush and mop the bottom of the oven, cleaning it completely. You don't want your pizza to pick up any cinders from the fire.

6. There should always be flames hugging the side and going partway up the dome of the oven, which will cook the top of the pizza while the oven floor cooks the bottom. To get the flames going, throw some wood shavings, thin wood chips, or kindling onto the embers before you put your pizza in the oven. If it's been a while between pizzas and your oven is not hot enough, add a log and let it burn to bring the oven back to temperature.

I suggest you cook one wood-fired pizza at a time, since juggling multiple pizzas in the oven is tricky and a single pizza cooks in less than 2 minutes.

Wood-Fired Oven Tips

- *The first time you cook pizza in a wood-fired oven, make some extra dough to practice with.*

- *If ingredients get stuck on the oven floor, use the ash scraper to move some coals over them and then let them burn for about 3 minutes. Be sure to move the coals back into the fire, and brush the oven floor well before making the next pizza.*

- *If you've used your oven within the last 24 hours, you'll find that it will take less time to come to temperature.*

WOOD-FIRED OVEN BAKING

MAKES ONE 12-INCH PIZZA; 6 SLICES

1 (9-ounce/255 gram) ball
Napoletana Dough (page 187)

Flour, for dusting

Make a fire in a wood-fired oven (see Building Your Fire, page 195). After you have moved the fire from the front of the oven toward the back (step 3), remove the dough ball from the refrigerator and leave wrapped at room temperature until the dough warms to 60°F to 65°F. This is about 1½ hours before the oven is ready for baking.

Dust the work surface with flour, then move the dough to the surface and dust the top (see Transferring the Dough to the Work Surface, page 30).

Sprinkle a wooden peel with flour. Open the dough on the work surface to a 12-inch round with a slightly raised edge (see Opening and Stretching the Dough, page 33).

Move the dough to the peel. As you work, shake the peel forward and backward to ensure the dough isn't sticking.

Top the pizza according to the recipe you're following. Shake the peel a final time to ensure the dough isn't sticking. If it is, lift up the edge that is sticking and dust the peel with more flour. Do not try to move it to the oven if it's sticking or you'll end up with a misshapen pizza and ingredients spilled onto the oven floor.

Give your fire a final check. You want to be sure that flames are reaching up the sides of the oven and partway across the dome. If necessary, add wood shavings or chips or kindling to get the flames going.

Transferring the pizza to the oven: Choose a spot near the fire, toward the center of the oven, to land your pizza. You will use this same spot throughout the cooking process. Reach in with the peel and tilt it down so that its front edge touches the oven floor. Give the peel a quick, short forward push to move the pizza off the front of it, then level the peel and pull it back with a long, smooth motion, leaving the pizza in place on the oven floor. Do not move the pizza at this point. If you aren't happy with the position, wait for about 15 seconds, until the dough sets enough to move it without tearing the bottom.

Rotating the pizza: As soon as the pizza is in the oven, put your wooden peel aside and pick up your metal *palino*, which you will use to move and rotate the pizza. You'll see that the side of the pizza closest to the fire will become browned and speckled (even a bit charred), usually after

continued

PRO TIP

STAGING WOOD Instead of throwing a log right on the fire. I stage it, by first putting it just inside the oven to the left of the mouth and leaving it it there for about 3 minutes. This helps the wood catch immediately and then burn more consistently when it's added to the fire. Note that you need a fairly large professional oven to have the space to do this. With a small home oven, your wood may be too close to the flames and might catch fire.

about 20 seconds. It's important to rotate the pizza as soon as this happens, as it will burn very quickly. Working between the pizza and the fire, position half of the metal peel under the side of the pizza closest to the fire. Lift the peel at a slight angle and pull it toward you to rotate the pizza 90 degrees counterclockwise ❶. Set the pizza on the oven floor again, then immediately center the peel under it and move the pizza back into its original spot. In order to brown the sides evenly, you'll need to rotate the pizza four times in this way, always keeping it in its original spot ❷. I recommend practicing this rotating maneuver with an untopped dough round (which you can ultimately throw away) several times until you get the hang of it.

Doming the pizza: If you want to char the crust a bit more just before you remove the pizza from the oven, center the palino under the pizza and carefully lift it up toward the roof of the oven, a technique known as doming (shown here on a Quattro Forni pizza) ❸. Keep the pizza moving with a gentle rocking motion, being careful that it remains centered and balanced on the peel. Dome the pizza for no more than a few seconds, checking constantly to make sure it isn't getting too black. If one side is getting too dark, pull the *palino* out of the oven completely, rotate the pizza, and then dome it again.

Finishing the pizza: Using the *palino*, remove the pizza from the oven and transfer it to a cutting board. Slice and garnish the pizza as directed in the recipe you are following.

Shutting down: When you're finished making pizzas for the day, use the ash scraper to spread the embers evenly across the oven floor, then close the oven door and let the oven cool completely. This can take up to 24 hours and sometimes even longer. Once the oven is cool, use your ash scraper and brush to scrape the ashes into a metal bucket. Be sure to let the ashes cool completely before you dispose of them.

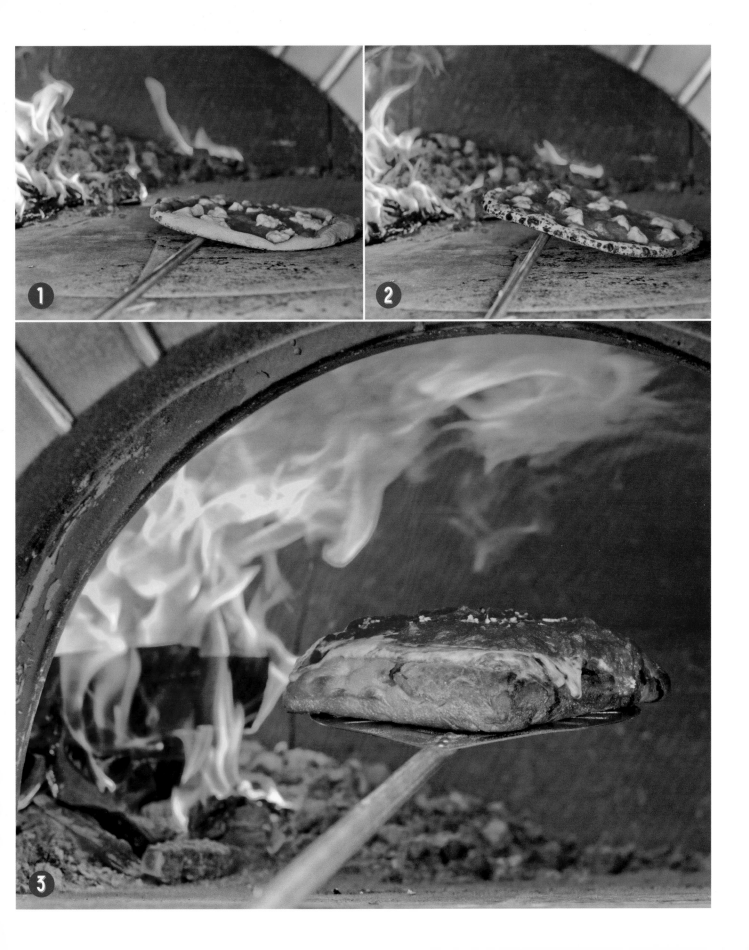

Troubleshooting

- *If the pizza looks like it's cooking too quickly at any time, move it farther away from the fire.*

- *If the pizza is not cooking quickly enough, move it closer to the fire and check to be sure a flame is curving up the sides of the oven and over the pizza.*

- *If the bottom of the pizza doesn't look like it's browning enough, move the pizza to a new spot on the oven floor. This may also be a sign (for future reference) that you have too much flour on the bottom of your pizza. Before you make your next pizza, add more wood to the fire. If that doesn't help, spread some hot embers over the area where you're cooking your pizzas and let the floor heat for 10 to 15 minutes; then rake the embers back into the fire and clean the floor with your oven brush and damp towel.*

- *If the bottom is brown enough but the edges aren't, pick up the pizza with the metal peel and hold the edge that needs browning toward the fire.*

- *If the area of the floor on which you are baking your pizzas is too hot, you can use a "dummy dough" (a dough round the size of a pizza with no topping on it) to cool the floor down. To do this, let the dummy dough cook on the floor until it's quite dark, flip it, and cook the second side until it's also dark, then discard the dough. The area where you cooked it will now be cooler for making your next pizza.*

- *If the black ring around the edge of the oven dome begins to creep up and you find that your pizzas start taking more than 90 seconds to bake, your oven is losing heat and you need to add more wood. Once you are baking pizzas, always add just one log at a time.*

HOME-OVEN BROILER METHOD

MAKES ONE 12-INCH PIZZA; 6 SLICES

This technique uses the broiler to create the charred effect of wood-fired oven pizza in a way that the oven alone can't do. I think it works best with baking steels, but pizza stones will also work. Here's the basic concept: you preheat the oven for an hour with two steels or stones to get them up to temperature, then you switch to the broiler setting for a few minutes while you get the pizza ready for baking. The pizza cooks on the upper steel or stone with the heat of the steel or stone below it and the charring heat of the broiler above it—just as it would cook both from above and below in a wood-fired oven—and then gets a final toasting on the lower steel to crisp the bottom.

If your oven has multiple broiler settings, set it to high the first time you try this. If you find that the top of your pizza is getting too dark before the crust is fully baked, switch to the medium setting.

---

1 (9-ounce/255 gram) ball Napoletana Dough (page 187)

Flour, for dusting

Remove the dough ball from the refrigerator and leave wrapped at room temperature until the dough warms to 60°F to 65°F. Meanwhile, set up the oven with two baking steels or pizza stones and preheat to 500°F for 1 hour (see Getting Started, page 29).

When you are ready to open the dough, switch the oven setting to broil, so that the broiler preheats for about 5 minutes while you prepare your pizza.

Dust the work surface with flour, then move the dough to the surface and dust the top (see Transferring the Dough to the Work Surface, page 30).

Sprinkle a wooden peel with flour. Open the dough on the work surface to a 12-inch round with a slightly raised edge (see Opening and Stretching the Dough, page 33).

Move the dough to the peel. As you work, shake the peel forward and backward to ensure the dough isn't sticking. Top the pizza according to the recipe you're using.

Slide the pizza onto the top steel (see Moving the Dough to the Oven, page 34). Close the door and broil for about 1½ minutes. (The first time you do this, check the progress of the pizza after about 1 minute, to make sure it's not cooking too fast or burning.) Slide the peel under the pizza (at this point, I like to switch to a perforated metal peel), then rotate it 180 degrees and return it to the top steel to continue broiling for another 1½ minutes. The top crust should be speckled, even charred, and the bottom should be browned and speckled. Slide the peel under the pizza, lifting the pizza onto the peel, then rotate the pizza 180 degrees and transfer it to the bottom steel to cook for about 30 seconds, to complete the cooking.

Transfer the pizza to a cutting board to slice or garnish it as directed in the recipe.

MARGHERITA

MAKES ONE 12-INCH PIZZA; 6 SLICES

The legend, which may or may not be entirely true, begins with the most famous take-out pizza order in history. In 1889, a renowned Neapolitan *pizzaiolo* named Raffaele Esposito was summoned to the city's splendid Capodimonte palace, where the visiting queen of Italy, Margherita of Savoy, wanted to taste the local pie. Eager to impress, Esposito served three kinds: a traditional marinara, one covered in whitebait (tiny young fish), and a third that he created for the occasion with tomato, mozzarella, and basil to represent Italy's national colors. Allegedly, this was the world's first cheese pizza, which makes it one of the most important moments in human history. The tricolor was the one Queen Margherita liked best, so guess what he named it?

Trust the quantities of sauce, cheese, and basil I've provided, even though they might look a bit skimpy.

---

1 (9-ounce/255-gram) ball
Napoletana Dough (page 187)

Flour, for dusting

Generous ⅓ cup (100 grams)
**Napoletana Tomato Sauce
(page 189)**

3 fresh basil leaves, torn in half

**4 ounces (115 grams) fresh whole-milk
mozzarella cheese, homemade
(page 190) or store-bought fior di latte,
preferably Grande, well drained**

Fine sea salt

**Extra virgin olive oil in a spouted
container, for drizzling**

Make a fire in a wood-fired oven (see Building Your Fire, page 195). Or, if you will be using a home oven, ready the oven as instructed in Home-Oven Broiler Method (see page 202).

Prepare the dough according to the instructions on page 197 for Wood-Fired Oven Baking or, if using a home oven, according to the instructions for Home-Oven Broiler Method.

Spoon the tomato sauce onto the center of the dough. Then, using the back of the spoon in a circular motion and working outward from the center, spread the sauce evenly over the surface, leaving a ½-inch border. (This will be a thin layer of sauce.) Arrange the basil, shiny side up, evenly over the sauce. Pinch the cheese into pieces slightly larger than a quarter and place them, skin side down, on the pizza, using some of the cheese to cover part of each piece of basil. This helps prevent the basil from burning. Sprinkle the pizza lightly with salt. Then, working from the center outward, drizzle a spiral of oil (about 1 ½ teaspoons) over the surface.

Bake the pizza as directed for Wood-Fired Oven Baking or the Home-Oven Broiler Method.

Transfer the pizza to a cutting board and cut into 6 wedges.

NAPOLETANA

Wood Fire–Roasted Cherry Tomatoes

Cherry tomatoes roasted in a wood-fired oven have an amazingly intense flavor. Toss them—on or off the stems—with olive oil to coat lightly, then season with salt and pepper and place in a cast-iron pan. Once the fire has been moved toward the back of the oven (see Building Your Fire, page 195, step 3), put the pan in the oven and roast the tomatoes until they have softened. It should take about 10 minutes but will depend on the intensity of the fire. If you will be using the tomatoes on a pizza, don't let them char too much since they will cook again. If you will be serving them alone or using them as a garnish, let them char slightly.

To use the tomatoes on pizza, pull off the stems if they're still attached and continue with the recipe. You don't need to cut the tomatoes, since they won't roll on the pizza.

These tomatoes also make a beautiful garnish, served on the stem alongside roasted or grilled meats or fish.

MARGHERITA EXTRA

MAKES ONE 12-INCH PIZZA; 6 SLICES

At my restaurants, we call this pizza the Spacca Napoli, named for the famous street that cuts through the heart of old Naples. In Italy, it's officially known as the margherita extra—the "extras" being *mozzarella di bufala* rather than *fior di latte*, and fresh cherry tomatoes instead of sauce. Look for *mozzarella di bufala* from Italy, which has a creamier flavor and better texture for pizza than American or Spanish buffalo mozzarella. This pizza is a great choice for summer, when you can buy or grow great cherry tomatoes. In the winter, you can give less-than-stellar cherry tomatoes a quick sauté with olive oil, garlic, and sea salt to add a bit more flavor action.

1 (9-ounce/255-gram) ball Napoletana Dough (page 187)

Flour, for dusting

12 raw cherry tomatoes or wood fire–roasted cherry tomatoes (see page 206)

1/2 teaspoon (1.5 grams) finely chopped garlic

Olive oil, for tossing

Fine sea salt and freshly ground black pepper

5 fresh basil leaves, torn in half

2 1/2 ounces (70 grams) mozzarella di bufala, well drained

Extra virgin olive oil in a spouted container, for drizzling

Make a fire in a wood-fired oven (see Building Your Fire, page 195). Or, if you will be using a home oven, ready the oven as instructed in Home-Oven Broiler Method (see page 202).

Prepare the dough according to the instructions on page 197 for Wood-Fired Oven Baking or, if using a home oven, according to the instructions for Home-Oven Broiler Method.

Cut large cherry tomatoes into quarters and smaller tomatoes in half and put them in a bowl. (All of the tomatoes must be cut to keep them from rolling around as you slide the pizza into the oven.) Toss the tomatoes with the garlic and a light coating of olive oil and season with salt and pepper. Set aside.

Arrange the pieces of basil, shiny side up, evenly over the dough. Pinch the cheese into pieces slightly larger than a quarter and place them, skin side down, on the pizza, using some of the cheese to cover part of each piece of basil. This helps prevent the basil from burning.

Scatter the tomatoes over the pizza and sprinkle the pizza lightly with salt. Then, working from the center outward, drizzle a spiral of extra virgin oil (about 1 1/2 teaspoons) over the surface.

Bake the pizza as directed for Wood-Fired Oven Baking or Home-Oven Broiler Method.

Transfer the pizza to a cutting board and cut into 6 wedges.

NAPOLETANA

MARINARA

MAKES ONE 12-INCH PIZZA; 6 SLICES

In the 1700s, Neapolitan sailors began topping their bland bread with tomatoes and herbs during long sea voyages. The idea caught on among their hometown's bakeries, and *pizza alla marinara* (mariner-style) was born. Today a traditional *pizza alla marinara* is topped with nothing more than pureed tomatoes, thinly sliced garlic, oregano, and extra virgin olive oil. That's right, no cheese. I like to roast the garlic to mellow its flavor. Even though I suggest cutting this pizza into six slices, I use only three garlic cloves—a nod to the idea that in Naples, and throughout Italy, pizzas like this are served whole as a meal for one person.

1 (9-ounce/255-gram) ball Napoletana Dough (page 187)

Flour, for dusting

3/4 cup (200 grams) Napoletana Tomato Sauce (page 189)

3 Roasted Garlic Cloves (page 209)

Fine sea salt

Extra virgin olive oil in a spouted container, for drizzling

Dried oregano, for dusting

Make a fire in a wood-fired oven (see Building Your Fire, page 195). Or, if you will be using a home oven, ready the oven as instructed in Home-Oven Broiler Method (see page 200).

Prepare the dough according to the instructions on page 197 for Wood-Fired Oven Baking or, if using a home oven, according to the instructions for Home-Oven Broiler Method.

Spoon the tomato sauce onto the center of the dough. Then, using the back of the spoon in a circular motion and working outward from the center, spread the sauce evenly over the surface, leaving a 1/2-inch border. Space the garlic cloves evenly around the pizza.

Sprinkle the pizza lightly with salt. Then, working from the center outward, drizzle a spiral of oil (about 1 1/2 teaspoons) over the surface.

Bake the pizza as directed for Wood-Fired Oven Baking or Home-Oven Broiler Method.

Transfer the pizza to a cutting board, dust the top with oregano, and drizzle with a bit more oil. Cut into 6 wedges.

ROASTED GARLIC CLOVES

Peeled garlic cloves, in number desired

Olive oil, to cover

Here's a handy way to make "roasted" garlic on the stove top. Make any quantity you need, just be sure the cloves are completely covered in oil.

Trim the root end of the garlic cloves and discard. Put the cloves in a small saucepan and add oil to cover. Set the pan over very low heat (see note); you should see small bubbles rising but no bubbles should break on the surface. If the heat is still too high, place the pan over a diffuser.

Cook the garlic for about 30 minutes, then check the cloves with the tip of a paring knife. They should be golden and completely tender. If they are not, continue to cook until they are ready.

Using a slotted spoon, transfer the garlic cloves to a heatproof jar or other container with a tight-fitting lid. Strain the cooking oil over the cloves and let cool to room temperature. Cover and refrigerate for up to 1 week. Bring to room temperature before using.

Note: If you will be using a wood-fired oven to cook the pizza, you can place the saucepan at the mouth of the oven as the oven heats. The garlic will cook from the radiating heat. It will probably take 20 to 30 minutes, but check the cloves often and turn the pan from time to time. The cooking time can vary significantly, depending on the intensity of the fire.

NAPOLETANA

Wine: A Match for Margherita

I like to serve Napoletana pizzas with wines from the region. At my restaurants, our recommended wine pairing with our pizza margherita is Grotta del Sole's Gragnano delle Penisola Sorrentina, a midpriced red made from a blend of Piedirosso, Aglianico, and Sciascinoso grapes. It has a slightly effervescent quality and a hint of sour cherry flavor.

MASTUNICOLA

MAKES ONE 12-INCH PIZZA; 6 SLICES

A classic of Naples, this pie was born as a thrifty *pizza bianca* (no tomatoes) that was traditionally topped with basil (which is *vasunicola* in Neapolitan dialect and probably the source of the pizza's name), a bit of cheese, and lard. I make my version with thinly sliced *lardo* (salt-cured pork fat), added after the pizza comes out of the oven. Although it's not cooked, the lardo melts a bit, becoming soft and translucent and adding some serious bacony richness.

1 (9-ounce/255-gram) ball Napoletana Dough (page 187)

Flour, for dusting

5 fresh basil leaves, torn in half

3 ounces (85 grams) mozzarella di bufala, well drained

Fine sea salt

Extra virgin olive oil in a spouted container, for drizzling

6 paper-thin strips (3 grams each) lardo

Make a fire in a wood-fired oven (see Building Your Fire, page 195). Or, if you will be using a home oven, ready the oven as instructed in Home-Oven Broiler Method (see page 202).

Prepare the dough according to the instructions on page 197 for Wood-Fired Oven Baking or, if using a home oven, according to the instructions for Home-Oven Broiler Method.

Arrange the pieces of basil, shiny side up, over the dough. Pinch the cheese into quarter-size pieces and place them, skin side down, on the pizza, using some of the cheese to cover part of each piece of basil. This helps prevent the basil from burning.

Sprinkle the pizza with salt. Then, working from the center outward, drizzle a spiral of oil (about 1 1/2 teaspoons) over the surface.

Bake the pizza as directed for Wood-Fired Oven Baking or Home-Oven Broiler Method.

Transfer the pizza to a cutting board. Arrange the *lardo* strips from the center toward the edges, spacing them evenly like the spokes on a wheel. Cut between the strips into 6 wedges and drizzle with a bit more oil.

Regional Italian

Americans who visit Italy are often surprised by the pizza. First there's the single-serve factor. No big pies in the center of the table with everybody sharing. Each person gets their own pizza, the size of a large dinner plate, unsliced, with a fork and knife to eat it with. Most Italians carve bite-size pieces and spear them with their fork,

⇒⇒⟶

but it's socially acceptable to cut a larger slice and eat it with your hands.

Then there's the crust, which is usually fairly chewy and quite crunchy on the bottom. And you really taste it because the cheese, sauce, and toppings are all used with a lot more restraint than what you'd find on a typical American pizza.

Even though the cooking of Italy's eighteen regions is infinitely varied, pizzerias tend to be quite similar from one end of the country to the other. In the same way New York style came to dominate the American pizza scene, Neapolitan is the model for pizzeria pizza in Italy. I'm not talking about official STG Neapolitan pizza, which *can* be found throughout Italy, but more about the universal popularity of pizza in the Neapolitan style, known generically as *pizza tonda* (round pizza).

Most Italian pizzerias use wood-fired ovens, so a pizza usually has a few spots of blackened char around the edge. In any Italian pizzeria, you'll always find a margherita and a marinara, along with a list of other classic options, like *quattro stagioni* ("four seasons," usually with marinated artichokes, ham, mushrooms, and black olives, each in its own quadrant); *capricciosa* ("whimsical," with toppings similar to those of the

quattro stagioni but scattered, and sometimes a sunny-side-up egg cooked on top); and *quattro formaggi* ("four cheeses," with mozzarella, Gorgonzola, and other cheeses like Fontina, Swiss, or pecorino). Alongside those, you'll usually find several signature creations of the house, as well as a calzone or two with a simple filling like mozzarella and ham or prosciutto.

Of course, there's plenty of pizza outside the world of pizzerias in Italy, too. You'll find big rectangular pizzas, called *pizza in teglia* (pan pizza) or *pizza al taglio* (pizza by the slice), sold in bakeries, take-out windows, and cafés throughout the country. These tend to be more like what we'd call Sicilian pizzas. Rome has its own version, *pizza in pala*, which you can read about and try on page 227.

The recipes in this chapter aren't meant to be exact replicas of specific Italian regional pizzas. They're more like my personal tributes to some of my favorite places in the country. I use my Master Dough (for all but the Romana) because the texture and flavor work well with these toppings and a single ball gives you a nice-size pie if you're planning to eat the whole thing yourself, Italian-style.

LUCCA

MAKES ONE 13-INCH PIZZA; 6 SLICES

When my wife, Julie, and I got married, we knew there was only one place to go for our honeymoon: Italy. I was excited to take her to Gombitelli, the tiny town in the mountains near Lucca where my dad's side of the family came from. My great-grandparents, Angelo and Olimpia Gemignani, had left Gombitelli for America at the turn of the last century, and my Grandpa Frank was born right after they got off the boat.

We meandered through the Tuscan countryside, following increasingly sketchy gravel roads and finally ending up on a narrow donkey trail that wound up the side of a steep mountain. I remembered this road from a visit I'd made seven years earlier. Since then, it seemed to have eroded and gotten even narrower. It was barely wide enough for a car, with a sheer drop along one side and, naturally, no guardrail. We came to a dead end, the front of the car facing a deep ravine, and an old man came out of his house, waving violently and screaming at us in Italian. I rolled down the window and said "Gemignani?" His expression changed from rage to joy as he motioned to follow him and raced off, back down the road, yelling "Gemignani! Gemignani!" I made the most terrifying U-turn of my life and followed him.

The minute I saw the little house and farm, I had the same overwhelming feeling I'd had the first time I'd been there. It was like stepping into my grandpa's farm in California. Although he'd never even been to Italy, he had the blood of a Tuscan *contadino*—and there in front of me was his backyard in every detail: the same flowers, the lemon tree, the dogwood, the fava beans, the big wine jugs wrapped in straw, the rusty tools scattered around. That California farm and my grandpa are long gone, but in that moment, I was home again.

My cousins had decided there was one thing they absolutely had to serve us for our welcome meal: pizza, of course. And this is the one they made. It was quite thin, almost like a toasted flatbread, and I've replicated that in this recipe by rolling the dough out and docking it, so you get a light, crisp crust that's just right with the gutsy *puttanesca*-style combination of crushed tomatoes, olives, garlic, and anchovies.

continued

1 (13-ounce/370-gram) ball Master Dough, preferably with starter (page 44), made with Poolish

2 parts flour mixed with 1 part semolina, for dusting

Scant 1/2 cup (100 grams) hand-crushed tomatoes (see page 28)

10 oil-cured black olives, pitted and halved

1 teaspoon (8 grams) minced drained oil-packed anchovies

1/4 teaspoon (0.7 grams) minced garlic

Extra virgin olive oil, for brushing and drizzling

6 ounces (170 grams) whole-milk mozzarella cheese, shredded (1 1/2 cups)

1 fresh basil leaf, rolled up lengthwise and cut crosswise into fine julienne

Dried oregano, for dusting

Remove the dough ball from the refrigerator and leave wrapped at room temperature until the dough warms to 60°F to 65°F. Meanwhile, set up the oven with two pizza stones or baking steels and preheat to 500°F for 1 hour (see Getting Started, page 29).

In a bowl, mix together the tomatoes, olives, anchovies, and garlic and set aside.

Dust the work surface with the dusting mixture, then move the dough to the surface and dust the top (see Transferring the Dough to the Work Surface, page 30).

Sprinkle a wooden peel with the dusting mixture.

Following the instructions in Rolling Pizza Dough (see page 103), roll out the dough into a round 14 to 15 inches in diameter. Using a pizza wheel, trim the dough to a 13-inch round. Brush the surface of the dough with oil, flatten the edge, then dock the surface.

Move the dough to the peel. As you work, shake the peel forward and backward to ensure the dough isn't sticking.

Mound the mozzarella in the center of the dough and use your fingertips to spread it out evenly over the surface, leaving a 3/4-inch border. Drizzle more oil over the top.

Slide the pizza onto the top stone (see Moving the Dough to the Oven, page 34). Bake for 4 minutes. Lift the pizza onto the peel, remove it from the oven, and scatter the tomato mixture over the top. Rotate the pizza 180 degrees and transfer it to the bottom stone. Bake for 5 minutes, until the bottom is browned and crisp and the top is golden brown.

If you would like the top of the pizza darker, transfer it to the top stone for 30 seconds.

Transfer the pizza to a cutting board and cut into 6 wedges. Scatter the basil over the top and finish with a dusting of oregano and a drizzle of oil.

RIMINI

MAKES ONE 12-INCH PIZZA; 6 SLICES

Mmm. Fried dough. On a trip to Rimini, a resort town on Italy's Adriatic coast, I had a memorable fried pizza topped with cheese and ham. To re-create it, I came up with this shallow-fry method in which you fry the dough, then flip it, top it with mozzarella, and cover it with a lid to melt the cheese. In honor of Rimini, I've topped this one with the region's famous *squacquerone* cheese, which is as deliciously soft and runny as it is difficult to pronounce. If you can't find it, you can use *crescenza* (also known as *stracchino*). It goes on after frying and quickly melts on the hot crust. I also add thin slices of the cooked ham sold in Italian delis as *prosciutto cotto*. Not to be confused with prosciutto, which is cured but not cooked, this is what we know as ham, but it's a bit paler, less smoky, and more delicate than typical American deli ham.

For this method, it's really helpful to roll your dough out as close to the stove top as possible and to have everything set up before you start cooking: your skillet on the stove top, a lid within easy reach, your cheeses and toppings measured out, and a plate lined with paper towels right next to the stove. Keep a close eye on the heat as you fry and adjust it as needed so the dough cooks all the way through without burning on the outside.

REGIONAL ITALIAN

---

1 (8-ounce/225-gram) ball Master Dough, preferably with starter (page 44), made with Poolish

Semolina, for dusting

1/2 cup (112 grams) olive oil, or more as needed

1 1/2 ounces (45 grams) whole-milk mozzarella cheese, shredded (1/4 cup plus 2 tablespoons)

Remove the dough ball from the refrigerator and leave wrapped at room temperature until the dough warms to 60°F to 65°F.

Line a large dinner plate with paper towels. Pour the oil into a 12-inch cast-iron skillet and have a lid and a pair of tongs nearby.

Dust a work surface near the stove with semolina, then move the dough to the surface and dust the top (see Transferring the Dough to the Work Surface, page 30).

Press out the dough into a flat disk and roll it out into an 11 1/2-inch round (see Rolling Pizza Dough, page 103).

continued

1 ounce (30 grams) thinly shaved lardo

1½ ounces (45 grams) squacquerone cheese

6 thin slices (2 ounces/55 grams) prosciutto cotto

Small piece young Pecorino Romano cheese, cold, for shaving

Heat the oil in the skillet over medium-high heat for about 3 minutes, until very hot with ripples covering the surface. Gently lift the dough and lower the bottom of one edge into the side of the pan closest to you, then lower the remaining dough into the pan. Cook for about 2 minutes, using tongs to check the bottom often and to rotate the dough as needed to brown evenly. If bubbles form on the top of the dough, pierce them gently with the tongs.

When the bottom is golden brown, turn the dough over. Immediately sprinkle the mozzarella evenly over the surface and cover the pan. Cook for 1 to 1½ minutes, until the cheese has melted and the bottom of the dough is a rich golden brown. Using the tongs, reach to the center of the pizza and transfer it to the towel-lined plate to drain briefly.

Transfer the pizza to the cutting board and cut into 6 wedges. Scatter the *lardo* and pinches of the *squacquerone* evenly over the top. Drape a slice of *prosciutto cotto* on each slice and garnish with shavings of the pecorino.

CALABRESE "DIAVOLA"

MAKES ONE 13-INCH PIZZA; 6 SLICES

Alla diavola—"devil's style"—is the Italian name for pizza topped with tomato sauce, mozzarella, and spicy salami (known as *soppressata piccante* or *salame piccante)*. Like all things spicy in Italy, it's associated with the south—regions like Calabria, Puglia, and Sicily that make up Italy's chile belt. *Alla diavola* is the Italian equivalent of pepperoni pizza, which, by the way, you won't find in Italy. Pepperoni is an American invention, originally inspired by southern Italian spicy salamis but ultimately quite different from them. Now, that inspiration is coming full circle, because more and more American pizzerias are adding spicy salamis and *soppressata* to their pies and talking about it as "the new pepperoni."

---

1 (13-ounce/370-gram) ball Master Dough, preferably with starter (page 44), made with Poolish

2 parts flour mixed with 1 part semolina, for dusting

2/3 cup (140 grams) ground tomatoes, preferably Tomato Magic or DiNapoli

1/2 teaspoon (2 grams) fine sea salt

3/4 teaspoon (.5 grams) dried oregano

7 ounces (200 grams) part-skim mozzarella cheese, shredded (1 3/4 cups)

12 large slices (2 ounces/60 grams) soppressata piccante

Red pepper flakes, for sprinkling

1 tablespoon (16 grams) Hot Pepper Oil (page 223)

Handful of arugula leaves

Small piece Parmigiano-Reggiano cheese, cold, for shaving

Remove the dough ball from the refrigerator and leave wrapped at room temperature until the dough warms to 60°F to 65°F. Meanwhile, set up the oven with two pizza stones or baking steels and preheat to 500°F for 1 hour (see Getting Started, page 29).

Put the ground tomatoes in a bowl and mix in the salt and oregano. Set aside.

Dust the work surface with the dusting mixture, then move the dough to the surface and dust the top (see Transferring the Dough to the Work Surface, page 30).

Sprinkle a wooden peel with the dusting mixture. Open the dough on the work surface to a 13-inch round with a slightly raised edge (see Opening and Stretching the Dough, page 33).

Move the dough to the peel. As you work, shake the peel forward and backward to ensure the dough isn't sticking.

Spoon the tomato sauce in the center of the dough. Then, using the back of the spoon in a circular motion and working outward from the center, spread the sauce evenly over the surface, leaving a 3/4-inch border. Mound the mozzarella in the center of the pizza and use your fingertips to spread it evenly over the sauce.

Slide the pizza onto the top stone (see Moving the Dough to the Oven, page 34). Bake for 7 minutes. Lift the pizza with the peel and remove it from the oven. Arrange the *soppressata* evenly over the top. Rotate the pizza 180 degrees and transfer it to the bottom stone. Continue to bake for another 7 minutes, until the bottom is browned and crisp and the top is golden brown.

Transfer the pizza to a cutting board and cut into 6 wedges. Finish with a sprinkling of pepper flakes, a drizzle of pepper oil, a scattering of arugula leaves, and shavings of Parmigiano-Reggiano.

HOT PEPPER OIL

MAKES 1 CUP (255 GRAMS)

1 tablespoon (14 grams) water

1 tablespoon (15 grams) crushed Calabrese peppers

2¹/₂ teaspoons (7 grams) chopped serrano chiles (with seeds)

2 teaspoons (5 grams) chopped Thai chile

¹/₂ small (.5 grams) Thai chile

¹/₄ teaspoon (.7 grams) smoked sweet paprika

¹/₄ teaspoon (1.5 grams) fine sea salt

¹/₄ teaspoon (.5 gram) freshly ground black pepper

1 cup (240 grams) olive or canola oil

Making your own hot pepper oil lets you customize the heat factor and the flavor. This is the recipe we use in my restaurants, and it goes with pretty much everything, from grilled fish, chicken, or steak to sautéed vegetables. It's great with warm bread for dipping, too. I like to store it in a widemouthed jar and use a spoon to drizzle it. That way I can spoon up some of the solids when I want a little extra chile heat.

Combine the water, Calabrese peppers, serrano chiles, Thai chiles, paprika, salt, and pepper in a heavy saucepan and place over medium-high heat. Heat, stirring, for about 30 seconds, then stir in the oil. When the oil comes to a boil, lower the heat to a simmer, and simmer for 1 minute.

Remove from the heat and pour into a heatproof container. Let cool completely, then cover. The oil can be stored at room temperature for up to 2 weeks.

QUATTRO ANCHOVY

MAKES ONE 13-INCH PIZZA; 4 SLICES

Anchovies have been part of Italian cooking since the ancient Romans used *garum* (fermented fish sauce) to flavor their food, and the earliest pizzas of Naples often featured anchovies or other small Mediterranean fish. Americans, of course, either love them or hate them, but it seems to me the tide is turning, and in my pizzerias, we get more requests for them all the time. So for all those die-hard anchovistas, I decided to come up with the ultimate anchovy pizza. It features a rich anchovy cream and four very different types of anchovies: salt packed (which have a rich, meaty flavor), white (mild, lightly pickled, and less fishy tasting), Calabrese (marinated with chiles and tomatoes) and brown (the familiar oil-packed type sold in cans and jars). Since anchovies aren't for everyone, this pie is not built for sharing. It's a pizza for one with four slices, each giving you a taste of a different kind of anchovy.

1 (13-ounce/370-gram) ball Master Dough, preferably with starter (page 44), made with Poolish

2 parts flour mixed with 1 part semolina, for dusting

ANCHOVY CREAM

1 tablespoon (24 grams) minced drained oil-packed anchovies

¼ cup (55 grams) mayonnaise

2 tablespoons (30 grams) sour cream

Squeeze of fresh lemon juice

2 tablespoons grated Pecorino Romano cheese

Pinch of freshly ground black pepper

Remove the dough ball from the refrigerator and leave wrapped at room temperature until the dough warms to 60°F to 65°F. Meanwhile, set up the oven with two pizza stones or baking steels and preheat to 500°F for 1 hour (see Getting Started, page 29).

Put the oil-packed anchovies, mayonnaise, sour cream, lemon juice, Pecorino, and black pepper in the bowl of a food processor and process until smooth. Set aside.

Salt-packed anchovies are whole anchovies with the spine intact, so you must fillet each anchovy. First, rinse the anchovies under cold running water, then soak them in a bowl of cold water to cover for 30 minutes, changing the water every 10 minutes. Drain and rinse well again. To fillet each fish, starting at the spine, gently pull off the top fillet. It should come off easily; if it doesn't, soak the anchovies a bit longer. Pull the other fillet away from spine and discard the spine. Remove and discard any small bones you feel in the fillets, then dry the fillets on a paper towel.

Dust the work surface with the dusting mixture, then move the dough to the surface and dust the top (see Transferring the Dough to the Work Surface, page 30).

2 whole (25 grams) salt-packed giant anchovies, preferably Agostino Recca

7 ounces (200 grams) whole-milk mozzarella cheese, shredded (1¾ cups)

4 fillets (18 grams) vinegar-packed Italian white anchovies, preferably Agostino Recca, drained

4 fillets (16 grams) Calabrese anchovies, preferably Tutto Calabria, drained

4 fillets (14 grams) oil-packed brown anchovies, preferably Agostino Recca, drained

Handful of small arugula leaves

Small piece Piave cheese, cold, for shaving

Lemon wedges, for serving

Sprinkle a wooden peel with the dusting mixture.

Following the instructions in Rolling Pizza Dough (see page 103), roll out the dough into a round 14 to 15 inches in diameter. Using a pizza wheel, trim the dough to a 13-inch round, brush the surface of the dough with oil, flatten the edge, and then dock the surface.

Move the dough to the peel. As you work, shake the peel forward and backward to ensure the dough isn't sticking.

Mound the mozzarella in the center of the dough and use your fingertips to spread it evenly over the surface, leaving a ¾-inch border.

Slide the pizza onto the top stone (see Moving the Dough to the Oven, page 34). Bake for 4 minutes. Lift the pizza onto the peel, rotate it 180 degrees, and then transfer it to the bottom stone. Bake for 5 minutes, until the bottom is browned and crisp and the top is golden brown.

Transfer the pizza to a cutting board. Spoon the anchovy cream onto the center of the pizza. Then, using the back of the spoon or a small offset spatula, spread the cream evenly over the surface almost to the edges. Cut the pizza into 4 wedges.

Garnish each slice decoratively with a different type of anchovy. The fillets can be placed side by side or crisscrossed to form Xs. Sometimes Calabrese anchovies are already broken up. If they are, spoon them onto the slice in small dollops. Scatter the arugula over the top and finish with shavings of Piave.

Serve the pizza with the lemon wedges, squeezing the juice over the slices just before eating.

SARDINIA

MAKES ONE 13-INCH PIZZA; 6 SLICES

This is my homage to the famous sheep's milk cheeses of Sardinia. I use young, soft Sardinian pecorino along with mozzarella for melting, and then shave two harder cheeses on top: *Fiore Sardo*, and a longer aged *Pecorino Sardo*. Sardinian pecorinos have a rich, creamy flavor that's ideal for pizzas. They're usually milder and less salty than *Pecorino Romano*, which I tend to use more sparingly as a garnishing cheese.

1 (13-ounce/370-gram) ball Master Dough, preferably with starter (page 44), made with poolish

4 parts flour mixed with 1 part semolina, for dusting

4 ounces (115 grams) whole-milk mozzarella cheese, shredded (1 cup)

3 ounces (85 grams) young Sardinian pecorino cheese, shredded (3/4 cup)

Small piece Fiore Sardo, cold, for shaving

Small piece aged Pecorino Sardo, cold, for shaving

Extra virgin olive oil, for drizzling

Remove the dough ball from the refrigerator and leave wrapped at room temperature until the dough warms to 60°F to 65°F. Meanwhile, set up the oven with two pizza stones or baking steels and preheat to 500°F for 1 hour (see Getting Started, page 29).

Dust the work surface with the dusting mixture, then move the dough to the surface and dust the top (see Transferring the Dough to the Work Surface, page 30).

Sprinkle a wooden peel with the dusting mixture.

Following the instructions in Rolling Pizza Dough (see page 103), roll out the dough into a round 14 to 15 inches in diameter. Using a pizza wheel, trim the dough to a 13-inch round, brush the surface of the dough with oil, flatten the edge, and then dock the surface.

Move the dough to the peel. As you work, shake the peel forward and backward to ensure the dough isn't sticking.

Mound the mozzarella in the center of the dough and use your fingertips to spread it evenly over the surface, leaving a 3/4-inch border. Do the same with the young pecorino.

Slide the pizza onto the top stone (see Moving the Dough to the Oven, page 34). Bake for 4 minutes. Lift the pizza onto the peel, rotate it 180 degrees, and then transfer it to the bottom stone. Bake for 2½ minutes, rotate it again 180 degrees, and bake for a final 2½ minutes, until the bottom is browned and crisp and the top is golden brown.

Transfer the pizza to a cutting board and cut into 6 wedges. Finish with shavings of *fiore sardo* and aged pecorino and a drizzle of oil.

PIZZA ROMANA

MAKES ONE 12 BY 24-INCH PIZZA; EIGHTEEN 4-INCH SQUARES

In Rome, pizza is huge. Literally. The city's own style, known as *pizza romana*, *pizza al metro* (pizza by the meter), or *pizza in pala* (paddle pizza), is baked in meter-long rectangular strips, which are sliced and sold by weight in bakeries and specialty food shops. There's thick-crust and thin (which is what I like best and what we serve at my restaurants), and in recent years, more innovations and variations have been added to the mix at places like Pizzarium, where Gabriele Bonci makes an innovative upside-down pan pizza made with toppings first baked on the bottom, then flipped over and finished.

At my restaurants, we feature whole, huge Romana pizzas, which come to your table as a showstopping shared meal. We cut them into eighteen squares, and top each set of six squares in a different way. I like to tell people to eat their way from one end to the other in "courses." There's always an "antipasto" section, a "main dish" section with protein, and a section with sweeter ingredients for "dessert." In this recipe, that would be the tomatoes, basil, and olives; the *soppressata piccante*, Parmigiano-Regiano, and arugula; and the fig, prosciutto, and Gorgonzola.

A home oven—even a large one—can't accommodate a pizza this size, so I worked out a simple method for baking the pizza in two parts: you bake them one after the other, then trim the edges, and once you line up the two halves end to end and add the toppings, you end up with a giant "wow" presentation.

But even though it looks super-colorful and dramatic, this pizza is actually quite foolproof because you bake the two halves with just cheese and then add all the toppings after they come out of the oven. By the time you get both halves baked and the whole thing assembled and topped, your pizza will be room temperature or slightly warm, but don't worry. That's the effect you're going for, and the room-temperature ingredients on top will taste great this way. You can use the three topping combos I've suggested here, or you can simply go with a single topping. To feed a crowd as a finger-food, just cut smaller pieces.

continued

You'll need a large peel and pizza stones or baking steels that can accommodate a 12 by 14-inch pizza. This looks very cool served on a giant pizza paddle or a very long cutting board.

1 (26-ounce/740-gram) ball Romana Dough (page 232)

Semolina, for dusting

12 ounces (340 grams) whole-milk mozzarella cheese, shredded (3 cups)

TOPPING NO. 1

18 cherry tomatoes, halved

12 oil-cured black olives, pitted and halved

3 large fresh basil leaves, rolled up lengthwise and cut crosswise into fine julienne

Extra virgin olive oil, for drizzling

Fine sea salt and freshly ground black pepper

TOPPING NO. 2

6 small slices (1 ounce/30 grams) soppressata piccante

Small handful of small arugula leaves

Small piece Parmigiano-Reggiano cheese, cold, for shaving

2 teaspoons crushed Calabrese peppers

Hot Pepper Oil (page 223), for drizzling (optional)

Set up the oven with two rectangular pizza stones or baking steels (see headnote) and preheat to 500°F one hour before the dough will be ready to roll (see Getting Started, page 29).

Dust the work surface with a generous amount of semolina, then move the dough to the surface and coat both sides with the semolina (see Transferring the Dough to the Work Surface, page 30).

Sprinkle a large wooden peel generously with semolina.

Rolling lengthwise (see photo ❶, page 230) and horizontally ❷, roll the dough into a 13 by 30-inch rectangle (see Rolling Pizza Dough, page 103). If the dough contracts, let it rest for a minute and then roll again (be sure it is dusted generously to keep it from sticking). You can also stretch the dough to help form it into a rectangle ❸. If the rectangle ends up a bit larger, don't worry, as it will be trimmed. Dock the entire surface of the dough ❹.

Using a pizza cutter, cut the dough rectangle in half crosswise ❺.

Move half of the dough to the peel and straighten the edges as necessary ❻. Don't worry if the dough overhangs the peel at this point, as it will be trimmed. As you work, shake the peel forward and backward to ensure the dough isn't sticking.

Mound half of the mozzarella in the center of the dough and use your fingertips to spread it evenly over the surface, leaving a border ❼. Keep in mind that the dough will be trimmed to a 12 by 14-inch rectangle, and that after trimming it, you want to have a 1/2-inch border around the cheese to prevent it from falling off as you move the dough to the stone.

Trim the dough to a 12 by 14-inch rectangle with a pizza wheel ❽. The edges will be squared off by the cutter. Press them gently with your fingertips to flatten them and keep them from curling up as the pizza bakes (see trimming and flattening the dough in Rolling Pizza Dough, page 103). Shake the peel often to ensure the dough isn't sticking. Just before the pizza is ready to go into the oven, check it and, if necessary, use your hands to restretch it into shape.

TOPPING NO. 3

12 slices fig, cut ¼ inch
(from 3 to 4 small figs)

3 thin slices (1.5 ounces/45 grams)
prosciutto, torn in half lengthwise
(optional)

1 tablespoon crumbled Gorgonzola
cheese, at room temperature

Balsamic Glaze (page 131),
for drizzling

Slide the dough onto the bottom stone (see Moving the Dough to the Oven, page 34). Take a peek at the pizza after 30 seconds. If it is puffing up in any area, prick the dough with a paring knife to flatten the puffed area and continue to bake for 5 minutes. Lift the pizza onto the peel, rotate it 180 degrees, and then transfer it to the top stone. Bake for 4 minutes. Lift a corner and check the bottom. It should be crisp and a rich golden brown. If it isn't ready, continue to bake for 1 to 2 minutes.

When the first half is removed from the oven, move the second piece of dough to the peel, top with the remaining cheese, and trim as you did the first piece of dough. Slide the second piece of dough onto the bottom stone and bake, rotate, and transfer the same way as the first half.

Set the dough halves next to each other on a large cutting board or directly on the work surface. Putting the straightest edges on the outside (because they will not be cut), match the other two short sides together. Trim the butting edges as needed to straighten them **9**. The long sides can be trimmed if you like. Move both pieces to a long serving board, butting them end to end to create the illusion of a single long pizza. Make 2 evenly spaced cuts lengthwise through the pizza (to make 3 strips of equal width) and then make 5 evenly spaced cuts horizontally through the pizza (to make 6 strips of equal width), to make 18 squares **10**.

Starting at one short end of the pizza and working across the width to the other, garnish 2 rows of 3 squares each (a total of 6 squares) with each of the following toppings, in order. Don't arrange the ingredients too carefully, as the pizza looks best with a more rustic presentation.

Topping No. 1: Scatter the cherry tomatoes and olives on the crust. Garnish with the basil and a drizzle of olive oil. Sprinkle with salt and pepper.

Topping No. 2: Place a slice of soppressata on each square. Scatter arugula leaves and Parmesan shavings over the soppressata. Spoon small bits of the Calabrese peppers over the top and drizzle lightly with the pepper oil.

Topping No. 3: Arrange 2 fig slices on each square and drape a halved prosciutto slice around the fig slices. Garnish with small pieces of Gorgonzola and drizzle the balsamic glaze over the top.

The pizza is best eaten in progression (from topping No. 1 to topping No. 3), from the lightest to the most robust to the sweet ending.

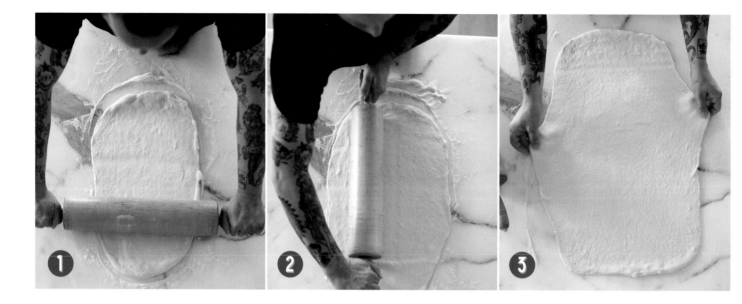

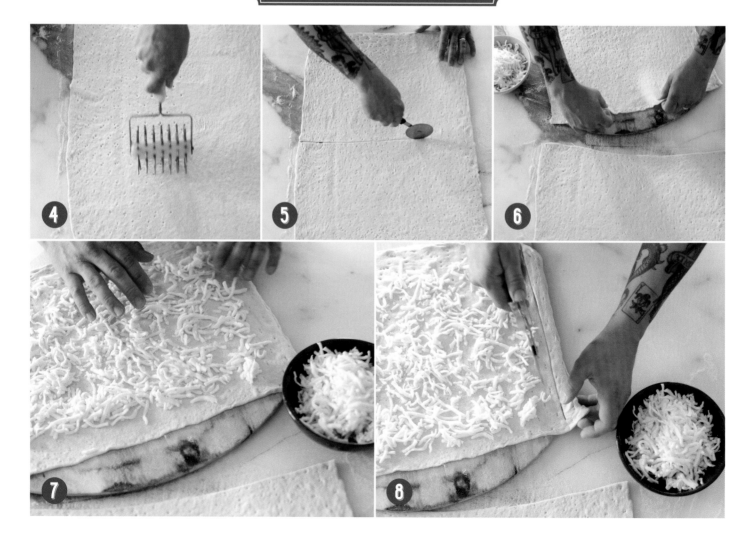

ROMANA DOUGH

MAKES 26 OUNCES (740 GRAMS) DOUGH, ENOUGH FOR 1 ROMANA PIZZA

1 gram (¼ plus ⅛ teaspoon) active dry yeast

70 grams (¼ cup plus 1 tablespoon) warm water (80°F to 85°F)

453 grams (3¾ cups) flour with 13 to 14 percent protein, preferably Pendleton Flour Mills Power or Giusto High-Performer

9 grams (1 tablespoon) diastatic malt

237 grams (1 cup) ice water

23 grams Poolish (page 47)

14 grams (1 tablespoon) fine sea salt

Semolina or flour, for dusting

For baker's percentages, see page 302.

Put the yeast in a small bowl, add the warm water, and whisk vigorously for 30 seconds. The yeast should dissolve in the water and the mixture should foam. If it doesn't and the yeast granules float, the yeast is "dead" and should be discarded. Begin again with a fresh amount of yeast and water.

Combine the flour and malt in the bowl of a stand mixer fitted with the dough hook. With the mixer running on the lowest speed, pour in most of the ice water, reserving about 2 tablespoons, followed by the yeast-water mixture. Pour the reserved water into the yeast bowl, swirl it around to dislodge any bits of yeast stuck to the bowl, and add to the mixer. Mix for about 15 seconds, stop the mixer, and add the poolish.

Continue to mix the dough at the lowest speed for about 1 minute, until most of the dough comes together around the hook. Stop the mixer. Use your fingers to pull away any dough clinging to the hook, and scrape the sides and bottom of the bowl with a bowl scraper or rubber spatula. Check the bottom of the bowl for any unincorporated flour. If there is still unincorporated flour, add ½ teaspoon of water and mix again. Turn the dough over and press it into the bottom of the bowl to pick up any stray pieces. All of the water will be absorbed, but the dough may not look completely smooth.

Add the salt and mix for 1 to 2 more minutes on the lowest speed to combine.

Use the bowl scraper to transfer the dough to an unfloured work surface, then knead for 2 to 3 minutes, until smooth (see Kneading the Dough, page 24).

Lift the dough into a large bowl, press it down slightly, and rub a little water over the top. Cover the bowl with a double layer of plastic wrap and refrigerate for 24 to 48 hours.

Dust the work surface with semolina. Uncover the dough and dust the top. Using the bowl scraper, loosen the dough from the sides and bottom of the bowl, turn the dough out onto the surface, and dust the top. Turn the dough over so that what was the top side in the bowl is the top side on the work surface.

Cup your hands around the dough and form it into a football shape. Transfer the dough to a half sheet pan and pat into an 8 by 4-inch oval. Cover with a damp dish towel and let rise at room temperature for 8 hours. If the towel dries out, dampen it again and re-cover the dough.

WINNER

Four Regions, One Winning Pizza

In 2011, I was the first American to win the Pizza Romana category at the World Championships of Pizza Makers in Naples, Italy. My entry was a play on the classic quattro stagioni *(four seasons). I made a* quattro regioni, *with sections that showcased the cuisines of four regions of Italy: Rome (a carbonara- style topping of cooked pancetta and lightly scrambled eggs, added at the last second), Naples (a caprese topping of* mozzarella di bufala, *sliced tomatoes, and basil), Puglia (with* burrata, *white anchovies, and lemon), and Calabria (a* diavola *with* soppressata piccante *and Calabrese peppers).*

Global

When I started messing around tossing pizzas in my brother's pizzeria, I never imagined that throwing dough could be my key to the world.

I won my first pizza acrobatics championship at twenty-one, but everything really started taking off two years later when I was invited to appear on *The Tonight Show with Jay Leno.* I immediately started getting offers to do TV appearances, competitions, and shows all over the world.

For a kid who had never been overseas, the next few years were like a crazy dream. I spent time in Italy, Germany, Spain, France, Belgium, the Netherlands, Canada, Mexico, the Dominican Republic, and all over the United States. I even ended up doing an extended tour of Thailand with an acrobatics team from Bangkok. And everywhere I went, I didn't just try the local pizza, I introduced myself to the people behind it and worked in their kitchens.

Pizzaiolos are like a secret society. We can spot each other a mile away. We know who's for real and who isn't. Within minutes of meeting, we're laughing and arguing and insulting each other like lifelong friends. So as I hopped from country to country, I used my downtime to meet many of the greatest *pizzaiolos* on the planet

and work alongside them. It was a world-class Pizza University that shaped everything I've done since.

But it was more of an education in methods, techniques, and variations than an immersion in world cuisines. What I discovered was that wherever you go, pizza is its *own* cuisine—a cuisine that may or may not reflect the foods and ingredients of the country where you're eating it.

So here are five pizzas inspired by the flavors I've experienced in my globe-trotting adventures—and by the pizzas from all over the world that I've tasted competing and judging in Italy and France since 2000. These aren't pizzas I actually tasted in any of the countries they represent. Think of them as my taste memories from those places, reinvented as pizzas. That's one of the coolest things about a disk of pizza dough. Whether you're going authentic or crazy creative, it's a perfect canvas for presenting the taste of a place.

BARCELONA

MAKES ONE 13-INCH PIZZA; 6 SLICES

When Julie and I ate our way across Barcelona, we got addicted to *bocadillos*, the tasty sandwiches served in tapas bars and cafés. We ate them every day at the incredible Boqueria market on the Ramblas. And it seemed like every one we tried one had a bit of scrambled egg spooned on top. So that got me thinking about a *bocadillo*-style pizza featuring the best of the Boqueria. I start with a quick tomato sauce made with saffron, fresh chorizo (buy it in bulk rather than in links), hot peppers, and a touch of cream. This rich sauce tastes like a Spanish version of Bolognese, and it's great on pasta, too. If you make one pizza, you'll have $1^1/4$ cups of sauce left over. Add a little extra cream if you like and toss the sauce with some *bucatini*. Or, for an incredible Spanish seafood experience, steam some mussels in white wine, toss them in the warm sauce, and serve over grilled bread.

In this pizza, the sauce gets topped with provolone and cured chorizo, and the whole thing gets finished just before serving with *jamón serrano*, shaved Manchego, serrano chiles, and dollops of creamy freshly scrambled eggs. Just like in all those *bocadillos*, it's that touch of egg that ties everything together.

1 (13-ounce/370-gram) ball Master Dough, preferably with starter (page 44), made with Poolish

4 parts flour mixed with 1 part semolina, for dusting

BARCELONA SAUCE

MAKES 2 CUPS (550 GRAMS)

2 tablespoons (28 grams) warm water

$1/8$ teaspoon (.6 grams) Spanish saffron threads

Olive oil, for sautéing

To make the sauce, put the warm water in a small bowl, sprinkle the saffron over the top, and let steep for 30 minutes.

Heat a film of oil in a skillet over medium heat and add the butter. When the butter has melted, pinch nickel-size pieces of the fresh chorizo and add them to the pan. Season with a pinch each of salt and pepper and then stir with a wooden spoon to break up the larger pieces. Adjust the heat if needed to keep the meat from browning.

When the chorizo is half-cooked, after about $1^1/2$ minutes, stir in the Calabrese and ñora peppers, paprika, and garlic. Cook for 30 seconds, then stir in the saffron and saffron water, the ground tomatoes, and the tomato paste. Simmer, stirring often, for 5 minutes. Stir the cream into the sauce and simmer gently for 3 to 4 minutes. If you want to make the

continued

1 tablespoon (14 grams) unsalted butter

3 ounces (85 grams) fresh bulk chorizo

Fine sea salt and freshly ground black pepper

1½ teaspoons (5 grams) crushed Calabrese peppers

½ teaspoon (1.5 grams) ground ñora pepper

½ teaspoon sweet (1.5 grams) smoked Spanish paprika

1 teaspoon (3 grams) minced garlic

8.5 ounces (240 grams/1 cup) ground tomatoes, preferably Tomato Magic or DiNapoli

8.5 ounces (250 grams/1 cup) tomato paste, preferably Bontá or Saporito Super Heavy Pizza Sauce

¼ cup (60 grams) heavy cream

5 ounces (140 grams) provolone cheese, thinly sliced (about 7 slices)

1 ounce (30 grams) cured Spanish chorizo, thinly sliced

2 farm-fresh eggs

1 tablespoon (15 grams) heavy cream

1 tablespoon (14 grams) unsalted butter

Fine sea salt and freshly ground black pepper

Sweet Smoked Spanish paprika, for dusting

Ground ñora peppers, for dusting

6 thin slices (about 1 ounce/30 grams) jamón serrano

Small piece Manchego cheese, cold, for shaving

1 small serrano chile, sliced into thin rounds (with seeds)

sauce ahead, at this point, it can be cooled, covered, and refrigerated for up to 1 day.

Rewarm ¾ cup (210 grams) of the sauce over medium heat as the pizza goes into the oven and reserve the remaining sauce for another use.

Meanwhile, remove the dough ball from the refrigerator and leave wrapped at room temperature until the dough warms to 60°F to 65°F. Set up the oven with two pizza stones or baking steels and preheat to 500°F for 1 hour (see Getting Started, page 29).

Dust the work surface with the dusting mixture, then move the dough to the surface and dust the top (see Transferring the Dough to the Work Surface, page 30).

Sprinkle a wooden peel with the dusting mixture. Open the dough on the work surface to a 13-inch round with a slightly raised edge (see Opening and Stretching the Dough, page 33).

Move the dough to the peel. As you work, shake the peel forward and backward to ensure the dough isn't sticking.

Arrange the provolone slices evenly over the surface, leaving a ¾-inch border.

Slide the pizza onto the top stone (see Moving the Dough to the Oven, page 34). Bake for 7 minutes. Remove the pizza from the oven and place it on a cutting board (or work directly on the peel if there is room to set it on the work surface). Spoon 8 dollops (about 1½ tablespoons each) of the sauce evenly around the pizza. Spread them slightly with the back of the spoon but do not cover the pizza; leave some open spaces. Arrange the chorizo slices evenly over the pizza.

Lift the pizza with the peel (if on a cutting board), rotate the pizza 180 degrees, and transfer it to the bottom stone. Bake for another 7 minutes, until the bottom is browned and crisp and the top is golden brown.

Meanwhile, in a bowl, whisk together the eggs and the 1 tablespoon cream until blended. Melt the butter in a small skillet over medium-high heat. Add the eggs, season with salt and pepper, and stir continuously with a rubber spatula to scramble. Move to a small bowl.

Transfer the pizza to a cutting board and cut into 6 wedges. Spoon pieces of the scrambled eggs onto each slice, then dust lightly with paprika and *ñora* pepper. Arrange the *jamón* and Manchego over the top. Sprinkle with the serrano chile.

MÜNCHEN

MAKES ONE 13-INCH PIZZA; 6 SLICES

When the Cooking Channel asked a number of chefs to come up with dishes for an episode of *Food(ography)* that was all about beer, I couldn't resist the challenge. Thinking back on my happiest beer memories, my mind went straight to Germany and beer-braised pork with apples, root vegetables, potatoes, and cabbage. First, I worked out the pork recipe, pulled the meat, and tossed it with the reduced braising liquid. Then I added the potato and cabbage elements to the pizza in the form of thinly sliced potatoes and a mixture of coleslaw and sauerkraut. To take it over the top, I added some crushed pretzels (who doesn't love beer and pretzels?) as a crunchy finishing touch. Then all it needed was a final drizzle of Jägermeister syrup to help digest it all!

The pork recipe makes much more than you'll need for one or even two pizzas, so serve it on another night, drenched in the reduced braising liquid, with the braised potatoes, carrots, and apples on the side. The meat is also great in a grilled sandwich with melted Swiss cheese, sauerkraut, and coleslaw.

1 (13-ounce/370-gram) ball Master Dough, preferably with starter (page 44), made with Poolish

3 parts flour mixed with 1 part semolina, for dusting

PORK

Olive oil, for browning

1 (4-pound/1.8-kilogram) bone-in pork shoulder

1 small white onion, cut into large chunks

1 large white or yellow potatoes, cut into large chunks

Position a rack in the bottom third of the oven, top the rack with a pizza stone or steel, and preheat the oven to 450°F.

To make the pork, heat a film of oil in a large sauté pan (big enough to hold the pork shoulder) over medium-high heat. When the pan is hot, add the pork shoulder, fat side down, and sear until browned, then turn the shoulder as needed to brown evenly on all sides. This step will take about 20 minutes total. Transfer the pork, fat side up, to a 6-quart Dutch oven, preferably enameled cast iron, then add the onion, potato, carrots, apple, sugar, salt, pepper, and beer. Pour in hot tap water to reach within 1 1/2 inches of the top of the meat and cover the pot.

Place the pot in the oven on the stone and cook the pork for 1 hour and 20 minutes. Check the level of the water, adding more hot water as necessary to maintain the original level, and then re-cover and continue to cook for about 1 hour longer, until fork-tender. If the pork is not tender, continue to cook, checking the meat every 15 minutes and adding more water as needed to maintain the original level, until fork-tender.

continued

2 carrots, peeled and cut into large chunks

1 large apple, preferably Fuji, cut into large chunks

2/3 cup (140 grams) firmly packed dark brown sugar

1/4 cup (55 grams) fine sea salt

2 tablespoons (14 grams) finely ground black pepper

2 (12–fluid ounce) bottles German beer, preferably Paulaner

1/2 cup Jägermeister

2 (55 grams) small yellow potatoes

1/4 cup (40 grams) Coleslaw (page 247)

1/4 cup (40 grams) sauerkraut, well drained

5 slices (5 ounces/140 grams) Muenster cheese

1/2 large (15 grams) hard pretzel

4 ounces (115 grams) part-skim mozzarella cheese, shredded (1 cup)

Remove the pot from the oven and let the meat cool in the liquid in the covered pot for 1 hour. Uncover, transfer the meat to a sheet pan, and let rest until cool enough to handle.

Meanwhile, strain the liquid through a fine-mesh strainer into a clean saucepan (the vegetables and apple can be reserved and eaten with the pork and sauce as a separate meal or they can be discarded). Place over medium-high heat, bring to a simmer, and cook for about 20 minutes, adjusting the heat as necessary, until reduced to 2½ cups.

Shred 1²/₃ cup (200 grams) of the pork and put it in a bowl. Pour in 1/4 cup (57 grams) of the reduced liquid and toss with the pork. (The pork can be covered tightly and refrigerated for up to 2 days and then warmed before using.) Shred the remaining pork and reserve with the remaining reduced liquid for another use.

Meanwhile, to make the Jägermeister syrup, pour the Jägermeister into a small saucepan, bring to a boil over high heat, and boil for 5 minutes. Remove the pan from the heat and check if the reduction is ready by lifting some on a spoon and drizzling it over a plate. It should have the consistency of maple syrup. If it is too thin, return it to the heat, checking it frequently. You should have 1 generous tablespoon. Pour the syrup into a small squeeze bottle. It will keep at room temperature for up to 3 days.

Remove the dough ball from the refrigerator and leave wrapped at room temperature until the dough warms to 60°F to 65°F. Meanwhile, set up the oven with two pizza stones or baking steels and preheat to 500°F for 1 hour (see Getting Started, page 29).

While the oven heats, using a mandoline, cut the potatoes into paper-thin slices and drop them into a bowl of very cold salted water. Let soak for 30 minutes, drain, and repeat with a new batch of salted water. Drain again and dry on paper towels.

Mix the slaw and sauerkraut together. Cut 3 slices of Muenster in half on the diagonal to form 6 triangles. Tear the remaining 2 slices into 12 smaller pieces. Finely crush the pretzel in a mortar with a pestle or with a rolling pin. Set aside.

Dust the work surface with the dusting mixture, then move the dough to the surface and dust the top (see Transferring the Dough to the Work Surface, page 30).

Sprinkle a wooden peel with the dusting mixture. Open the dough on the work surface to a 13-inch round with a slightly raised edge (see Opening and Stretching the Dough, page 33).

Move the dough to the peel. As you work, shake the peel forward and backward to ensure the dough isn't sticking.

Mound the mozzarella in the center of the dough and use your fingertips to spread it evenly over the surface, leaving a 3/4-inch border. Arrange the sliced potatoes evenly over the top.

Slide the pizza onto the top stone (see Moving the Dough to the Oven, page 34). Bake for 7 minutes. Lift the pizza onto the peel and remove it from the oven. Arrange the broken pieces of Muenster cheese around the pizza and scatter the pork evenly over the top. Rotate the pizza 180 degrees and transfer it to the bottom stone. Bake for 5 minutes, until the bottom is browned and crisp and the crust is golden brown.

Transfer the pizza to a cutting board and cut into 6 wedges. Place a Muenster triangle on each slice, arranging them so they are all facing the same direction to resemble the spokes of a wheel. Garnish each cheese triangle with a spoonful of the slaw mixture. Drizzle the pizza with a spiral of the Jägermeister syrup and finish with a dusting of the pretzel.

DUBLINER

MAKES ONE 13-INCH PIZZA; 6 SLICES

At our take-out Slice House, we serve awesome deli sandwiches, and our house-made corned beef, pastrami, and Italian beef have been written up all over the place. We brine our corned beef for a week and then braise it in Anchor Steam, San Francisco's most famous brew. For home cooks, I recommend starting with a store-bought brined brisket and then seasoning the cooking liquid as directed here. You might be surprised that I boil the beef rather than simmering it. Don't worry. It will end up fork-tender and just right for shredding. For this pizza, I combine it with Dubliner, a nutty white Cheddar–style cheese, and our classic house-made coleslaw.

1 (13-ounce/370-gram) ball Master Dough, preferably with starter (page 44), made with Poolish

3 parts flour mixed with 1 part semolina, for dusting

CORNED BEEF

1 (6 pound/2.7 kilogram) brined beef brisket

1 cup (220 grams) firmly packed light brown sugar

3 tablespoons (20 grams) whole allspice

2 tablespoons (15 grams) juniper berries

2 tablespoons (13 grams) whole cloves

2 tablespoons (10 grams) ground ginger

2 tablespoons (20 grams) yellow mustard seeds

To make the corned beef, drain the brisket and discard the brine and spices. Place the brisket in an 8- to 10-quart stockpot or Dutch oven and add the brown sugar, allspice, juniper, cloves, ginger, mustard seeds, salt, peppercorns, bay leaves, and beer. Pour in cold water to cover the brisket by 2 inches. Place over high heat and bring to a boil. Turn down the heat to a gentle boil and cook, uncovered for 4 hours, checking the liquid level every 30 minutes and adding more water as necessary to maintain the original level. Test the meat for doneness with a fork and continue to cook for 5 to 6 hours total, until the meat is fork-tender. Reserve the remaining corned beef for another use.

Remove the pot from the heat and let the meat rest in the liquid for 30 minutes. Transfer the corned beef to a cutting board (reserving the liquid) and trim away any fat. When the meat is cool enough to handle, using your hands, shred 6 ounces (170 grams) of the corned beef with the grain and put in a bowl. Strain enough of the cooking liquid through a fine-mesh strainer held over the meat to moisten it. The meat can be refrigerated for up to 2 days and warmed before using. Reserve the remaining corned beef for another use.

To make the Russian dressing, combine all of the ingredients in a bowl and stir to mix well. Cover and refrigerate for up to 3 days. Bring to room temperature and transfer to a squeeze bottle before using.

continued

GLOBAL

2 tablespoons (28 grams) fine sea salt

2 tablespoons (18 grams) black peppercorns

6 bay leaves

3 (12–fluid ounce/340-gram) bottles beer, preferably Anchor Steam

RUSSIAN DRESSING

MAKES 1 CUP (215 GRAMS)

$^1/_2$ cup (110 grams) mayonnaise

$^1/_4$ cup (68 grams) ketchup

1 tablespoon (12 grams) granulated sugar

1 tablespoon (15 grams) Worcestershire sauce

$^1/_2$ teaspoon (2.5 grams) drained prepared horseradish

$^1/_2$ teaspoon (1.5 grams) finely chopped white onion

$^1/_2$ teaspoon (1.5 grams) finely chopped garlic

$^3/_4$ teaspoon (3.5 grams) fine sea salt

$^1/_2$ teaspoon (1 gram) freshly ground black pepper

$^1/_2$ teaspoon (1.5 grams) chili powder

$^1/_2$ tablespoon (2.5 grams) finely chopped parsley

$^1/_2$ teaspoon (2.5 grams) hot pepper sauce (optional)

7 ounces (200 grams) Dubliner cheese, shredded (1$^3/_4$ cups)

$^1/_3$ cup (50 grams) Coleslaw (page 247)

2 (30 grams) Peppadew peppers, coarsely chopped

Remove the dough ball from the refrigerator and leave wrapped at room temperature until the dough warms to 60°F to 65° F. Meanwhile, set up the oven with two pizza stones or baking steels and preheat to 500°F for 1 hour (see Getting Started, page 29).

Dust the work surface with the dusting mixture, then move the dough to the surface and dust the top (see Transferring the Dough to the Work Surface, page 30).

Sprinkle a wooden peel with the dusting mixture. Open the dough on the work surface to a 13-inch round with a slightly raised edge (see Opening and Stretching the Dough, page 33).

Move the dough to the peel. As you work, shake the peel forward and backward to ensure the dough isn't sticking.

Mound the Dubliner cheese in the center of the dough and use your fingertips to spread it evenly over the surface, leaving a $^3/_4$-inch border.

Slide the pizza onto the top stone (see Moving the Dough to the Oven, page 34). Bake for 6 minutes. Lift the pizza onto the peel, rotate it 180 degrees, and then transfer it to the bottom stone. Bake for 4 minutes.

Remove the pizza from the oven and place on a cutting board (or work directly on the peel if there is room to set it on the work surface). Arrange the corned beef evenly over the top. Rotate the pizza 180 degrees, slide it onto the top stone, and bake for 2 minutes, until the bottom is browned and crisp and the crust is golden brown.

Transfer the pizza to a cutting board and cut into 6 wedges. Spoon some slaw over each slice and finish with the Peppadew peppers and a squeeze of Russian dressing.

DRESSING

3 tablespoons (40 grams) mayonnaise

2 tablespoons (24 grams) granulated sugar

2 tablespoons (28 grams) distilled white vinegar

2 tablespoons (28 grams) buttermilk

1 teaspoon (5 grams) freshly squeezed lemon juice

Fine sea salt and freshly ground black pepper

1 cup (80 grams) packed shredded green cabbage

2 tablespoons (12 grams) peeled and shredded carrot

1 tablespoon (9 grams) thinly sliced red onion

2 teaspoons (10 grams) coarsely chopped Peppadew peppers

Fine sea salt and freshly ground black pepper

COLESLAW

MAKES 1 CUP (150 GRAMS)

We all know coleslaw as a side and sandwich ingredient. But wait till you experience what its cool, crunchy creaminess does for a slice of pizza. This is the classic version we serve at Slice House and in my restaurants.

To make the dressing, in a small bowl, whisk together the mayonnaise and sugar until thoroughly mixed, then whisk in the vinegar, buttermilk, and lemon juice. Season with salt and pepper, then taste and adjust with more salt, pepper, and lemon juice if needed. Cover and refrigerate for at least 2 hours before using. The flavor of the dressing is at its best after 8 hours.

In a bowl, toss together the cabbage, carrot, onion, and Peppadew peppers. Add about half of the dressing and stir to coat all of the ingredients evenly. Add more dressing to taste, then season with salt and pepper. Cover and refrigerate for at least 2 hours or up to 1 day. Stir the coleslaw before using.

PARISIAN

MAKES ONE 13-INCH PIZZA; 6 SLICES

In 2013, I was a judge at a big pizza competition in Paris. In two days, I tasted seventy-three pizzas, most of them too rich and fussy for my taste. Let's just say that almost every entry featured smoked fish, foie gras, gold leaf, or edible flowers. But one extravagant ingredient that I thought really did work was truffles, and that inspired me to come up with this pizza that makes the most of truffle paste, wild mushrooms, and two of my favorite French cheeses: nutty Comté and triple-cream Saint André. If you like, you can top the fully baked pizza with paper-thin slices of prosciutto or *speck*. And if you can get your hands on a fresh truffle, shave it on top right at the table. That's the kind of simple, earthy luxury I can really get behind.

---

1 (13-ounce/370-gram) ball Master Dough, preferably with starter (page 44), made with Poolish

Flour, for dusting

8 ounces (225 grams) assorted mushrooms (such as pioppini, oyster, shiitake, and trumpet)

Olive oil, for sautéing

Fine sea salt and freshly ground black pepper

5 ounces (140 grams) part-skim mozzarella cheese, shredded (1¼ cups)

1½ teaspoons (6 grams) truffle paste, or 1 fresh truffle (to taste)

1½ ounces (45 grams) Saint André cheese

Remove the dough ball from the refrigerator and leave wrapped at room temperature until the dough warms to 60°F to 65°F. Meanwhile, set up the oven with two pizza stones or baking steels and preheat to 500°F for 1 hour (see Getting started, page 29).

Meanwhile, clean and trim the mushrooms so that they will all cook in about the same amount of time. Leave the *pioppini* and other small, delicate mushrooms whole. Slice the trumpets lengthwise into slices ⅛ inch thick.

Heat a generous film of oil in a skillet over medium-high heat until very hot. Add the larger mushroom pieces and sauté for 1 minute. Add the remaining mushrooms, season with fine sea salt and pepper, and sauté, stirring often, for 2 to 3 minutes, until the mushrooms are softened but not browned. Remove from the heat and set aside.

Dust the work surface with the dusting mixture, then move the dough to the surface and dust the top (see Transferring the Dough to the Work Surface, page 30).

Dust a wooden peel with the flour. Open the dough on the work surface to a 13-inch round with a slightly raised edge (see Opening and Stretching the Dough, page 33).

continued

Small piece Comté cheese, cold, for shaving

Handful of arugula leaves

Extra virgin olive oil, for drizzling

Maldon sea salt, for finishing

Move the dough to the peel. As you work, shake the peel forward and backward to ensure the dough isn't sticking.

Mound the mozzarella in the center of the dough and use your fingertips to spread it evenly over the surface, leaving a 3/4-inch border. Scatter the mushrooms evenly over the top.

Slide the pizza onto the top stone (see Moving the Dough to the Oven, page 34). Bake for 7 minutes. Lift the pizza onto the peel, rotate it 180 degrees, and then transfer it to the bottom stone. Bake for 6 minutes, until the bottom is browned and crisp and the top is golden brown.

Transfer the pizza to a cutting board and cut into 6 wedges. Garnish each wedge with 1/4 teaspoon dollops of truffle paste, pinches of the Saint André, and shavings of Comté. Scatter the arugula over the top and finish with a drizzle of extra virgin oil and a pinch each of pepper and Maldon salt.

GRECO

MAKES ONE 13-INCH PIZZA; 6 SLICES

Feta, Kalamata olives, oregano, and a squeeze of fresh lemon juice give this grilled-squash pizza its unmistakably Greek flavor. I use a panini press to grill the slices of yellow squash and zucchini because I love the look and slightly charred flavor this method produces. You can also cook the squash in the oven or on a grill or stove-top grill pan. Grilling the cut face of a lemon half in the same way gives it a beautiful appearance and tones down its acidity a bit.

---

1 (13-ounce/370-gram) ball Master Dough, preferably with starter (page 44), made with Poolish

1 part flour mixed with 1 part semolina, for dusting

1 to 2 medium (about 6 ounces/ 170 grams each) zucchini

1 to 2 medium (about 6 ounces/ 170 grams each) straight-neck yellow squash

Olive oil, for brushing

Fine sea salt and freshly ground black pepper

7 ounces (200 grams) part-skim mozzarella cheese, shredded (1¾ cups)

1-ounce (30-gram) piece Feta cheese, preferably water-packed Greek

6 pitted Kalamata olives, quartered lengthwise

1 large (18 grams) Peppadew pepper, cut into strips

Remove the dough ball from the refrigerator and leave wrapped at room temperature until the dough warms to 60°F to 65°F. Meanwhile, set up the oven with two pizza stones or baking steels and preheat to 500°F for 1 hour (see Getting Started, page 29).

Cut off the ends of the zucchini and yellow squash and discard. Trim away one long side (it won't be used) of the zucchini and cut the remaining zucchini lengthwise on a mandoline or by hand into thin, even slices ⅛ inch thick, discarding the other long side. You will need a total of 6 slices.

Cut the yellow squash crosswise on a slight diagonal into slices ⅛ inch thick, discarding the end slice. You will need a total of 12 slices.

To cook the squash slices on a panini press, heat the press according to the manufacturer's instructions. Brush both sides of the zucchini and yellow squash slices with olive oil and season lightly with salt and pepper. Arrange on the press, close the lid, and cook for 30 seconds. Lift the lid and check to see if the slices are etched with grill marks and tender. If not, continue to cook as needed. Transfer the slices to a flat plate and season with additional salt and pepper.

To cook the squash slices in the oven, coat a half sheet pan with a generous film of olive oil. Arrange the zucchini and yellow squash slices in a single layer, turning to coat both sides with oil, and season with salt and pepper. Set the pan on the top stone and cook for 4 to 5 minutes. The slices will cook and sizzle in the oil but should not brown (this would toughen the edges). Transfer the slices to a flat plate and season with additional salt and pepper.

continued

Grated Pecorino Romano cheese, for dusting

Dried oregano, for dusting

Garlic Oil (page 29), for drizzling

1/2 lemon, grilled (see headnote)

Dust the work surface with the dusting mixture, then move the dough to the surface and dust the top (see Transferring the Dough to the Work surface, page 30).

Sprinkle a wooden peel with the dusting mixture. Open the dough on the work surface to a 13-inch round with a slightly raised edge (see Opening and Stretching the Dough, page 33).

Move the dough to the peel. As you work, shake the peel forward and backward to ensure the dough isn't sticking.

Mound the mozzarella in the center of the dough and use your fingertips to spread it evenly over the surface, leaving a 3/4-inch border.

Slide the dough onto the top stone (see Moving the Dough to the Oven, page 34). Bake for 7 minutes.

Remove the pizza from the oven and place on a cutting board (or work directly on the peel if there is room to set it on the work surface). Place the zucchini slices on the pizza, arranging them like the spokes of a wheel. Then put the yellow squash slices between the zucchini slices, placing 2 slices in each section.

Lift the pizza with the peel (if on a cutting board) rotate it 180 degrees and then transfer. Bake for 6 minutes, until the bottom is browned and crisp and the top is golden brown.

Transfer the pizza to a cutting board and cut into 6 wedges. Crumble the Feta over the pizza, then scatter the olives and Peppadew peppers evenly over the top. Finish with a dusting of pecorino and oregano and with a drizzle of garlic oil over the surface and the crust.

Just before serving, squeeze the lemon over the top.

Grilled

The grilled pizza craze got its start back in the 1980s, at Al Forno in Providence, Rhode Island, where George Germon and Johanne Killeen put it on the map. The basic method is simple: You lay the dough right on the grill grates until it's half-cooked and has grill marks on the bottom. Then you flip it, top the grill-marked side, finish cooking, and, in some cases, add more toppings when the pizza comes off the grill.

Why make pizzas this way? Two reasons: You don't have to heat up the oven—and your entire house. And you get an extra-tasty crust with just a bit of char and smoky flavor. If you love wood-fired pizza but don't have a wood-burning oven, this method will get you close. In fact, I based my recipe for dough for grilled pizza on my Napoletana Dough (page 187), opting for soft Caputo or San Felice double zero flour and no malt.

Grilled Pizza Tips

- For grilled pizzas, I prefer to roll the dough with a rolling pin to create a uniformly thin crust, which will show pronounced grill marks. You can also open up and stretch your dough by hand without using a rolling pin (page 33), which will give you a thicker crust with less distinct grill marks and a look and chewy texture that's more like wood-fired pizza.

- I like to use just flour for dusting here, rather than a mix of flour and semolina, because the high heat of the grill can cause semolina to burn. But if you find your dough is not sliding on and off the peel easily, you can throw a little semolina under it.

- Because grills vary widely in temperature, you'll need to keep a watchful eye on your pizza, especially the first few times you try this. If you have a large grill, I suggest keeping lower heat in part of the grill, so you can move your pizza there if you sense that the underside is cooking too fast.

- The first side of your pizza (which will end up being the top) will show grill marks because the soft dough will stretch down a bit between the grates; but the second side will be firmer and won't have prominent grill marks. It will look toasted and speckled like the bottom of a wood-fired crust. Wait until the grill marks are fairly dark on the first side before you flip the pizza.

- You can serve grilled pizzas open-faced in the traditional way, or put all the toppings on one side, fold the other side over, and cut your folded pizza into three or four wedges to eat sandwich-style. I really like the folded presentation because the crust has just the right balance of crispness and softness for the purpose.

- This dough makes really nice grilled flatbreads, which are a lot like Indian naan. To make them, portion the dough into 4- to 5-ounce (115- to 140-gram) balls, roll them out, and grill them on both sides until they're cooked through. You can serve them with dips, spreads or cheeses, or you can drizzle them with olive oil, melted butter, or Garlic Oil (page 29) and sprinkle them with herbs to serve as a party snack.

DOUGH FOR GRILLING

MAKES 27 OUNCES (765 GRAMS), ENOUGH FOR THREE 9-OUNCE (255-GRAM) BALLS

4.5 grams (1½ teaspoons) active dry yeast

85 grams (⅓ cup plus 1 teaspoon) warm water (80°F to 85°F)

453 grams (3¾ cups) 00 flour, preferably Caputo or San Felice, plus more for kneading

210 grams (¾ cup plus 2 tablespoons) ice water

9 grams (2 teaspoons) fine sea salt

For baker's percentages, see page 302.

Put the yeast in a small bowl, add the warm water, and whisk vigorously for 30 seconds. The yeast should dissolve in the water and the mixture should foam. If it doesn't and the yeast granules float, the yeast is "dead" and should be discarded. Begin again with a fresh amount of yeast and water.

Put the flour in the bowl of a stand mixer fitted with the dough hook. With the mixer running on the lowest speed, pour in most of the ice water, reserving about 2 tablespoons, followed by the yeast-water mixture. Pour the reserved water into the yeast bowl, swirl it around to dislodge any bits of yeast stuck to the bowl, and add to the mixer.

Continue to mix the dough on the lowest speed for about 1 minute, until most of the dough comes together around the hook. Stop the mixer. Use your fingers to pull away any dough that clings to the hook, and scrape the sides and bottom of the bowl with a bowl scraper or rubber spatula.

Add the salt and continue to mix on the lowest speed for 1 minute to combine. Stop the mixer, pull the dough off the hook, and continue to mix the dough for about 1 minute. The dough won't look completely smooth, but if you rub some between your fingers, you shouldn't feel any undissolved salt. If you do, continue to mix for another minute.

Using the bowl scraper, transfer the dough to an unfloured work surface, then knead for 2 to 3 minutes, until smooth (see Kneading the Dough, page 24). If the dough is too sticky to knead, sprinkle it with just enough flour to allow you to work with it. Cover the dough with a damp dish towel and let rest at room temperature for about 1 hour.

Use your dough cutter to loosen the dough and to cut it into thirds. Weigh each piece, adjusting the quantity of dough as necessary to give you equal weights of 9 ounces (255 grams) each.

Form the dough into balls (see Balling the Dough, page 26). Set the balls on a half sheet pan, spacing them about 3 inches apart. Or, if you will be baking the balls on different days, place them on separate quarter sheet pans. Wrap the pan(s) airtight with a double layer of plastic wrap, sealing the wrap well under the sheet pan(s). Put the pan(s) in a level spot in the refrigerator and refrigerate for 24 to 48 hours.

GRILLED •

GRILLED PIZZA MASTER RECIPE

MAKES ONE 12- TO 13-INCH PIZZA

1 (9-ounce/255-gram) ball Dough for Grilling (page 257)

Flour, for dusting

Remove the dough ball from the refrigerator and leave wrapped at room temperature until the dough warms to 60°F to 65°F. This will be about 1½ hours before you begin grilling the pizza.

The pizza should be grilled on a preheated gas, wood, or charcoal grill over medium-high heat. If you are using a wood or charcoal grill, use indirect heat to avoid burning the bottom of the pizza. If you can set up two zones on your gas grill, heat one to medium-high and one to medium. That way, if the pizza is cooking too quickly over the medium-high zone, it can be moved to the medium zone.

If possible, set up a station near the grill with a cutting board, a sheet pan, a pair of tongs, your pizza cutter, and all the toppings for the pizza.

Dust the work surface with flour, then move the dough to the surface and dust the top (see Transferring the Dough to the Work Surface, page 30).

Sprinkle a wooden peel with flour.

Roll out the dough into a 12- to 13-inch round, press the edges with a rolling pin to keep them from puffing on the grill, and dock the surface of the dough (see Rolling Pizza Dough, page 103).

Move the dough to the peel. As you work, shake the peel forward and backward to ensure the dough isn't sticking.

For the first grilling: Slide the dough onto the grill and cook uncovered for about 1 minute. Lift an edge of the dough with a pair of tongs and check the bottom to make sure it isn't burning. If it is just beginning to brown, lower the edge and continue to grill for another 30 seconds to 1 minute, until browned and well marked. If it is too dark when you check, rotate the dough 90 degrees and continue grilling for another 30 seconds to 1 minute, until the dough is browned in a crosshatch pattern. If it's not brown enough when you check, increase the heat or move the dough to a hotter spot on the grill.

Lift the dough onto the peel. If you have space on the counter, you can work with the pizza directly on the peel; otherwise, slide it onto the cutting board. Flip the dough over and press down on the top to flatten it and burst any bubbles. Scatter the cheese listed in each recipe evenly over the crust, leaving a 3/4-inch border. Slide the dough back onto the peel (if it was moved to the cutting board).

For the second grilling: Hold the peel over the grill and use your hand to slide the pizza carefully back onto the grill grate. (If you shake the peel to remove the pizza, the cheese may fly off the crust onto the grill.) Cover the grill and cook for 30 seconds to 1 minute, rotating the pizza as necessary to brown the bottom evenly and melt the cheese. If the bottom browns before the cheese has melted, move the pizza to the sheet pan and return the pan to the grill just until the cheese has melted.

Transfer the pizza to the cutting board and complete according to the recipe. For a sandwich-style pizza, arrange the toppings on half of the pizza, fold the pizza in half, and cut into 3 wedges. For a traditional pizza, cover the entire top and serve open-faced.

GRILLED

STEAK LOVER'S

MAKES ONE 12- TO 13-INCH PIZZA; 3 SANDWICH-SIZE WEDGES OR 6 SLICES

Grilled steak with mango salsa is insanely good on a pizza—especially when the pizza is grilled, too. I like to cook a nice thick steak to make sure it stays juicy, so I recommend grilling a one-pounder, which, like the amount of mango salsa, will be enough for two pizzas. The salsa can be made several hours ahead of time. Be sure to check the heat of your serrano chiles—they can really vary in terms of spiciness—and adjust the quantity to suit your taste.

1 (9-ounce/255-gram) ball Dough for Grilling (page 257)

Flour, for dusting

MANGO SALSA
MAKES ³/₄ CUPS (176 GRAMS),
ENOUGH FOR 2 PIZZAS

²/₃ cup (140 grams) finely diced ripe mango

1 tablespoon (9 grams) finely diced red onion

1 tablespoon (8 grams) finely diced serrano chiles

1 tablespoon (2 grams) chopped cilantro

1 tablespoon (15 grams) freshly squeezed lime juice

Pinch of fine sea salt

To make the mango salsa, a few hours before making the pizza, stir together all of the ingredients in a bowl. Taste and adjust the seasoning. Cover and set aside at room temperature.

Prepare the dough and set up the grill (see Grilled Pizza Master Recipe, page 258).

About 10 minutes before you are ready to grill the pizza, rub the steak with oil and season both sides with salt and pepper. Grill the steak over medium-high heat, turning once, for a total of 7 to 8 minutes, until an instant-read thermometer inserted into the center registers 125°F to 130°F for rare to medium-rare. Transfer the steak to a cutting board and let rest while you grill the pizza.

The first grilling: Grill the pizza as instructed in the master recipe.

When the half-cooked pizza is removed from the grill, flip it over as directed, then mound the mozzarella in the center of the dough and use your fingertips to spread it evenly over the surface, leaving a ³/₄-inch border.

The second grilling: Return the pizza to the grill to cook and lightly brown the second side and melt the cheese as instructed in the master recipe.

1 (1-pound/455-gram) strip steak, at room temperature

Extra virgin olive oil, for rubbing

Fine sea salt and freshly ground black pepper

4 ounces (115 grams) whole-milk mozzarella cheese, shredded (1 cup)

Lemon wedges, for serving

Completing the pizza: Thinly slice the steak on the diagonal against the grain. Arrange half of the slices over half of the pizza (if you are folding it) or over the top (if you are serving it open-faced). Top the steak with half of the salsa. (Use the remaining steak and salsa for a second pizza or another purpose.) Drizzle with oil, sprinkle with salt and pepper, and squeeze a wedge of lemon over the top.

Fold the pizza in half and cut it into 3 wedges to serve sandwich-style, or cut the open-faced pizza into 6 wedges. Serve extra lemon wedges on the side.

INSALATA

MAKES ONE 12- TO 13-INCH PIZZA; 3 SANDWICH-SIZE WEDGES OR 6 SLICES

Sometimes what you really want is pizza and a salad. This is the pizza for those times. It's a great choice for an outdoor party in the summer.

---

1 (9-ounce/255-gram) ball Dough for Grilling (page 257)

Flour, for dusting

CITRUS VINAIGRETTE
MAKES ²/₃ CUPS (155 GRAMS)

¹/₄ cup plus 2 tablespoons (85 grams) freshly squeezed orange juice

2¹/₂ tablespoons (53 grams) honey

1¹/₄ teaspoons (7 grams) Dijon mustard

1 tablespoon (14 grams) extra virgin olive oil

Fine sea salt, freshly ground black pepper, and freshly ground white pepper

3 ounces (85 grams) whole-milk mozzarella cheese, shredded (³/₄ cup)

4 cups (scant 2 ounces/50 grams) loosely packed arugula or mixed baby greens

3 ounces (85 grams) fresh goat cheese, preferably Laura Chenel

16 raspberries

10 salted roasted Marcona almonds, coarsely chopped

Fleur de sel and freshly ground black pepper

Prepare the dough and set up the grill (see Grilled Pizza Master Recipe, page 258).

While the grill heats, make the vinaigrette. In a small bowl, whisk together the orange juice, honey, mustard, and oil. Season with the salt, black pepper, and white pepper. Set aside.

The first grilling: Grill the pizza as instructed in the master recipe.

When the half-cooked pizza is removed from the grill, flip it over as directed, then mound the mozzarella in the center of the dough and use your fingertips to spread it evenly over the surface, leaving a ³/₄-inch border.

The second grilling: Return the pizza to the grill to cook and lightly brown the second side and melt the cheese as instructed in the master recipe.

Completing the pizza: In a bowl, toss the arugula with a light coating of the vinaigrette. Mound the salad over half of the pizza (if you are folding it) or over the top (if you are serving it open-faced). Crumble the goat cheese over the arugula and garnish with the raspberries and almonds. Sprinkle with fleur de sel and black pepper.

Fold the pizza in half and cut it into 3 wedges to serve sandwich-style, or cut the open-faced pizza into 6 wedges. Serve the remaining dressing on the side.

GRILLED

ST-GERMAIN BBQ CHICKEN

MAKES ONE 12- TO 13-INCH PIZZA; 3 SANDWICH-SIZE WEDGES OR 6 SLICES

Even though it's not intentionally Asian, eating this pizza is a lot like enjoying a Vietnamese bánh mì sandwich because you get succulent sweet-savory grilled chicken and a crunchy, fresh pickled cucumber and carrot relish in every bite. St-Germain is a French elderflower liqueur that's showing up in hip cocktails everywhere. I like what its floral, perfumy flavor does for BBQ sauce. The chicken, by the way, is a totally legit main course on its own, too. Just slather the whole pieces with the BBQ sauce right after you take them off the grill and serve extra sauce on the side.

1 (9-ounce/255-gram) ball Dough for Grilling (page 257)

Flour, for dusting

BBQ SAUCE
MAKES 1²/₃ CUPS (450 GRAMS)

Olive oil, for cooking

¼ cup (40 grams) finely chopped white onion

1 teaspoon (3 grams) minced garlic

3 tablespoons (37 grams) St-Germain liqueur

1 teaspoon (2.5 grams) freshly ground white pepper

1 teaspoon (2.5 grams) freshly ground black pepper

½ teaspoon (1 grams) cayenne, or to taste

1 teaspoon (4.5 grams) dark brown sugar

1 teaspoon (7 grams) honey

To make the sauce, heat a film of oil in a saucepan over medium-high heat. Reduce heat to medium and add the onion and garlic and cook gently, stirring often, for 2 minutes, until softened. Stir in the liqueur; white, black, and cayenne peppers; brown sugar; honey; and ketchup. Turn up the heat to medium-high and bring to a simmer.

Turn down the heat to low and stir in the liquid smoke. Simmer gently for about 15 minutes to combine the flavors. The sauce can be refrigerated for up to 2 weeks and reheated before using.

To make the relish, peel the cucumber and cut it in half lengthwise. Cut off the end and discard. Using a teaspoon, scrape out the seeds. Slice the cucumber crosswise into thin half-moons and put them in a bowl. Add the onion, granulated sugar, vinegar, and carrots and toss to mix. Season with salt. The relish can be covered and refrigerated for up to 1 day.

To make the brine, bring the water to a boil in a small saucepan over high heat, add the salt and sugar, and stir until dissolved. Pour into a heatproof bowl large enough to hold the chicken and all of the liquid. Stir in the ice water. The water needs to be at room temperature or cooler before adding the chicken. Add the chicken and set aside at room temperature for 30 minutes.

Meanwhile, prepare the dough and set up the grill to medium-low heat (see Grilled Pizza Master Recipe, page 258).

Bring a saucepan of water to a boil over high heat. Add the corn, blanch for 1 minute, and drain.

continued

GRILLED

1¹/₂ cups (410 grams) ketchup

1 teaspoon (5 grams) liquid smoke (optional)

CUCUMBER RELISH
MAKES ¹/₂ CUPS (85 GRAMS)

¹/₄ English cucumber (85 grams)

1¹/₂ tablespoons (14 grams) diced red onion

1¹/₂ teaspoons (6 grams) granulated sugar

1 tablespoon (15 grams) rice vinegar

3 tablespoons (18 grams) peeled and shredded carrot

Fine sea salt

BRINE

1 cup (236 grams) water

3 tablespoons (45 grams) fine sea salt

2 teaspoons (8 grams) granulated sugar

2 cups (472 grams) ice water

3 (6-ounce/170-gram) bone-in, skin-on chicken thighs

1 large ear corn, shucked

¹/₂ teaspoon (2.5 grams) fine sea salt

¹/₄ teaspoon (0.6 grams) cayenne pepper

2 tablespoons (28 grams) unsalted butter, melted

Olive oil

4 ounces (115 grams) whole-milk mozzarella cheese, shredded (1 cup)

In a small bowl, stir together the salt and cayenne, then mix with the butter. Set aside for basting the corn.

The chicken and corn can be grilled at the same time. The corn should take only about 5 minutes and the chicken about 20 minutes. To grill the chicken, remove the thighs from the brine, dry well, and rub them with a little oil. Place them, skin side down, on the grill and cook for 5 minutes, adjusting the heat as necessary to keep the chicken from burning. Turn the pieces 90 degrees and cook for another 5 minutes. Turn them over and repeat on the second side for a total of 20 minutes, until cooked through. Check by gently moving the meat away from the bone to see that the meat is not pink. Remove the chicken from the grill and let rest until it is cool enough to handle.

Meanwhile, add the corn to the grill and cook, turning often and basting with the seasoned butter, for about 5 minutes, until the kernels are just tender. There may be some charred sections, which will add flavor to the pizza. Remove the corn from the grill and let it cool enough to handle. Cut the kernels from the cob and set aside. You will need about ¹/₃ cup (45 grams) for the pizza.

Pull the meat from the bones and discard the chicken skin or leave it on if you prefer. Cut the meat into slices ¹/₄ inch thick and put in a bowl to keep warm.

The first grilling: Preheat the grill to medium-high and grill the pizza as instructed in the master recipe.

When the half-cooked pizza is removed from the grill, flip it over as directed, then mound the mozzarella in the center of the dough and use your fingertips to spread it evenly over the surface, leaving a ³/₄-inch border.

The second grilling: Return the pizza to the grill to cook and lightly brown the second side and melt the cheese as instructed in the master recipe.

Completing the pizza: Spread a generous coating of warm BBQ sauce (about ¹/₄ cup/70 grams) over the surface, and arrange the chicken over half of the pizza (if you are folding it) or over the top (if you are serving it open-faced). Spoon the cucumber relish over the top and sprinkle with the corn. Fold the pizza in half and cut it into 3 wedges to serve sandwich-style, or cut the open-faced pizza into 6 wedges. Serve with additional BBQ sauce on the side.

Using a Stone on the Grill

A lot of people enjoy making pizza outdoors using a pizza stone on the grill. The result can be similar to wood-fired pizza. Not all stones are designed to work on a grill, though, so before you try this, be sure you check the package, the directions, or the manufacturer's website to make sure yours will work in this way.

Depending on your grill, it can be tricky to maintain a consistent temperature in the correct range because even with the lid closed, you're not getting radiant heat from above. You'll need to preheat the stone on the grill, directly over medium-high to high heat for about half an hour. Then, put the pizza on the hot stone, close the lid, and cook the pizza for about 10 minutes, rotating it after about 5 minutes and keeping an eye on it so the bottom doesn't burn. Since every grill is different, you'll need to experiment quite a bit. If you have a wok lid, you can put it over the pizza before you close your grill lid to concentrate the heat around the pizza even more.

Green Egg Technique

I've gotten the best results by using a pizza stone on a ceramic cooker. I love the one made by Big Green Egg, and they make a pizza stone specially designed for the cooker. It works much better than a gas or electric grill for two reasons: it holds its temperature for a long time, and the ceramic dome generates radiant heat from the top, so the pizza cooks from both the top and bottom. And you can use the vents and the built-in thermometer to regulate the heat. It's important to open the lid as little as possible, because the change in air circulation can affect the temperature significantly.

Once the fire is going, place the pizza stone over the plate setter for at least 30 minutes, until it heats to 575°F to 600°F. Transfer the pizza to the stone and close the lid. Keep your eye on the thermometer, and keep the heat at 550°F to 575°F. The pizza should be done in about 10 minutes. Take a quick peek after 5 minutes to see if the bottom is browning evenly, and if it's not, rotate the pizza 180 degrees.

To make a second pizza, let the temperature return to about 575°F before you transfer the pizza to the stone.

GRILLED

Wrapped and Rolled

With a little practice, you can turn my Master Dough into all kinds of wrapped, rolled, and stuffed creations. Start with a basic calzone to get the hang of it and from there, you can move on to the Calzonewich, the Bow Tie, and my two Stromboli-style rolls. I've also included some fun ways to use up any extra dough. Let's get rolling.

CALZONE WITH MEATBALLS OR SPINACH

MAKES ONE 10-INCH CALZONE (PHOTO PAGE 270)

An 8-ounce dough ball, rolled out with a rolling pin to give you a nice, uniform thickness, is just right for a calzone. To get you started, I've given you two fillings: meatballs and sautéed spinach. Once you get the hang of it, you can stuff a calzone with pretty much any pizza ingredients. As you experiment, use the cheese and filling quantities here as a guide. They might seem a bit small, but you always want to avoid overstuffing a calzone, which can create too much steam and cause a blowout.

One 8-ounce (225-gram) ball Master Dough, preferably with starter (page 44), made with Poolish

1 part flour mixed with 1 part semolina, for dusting

MEATBALL CALZONE

4 ounces (115 grams) cooked Meatballs (page 287), broken into quarter-size pieces (1 cup)

2¹/₂ ounces (70 grams) part-skim mozzarella cheese, shredded (²/₃ cup)

1¹/₂ ounces (45 grams/3¹/₂ tablespoons) whole-milk ricotta cheese, preferably New York–style Polly-O or Ricotta Cream, page 91

¹/₂ teaspoon (1.5 grams) minced garlic

Grated Pecorino Romano cheese, for dusting

Dried oregano, for dusting

Remove the dough ball from the refrigerator and leave wrapped at room temperature until the dough warms to 60°F to 65°F. Meanwhile, set up the oven with two pizza stones or baking steels and preheat to 500°F for 1 hour (see Getting Started, page 29).

Dust the work surface with the dusting mixture, then move the dough to the surface and dust the top (see Transferring the Dough to the Work Surface, page 30).

Sprinkle a wooden peel with the dusting mixture.

Roll out the dough into a 10-inch round (see Rolling Pizza Dough, page 103).

Move the dough to the peel. As you work, shake the peel forward and backward to ensure the dough isn't sticking.

To make the meatball calzone, arrange the meatballs over half of the dough, leaving a ¹/₂-inch border. Sprinkle the mozzarella over the meatballs, and spoon the ricotta evenly over the top. Scatter the garlic over the top and dust with pecorino and oregano.

For the spinach calzone, use your fingertips to spread the mozzarella over half of the dough, leaving a ¹/₂-inch border. Distribute the spinach in an even layer over the cheese. Drizzle with garlic oil and dust with pecorino and oregano.

1 egg (optional), for egg wash

Garlic Oil (page 29), for brushing

Red pepper flakes, for dusting

1/2 cup (125 grams) Meatball Marinara (page 290), warm

SPINACH CALZONE

2¹/2 ounces (70 grams) part-skim mozzarella cheese, shredded (2/3 cup)

1/2 cup (95 grams) well-drained Sautéed Spinach (page 83)

Garlic Oil (page 29), for drizzling and brushing

Grated Pecorino Romano cheese, for dusting

Dried oregano, for dusting

1 egg (optional), for egg wash

Red pepper flakes, for dusting

Fold the dough over to enclose the toppings. Using your fingers, push down around the outside of the filling to remove any air bubbles. Using the tip of a knife or the tines of a fork, press down around the open edges of the dough to seal with a decorative edge.

If you would like a shiny crust, brush the top and sides of the calzone with the egg wash. To make the egg wash, remove half the egg white from a large egg and put the yolk and the remaining egg white in a small bowl. Using a small whisk, whip to combine. Strain before using.

Slide the calzone onto the top stone (see Moving the Dough to the Oven, page 34). Bake for 4 minutes. Rotate the calzone 180 degrees and continue to bake for 4 to 6 minutes, until the bottom is browned and crisp and the top is golden brown.

Transfer the calzone to a cutting board. Brush with garlic oil and finish with a light dusting of pecorino, oregano, and pepper flakes. Let the calzone rest for about 3 minutes.

Using a serrated knife, cut the calzone in half crosswise. Serve the meatball calzone with the marinara on the side.

MORTADELLA AND CHEESE CALZONEWICH

MAKES ONE 10-INCH CALZONEWICH

We came up with this idea back in the day, when I worked at my brother's pizzeria, Pyzano's. It's a calzone stuffed with mortadella and mozzarella, baked, and then slit open and filled sandwich-style with prosciutto, lettuce, tomato, vinaigrette, mustard, and mayo. The result is a perfect cross between a calzone and a classic Italian deli sandwich, and the contrast between the warm crust and cheese and the cool filling ingredients is totally right.

1 (8-ounce/225-gram) ball Master Dough, preferably with starter (page 44), made with Poolish

1 part flour mixed with 1 part semolina, for dusting

1 tablespoon (14 grams) extra virgin olive oil

1 teaspoon (5 grams) red wine vinegar

Dried oregano, for seasoning

Fine sea salt and freshly ground black pepper

1½ ounces (45 grams) thinly sliced mortadella

2½ ounces (70 grams) part-skim mozzarella cheese, shredded (⅔ cup)

Remove the dough ball from the refrigerator and leave wrapped at room temperature until the dough warms to 60°F to 65°F. Meanwhile, position a rack in the center of the oven, place a pizza stone or baking steel on the rack, and preheat the oven to 500°F for 1 hour (see Getting Started, page 29).

To make the vinaigrette, in a small bowl, stir together the oil and vinegar and season with oregano, salt, and pepper. The dressing should be very flavorful, since this will season your calzonewich. Set aside.

Dust the work surface with the dusting mixture, then move the dough to the surface and dust the top (see Transferring the Dough to the Work surface, page 30).

Sprinkle a wooden peel with the dusting mixture.

Roll out the dough into a 10-inch round (see Rolling Pizza Dough, page 103).

Move the dough to the peel. As you work, shake the peel forward and backward to ensure the dough isn't sticking.

1 egg (optional), for egg wash

1¹/2 ounces (45 grams) thinly sliced prosciutto

Dijon or spicy brown mustard, for spreading

Mayonnaise, for spreading

4 small slices tomato

3 or 4 butter lettuce leaves

Fold the mortadella slices and arrange them on half of the dough, leaving a ¹/2-inch border. Sprinkle the mozzarella evenly over the mortadella.

Fold the dough over to enclose the toppings. Using your fingers, push down around the outside of the filling to remove any air bubbles. Using the tip of a knife or the tines of a fork, press down around the open edges of the dough to seal with a decorative edge.

If you would like a shiny crust, brush the top and sides of the calzone with the egg wash. To make the egg wash, remove half the egg white from a large egg and put the yolk and th remaining egg white in a small bowl. Using a small wisk, whip to combine. Strain before using.

Slide the calzone onto the top stone (see Moving the Dough to the Oven, page 34). Bake for 4 minutes. Rotate the calzone 180 degrees and continue to bake for another 4 to 6 minutes, until the bottom is browned and crisp and the top is golden brown.

Transfer the calzone to a cutting board and let it rest for 5 to 10 minutes. Using a serrated knife, cut the rounded edge horizontally from side to side. Do not cut all the way through the straight side.

Open the lid. The mortadella and cheese may have shifted toward the back. If needed, use a fork to move the filling carefully. Drape the prosciutto over the top. Spread mustard and mayonnaise to taste over the prosciutto, and top the filling with tomato slices and lettuce. Spoon the vinaigrette over the lettuce.

THE BOW TIE

MAKES ONE 11-INCH BOW TIE (PHOTO PAGE 271)

I created this calzone-with-a-twist as a date-night special for Valentine's Day. It's half meat and half veggie, with the two parts joined at the center like a bow tie. I make it directly on the work surface and then use my perforated metal peel to transfer it to the oven. But the first several times you make this calzone, I suggest you build it right on your wooden peel, so it's easier to maneuver.

---

1 (8-ounce/225-gram) ball Master Dough, preferably with starter (page 44), made with Poolish

1 part flour mixed with 1 part semolina, for dusting

1/4 cup (45 grams) Sautéed Onions (page 89)

4 small pieces (50 grams) marinated artichokes, drained and chopped

2 ounces (55 grams) whole-milk mozzarella cheese, shredded (1/2 cup)

1 oil-packed sundried tomato cut into slivers

1/2 ounce (15 grams) pepperoni slices, preferably in natural casing

2 slices (12 grams) Genoa salami

1/3 cup (85 grams) Meatball Marinara (page 290), warm

1/4 cup (40 grams) Basil Pesto (page 134), at room temperature

Remove the dough ball from the refrigerator and leave wrapped at room temperature until the dough warms to 60°F to 65°F. Meanwhile, set up the oven with two pizza stones or baking steels and preheat to 500°F for 1 hour (see Getting Started, page 29).

Dust the work surface with the dusting mixture, then move the dough to the surface and dust the top (see Transferring the Dough to the Work Surface, page 30).

Sprinkle a wooden peel with the dusting mixture.

Roll out the dough into an 11-inch round (see Rolling Pizza Dough, page 103).

Using a pizza wheel, make a cut on the edge of the dough round about 3/4 inch off center. Now continue to cut toward the center of the round, stopping about 3/4 inch short of the center ❶. Move the wheel 1½ inches over from where you stopped and cut outward from that point to the opposite edge of the round ❷. You will have a 1½-inch uncut area in the center of the dough.

Move the dough to the peel. As you work, shake the peel forward and backward to ensure the dough isn't sticking.

Picture the dough in quarters. Mound the onions and artichokes in the center of one of the quarters. Mound half of the mozzarella on top of the artichokes and onions and finish with the sun-dried tomatoes. On the quarter opposite the one just topped, lay the pepperoni slices in the center, mound half of the remaining mozzarella over the top, and drape the salami over the mozzarella ❸. Top the salami with the remaining mozzarella.

Lift the untopped side of dough that is on the same side of the cut as the vegetable filling, and fold it over to enclose the filling. Using the tip of a knife or the tines of a fork, press down around the open edges of the dough to seal with a decorative edge ❹.

Repeat lifting, enclosing, and sealing the filling on the opposite side ❺, to complete the bow-tie shape.

Slide the dough onto the top stone (see Moving the Dough to the Oven, page 34). Bake for 6 minutes. Carefully lift the calzone onto the peel, being especially careful of the middle section, rotate it 180 degrees, and then transfer it to the bottom stone. Bake for 4 minutes, until the bottom is browned and crisp and the top is golden brown. Lift the calzone onto the peel and transfer to the top stone for a final 1 to 2 minutes.

Transfer the calzone to a serving platter or serving board and serve the marinara and pesto on the side.

PEPPEROLI

MAKES ONE 12-INCH ROLL; 3 LARGE PIECES (PHOTO PAGE 270)

This is my pepperoni-filled version of a Stromboli, the jelly roll of the pizza world. To serve it as a finger-food appetizer, just cut it into thinner slices and arrange them around a bowl of the Meatball Marinara (page 290).

1 (8-ounce/225-gram) ball Master Dough, preferably with starter (page 44), made with Poolish

1 part flour mixed with 1 part semolina, for dusting

1½ ounces (45 grams) sliced pepperoni, preferably in natural casing

2½ ounces (70 grams) part-skim mozzarella cheese, shredded (2/3 cup)

½ teaspoon (1.5 grams) minced garlic

Grated Pecorino Romano cheese, for dusting

Dried oregano, for dusting

Extra virgin olive oil, for brushing

Garlic Oil (page 29), for brushing

½ cup (125 grams) Meatball Marinara (page 290), warm

Remove the dough ball from the refrigerator and leave wrapped at room temperature until the dough warms to 60°F to 65°F. Meanwhile, set up the oven with two pizza stones or baking steels and preheat to 500°F for 1 hour (see Getting Started, page 29).

Dust the work surface with the dusting mixture, then move the dough to the surface and dust the top (see Transferring the Dough to the Work Surface, page 30).

Roll out the dough into a rectangle about 10 by 12½ inches, then dock the entire surface of the dough (see Rolling Pizza Dough, page 103).

Position the dough with a long side facing you. Scatter the pepperoni evenly over the top, leaving a ½-inch border on the bottom and a 1-inch border at the top and on both sides. Mound the mozzarella in the center and use your fingertips to spread it evenly over the pepperoni. Sprinkle with the garlic and top with a dusting of pecorino and oregano.

Fold up the border of the dough nearest you and then continue to roll up as you would a jelly roll (see Sausage Roll photo ❶, page 280). Turn the roll seam side up and stretch the edge of the dough over to compact the roll as much as possible ❷. Press on the seam to seal and then pinch it closed ❸.

Trim both ends of the roll to straighten them, leaving about ¾ inch of unfilled dough on each end. Just as you would wrap a gift, fold in the two points of the dough on each end and then fold the end over them. Using the handle of a pizza wheel or the end or a wooden spoon, press along the folded edge for a tighter and more decorative seal ❹.

Brush the top of the roll with olive oil. Brushing the dough with oil will help soften it and prevent it from shattering when the roll is cut.

Pull out the top rack of the oven. Carefully lift the roll and transfer it to the stone. Bake for 7 minutes. Lift the roll onto a peel, rotate it 180 degrees, and then transfer it to the bottom stone. Bake for 7 minutes, until the dough is a rich golden brown.

Transfer the roll to a cutting board and let it rest for 2 to 3 minutes. Brush the top with garlic oil and sprinkle with pecorino and oregano. Using a serrated knife, cut crosswise on the diagonal into 3 equal pieces.

Arrange the pieces on a serving platter or board with the marinara on the side.

And They Called It Pepperoni

Pepperoni is far and away America's favorite pizza topping. It's estimated that 36 percent of pizzas sold in the United States are pepperoni pizzas. But did you know that pepperoni isn't actually Italian? If you order it in a pizzeria in Italy, you'll get a questioning look and possibly a pizza with bell peppers (peperoni) on it. Although it was inspired by spicy Italian salami, the sausage we know as pepperoni is an Italo-American invention dating back to the 1930s. A clue to its American origins is that it contains beef, an ingredient not often used in sausage in Italy and much more available in America. It's the beef—and particularly the beef fat—in pepperoni that helps it withstand the high heat of a pizza oven.

Like with any ingredient, I'm picky about pepperoni. The only brand I use in my restaurants is Swiss American, and the type I order, Capo Di Monte, has two special qualities that distinguish it from every

other pepperoni I've tried. It's made with a higher proportion of beef than what's typical, giving it a fuller flavor and a nice chew. And, most important, it's made with a natural casing. Most pepperoni is cured in an artificial casing, which is stripped away in the factory. Natural-casing pepperoni performs differently. As it cooks on a pizza, the casing shrinks, causing the pepperoni to "cup." Most pizzerias consider this a defect because they want their pepperoni to lie flat and create better "coverage," so customers feel they're getting more value for their money. But I use small slices of natural-casing pepperoni because I love the cupping effect. As the slices cup, the raised edges get crisp and develop an almost bacony flavor, while the center stays soft and moist. If you can find natural-casing pepperoni (I recommend Ezzo brand for home cooks), give it a try and you'll taste what I'm talking about.

SAUSAGE ROLL

MAKES ONE 12-INCH ROLL; 6 TO 8 PIECES (PHOTO PAGE 270)

The secret to getting a uniform spiral of sausage encased in dough is to roll out a thin sheet of sausage between pieces of plastic wrap and then lay that sheet over the dough. There's no cheese in this roll, but it's super-rich and flavorful without it.

1 (9-ounce/370-gram) ball Master Dough, preferably with starter (page 44), made with Poolish

1 part flour mixed with 1 part semolina, for dusting

5 ounces (140 grams) Sweet Fennel Sausage (page 54), cold

Extra virgin olive oil, for brushing

Garlic Oil (page 29), for brushing

Grated Pecorino Romano cheese, for sprinkling

Dried oregano, for sprinkling

Red pepper flakes, for sprinkling

1/2 cup (125 grams) Meatball Marinara (page 290), warm

Remove the dough ball from the refrigerator and leave wrapped at room temperature until the dough warms to 60°F to 65°F. Meanwhile, set up the oven with two pizza stones or baking steels and preheat to 500°F for 1 hour (see Getting Started, page 29).

Put the sausage in the center of a piece of plastic wrap 12 inches long. Top with a second piece of plastic wrap and press or roll the patty into an even rectangle about 9 by 6 inches and 1/8 inch thick. Remove the top piece of plastic wrap and trim the sausage as necessary to straighten the sides. Recover with plastic wrap and refrigerate until needed.

Dust the work surface with the dusting mixture, then move the dough to the surface and dust the top (see Transferring the Dough to the Work Surface, page 30).

Roll out the dough into a rectangle about 12 by 8 inches, then dock the entire surface of the dough (see Rolling Pizza Dough, page 103).

Position the dough with a long side facing you. Remove the top piece of plastic wrap from the sausage. Using the bottom piece of plastic wrap, flip and center the sausage on the dough, positioning it 1/2 inch from the edge nearest you, then remove the plastic wrap. Trim the other three sides of the dough, leaving a 1-inch border at the top and on both sides.

Fold up the border of the dough nearest you and then continue to roll up as you would a jelly roll ❶. Turn the roll seam side up and stretch the edge of the dough over to compact the roll as much as possible ❷. Press on the seam to seal and then pinch it closed ❸.

Trim the ends to straighten them, leaving about 3/4 inch of unfilled dough on each end. Just as you would wrap a gift, fold in the two points of dough on each end and fold the end over them. Using the handle of a pizza wheel or the end of a wooden spoon, press along the folded edge for a tighter and more decorative seal ❹.

continued

Brush the top with olive oil. Brushing the dough with oil will help soften it and prevent it from shattering when the roll is cut.

Pull out the top rack of the oven. Carefully lift the roll and transfer it to the stone. Bake for 7 minutes. Lift the roll onto the peel, rotate it 180 degrees, and then transfer it to the bottom stone. Bake for another 7 minutes, until a rich golden brown.

Transfer the roll to a cutting board and let it rest for 2 to 3 minutes. Brush the top with garlic oil and sprinkle with pecorino, oregano, and pepper flakes. Using a serrated knife, cut on a slight diagonal into 6 to 8 pieces.

Arrange the pieces on a serving platter or board with the marinara on the side.

TWO COOL THINGS TO DO WITH LEFTOVER DOUGH

If you've got a little extra pizza dough—a second or third ball you don't want to make into pizza or maybe some trimmings—here are two simple ways to use it. And if you don't have leftover dough, don't let that stop you. These nibbles are totally worth making from scratch.

1 (8-ounce/225-gram) ball Master Dough, preferably with starter (page 44), made with Tiga or Poolish

1 part flour mixed with 1 part semolina, for dusting

Canola oil, for deep-frying, if frying the knots

1 tablespoon (14 grams) unsalted butter, melted, for fried knots, or 1½ tablespoons (21 grams), melted, for baked knots

1 teaspoon (3 grams) finely chopped garlic, or to taste

1 teaspoon (4 grams) finely chopped flat-leaf parsley, or to taste

1 teaspoon (2 grams) grated Pecorino Romano cheese, or to taste

Generous pinch of fine sea salt

Pinch of red pepper flakes

Honey, for drizzling (optional)

GARLIC KNOTS

MAKES 12 KNOTS

I take this classic pizzeria appetizer one step further by drizzling the knots with honey just before serving. I like them fried, but they're also great baked right on the stone. They are an addictive sweet-savory party snack to go with beer, Prosecco, or cocktails.

Remove the dough ball from the refrigerator and leave wrapped at room temperature until the dough warms to 60°F to 65°F.

Meanwhile, if you are baking the knots, position a rack in the upper third of the oven, top it with a pizza stone or baking steel, and preheat the oven to 500°F for 1 hour (see Getting Started, page 29).

If you are frying the knots, when the dough has come to temperature, pour oil to a depth of 2 inches into a deep pot (at least 6 inches) and heat to 350°F, regulating the heat as needed to maintain the temperature.

Dust the work surface with the dusting mixture, then move the dough to the surface and dust the top (see Transferring the Dough to the Work Surface, page 30).

Roll out the dough into a rectangle about 6 by 12 inches and slightly less than ⅛ inch thick (see Rolling Pizza Dough, page 103).

Cut the dough into 12 strips each about 1 inch wide. Tie each strip into a knot.

To bake the knots: Pull out the oven rack, pat the knots to remove any excess flour, and quickly lay the knots on the stone. Bake for 6 minutes, then check the knots and move them around the stone as necessary to bake them evenly. Continue to bake for 2 minutes, until the knots are a rich golden brown.

To deep-fry the knots: Carefully drop 4 to 6 knots (depending on the width of your pot) into the hot oil and fry, moving them around the oil, for 3 to 4 minutes, until both sides are evenly browned. Using tongs, drain the knots briefly on paper towels and keep warm while you fry the remaining knots.

While the knots are hot, put them in a large bowl and toss them with the butter. Add the garlic, parsley, pecorino, salt, and pepper flakes and toss again to coat them evenly.

Pile the knots on a serving platter or in a serving bowl. Drizzle with honey and serve immediately.

BACON TWISTS

MAKES 6 TWISTS (PHOTO PAGE 271)

1 (8-ounce/225-gram) ball Master dough, preferably with starter (page 44), made with Tiga or Poolish

1 part flour mixed with 1 part semolina, for dusting

6 strips (220 grams) bacon, preferably regular or thin-cut

Maple syrup or honey, for brushing

Grated Pecorino Romano cheese, for dusting

If you've ever made cheese straws, you'll recognize this technique. You lay a strip of bacon on a strip of dough, twist them together to make a spiral, and bake on a sheet pan. I drizzle these with maple syrup or honey for a bacon-candy effect. You can serve them as an appetizer, and they're also perfect for dipping into soft-boiled eggs for breakfast or brunch. Avoid thick-cut bacon here. It doesn't twist well and it may not cook completely.

Remove the dough ball from the refrigerator and leave wrapped at room temperature until the dough warms to 60°F to 65°F. Meanwhile, position a rack in the center of the oven, top it with a pizza stone or baking steel, and preheat to 425°F for 1 hour (see Getting Started, page 29).

Dust the work surface with the dusting mixture, then move the dough to the surface and dust the top (see Transferring the Dough to the Work Surface, page 30).

Roll out the dough into a rectangle 1/8 inch thick and with one side just slightly longer than the length of the bacon strips (see Rolling Pizza Dough, page 103).

Have a half sheet pan at your side. Lay a strip of bacon along one end of the dough. Using a pizza wheel, trim the dough around the bacon, making the dough strip just slightly wider than the bacon strip.

Working outward from the center, twist together the dough and bacon. The finished twist will resemble a barbershop pole. Lay the twist on the pan. Use your thumbs to press the two ends of the dough down against the pan to secure them. This will help keep the twists from unraveling as they bake.

Set the pan on the stone and bake for 8 minutes. Rotate the pan 180 degrees and bake for another 8 minutes, until the twists are crisp and the bacon is cooked.

Remove the pan from the oven and, using a metal spatula, lift the twists. Blot them on paper towels, if you like, but don't forget that the bacon fat adds flavor. Place the twists on a cutting board and cut off the two flattened ends from each twist. Brush the twists lightly with maple syrup and finish with a dusting of pecorino.

MEATBALLS

**MAKES ABOUT 4 POUNDS (1.8 KILOGRAMS); FIVE 13-OUNCE (370-GRAM) MEATBALLS GIGANTES
OR SIXTEEN 4-OUNCE (115-GRAM) MEATBALLS**

Several little touches make these meatballs extra-moist, tender, and flavorful. I use both seasoned bread crumbs and a puree of fresh bread, cream, and ricotta (a mixture called a panade that helps the texture stay soft and light); a bit of our rooftop honey for caramelization and sweetness; and a blend of sausage, ground beef, and ground veal. These can be your go-to meatballs for any purpose.

We make the meatballs in two sizes. The smaller ones (about 2½ inches in diameter) get sliced or crumbled for pizzas and calzones or simmered in Meatball Marinara (page 290) for pasta and sandwiches.

The larger ones we serve as our signature Meatball Gigante shared appetizer. These weigh in at a whopping 13 ounces and measure about 4 inches across. We make only twenty-five a day, and they always sell out. I've given you the method for making them as well as our four most popular ways to serve them. For big groups, we'll do a trio or a quartet of gigantes or regular-size meatballs, each topped in a different way.

One rule of thumb (and fingers): you can mix the ingredients fairly aggressively, but be sure to use a light hand when you're shaping, so you don't compact the meat too much.

SEASONED BREAD CRUMBS

1½ slices (50 grams) artisanal white bread, crusts removed

½ teaspoon (0.7 grams) chopped flat-leaf parsley

¼ teaspoon (0.7 grams) garlic powder

¼ teaspoon (0.7 grams) onion powder

⅛ teaspoon (0.7 grams) fine sea salt

Pinch of freshly ground black pepper

To make the bread crumbs, position a rack in the center of the oven and preheat the oven to 300°F.

Arrange the bread slices on a sheet pan and place in the oven. After 15 minutes, turn the slices over and leave for about 20 minutes longer, until they are dry without coloring. Remove from the oven and let cool completely.

Tear the bread into 1-inch irregular pieces and put them in a food processor. Add the parsley, garlic and onion powders, salt, and pepper and pulse until coarse, evenly seasoned crumbs have formed. The crumbs can be used immediately or stored in an airtight container at room temperature for up to 3 days.

continued

MEATBALLS

1/2 cup (15 grams) lightly packed torn
artisanal white bread, crusts removed

1/4 cup plus 1 tablespoon (75 grams)
heavy cream

4 ounces (115 grams/scant 1/2 cup)
whole-milk ricotta cheese, preferably
New York–style Polly-O or Ricotta
Cream, page 91

11/2 teaspoons (3.5 grams)
cayenne pepper

2 tablespoons (28 grams) water

2 pounds (910 grams) Sweet Fennel
Sausage (page 54)

11/4 pounds (570 grams) ground
beef, preferably Niman Ranch with
20 percent fat

4 ounces (115 grams) ground veal

1 tablespoon (4 grams) chopped
flat-leaf parsley

21/2 teaspoons (8 grams) finely
chopped garlic

1/4 cup (20 grams) grated Parmesan
cheese

1 egg, lightly beaten

2 tablespoons plus 2 teaspoons
(56 grams) honey

To make the meatballs, leave the oven rack in the center of the oven and preheat the oven to 400°F. Line a sheet pan with parchment paper.

Put the torn bread, cream, and ricotta in the food processor and process until smooth. Set aside.

In a large bowl, combine the cayenne and water. (Mixing the cayenne with water will help to incorporate it more evenly into the meat mixture.) Break the sausage, beef, and veal into small chunks and add them to the bowl. Squeeze the meat through your hands to combine thoroughly and to mix in the cayenne water.

Continue to mix by hand, adding the parsley, garlic, and bread crumbs. When the ingredients are well combined, mix in the Parmesan, followed by the ricotta mixture.

Finally, mix in the egg and honey and continue to combine. This last step may take longer that you might think. You need to lift the mixture from the bottom, scrape it from the sides of the bowl, and work it through your fingers to ensure that all of the ingredients are evenly incorporated.

Weigh out 13-ounce (370-gram) portions for large meatballs or 4-ounce (115-gram) portions for small meatballs. Using your hands, gently shape each portion into a smooth ball. To keep a light texture, don't roll the meat on the work surface or put too much pressure on it as you shape the balls. As the meatballs are shaped, place them on a half sheet pan, spacing them apart so they don't touch.

Bake the large meatballs for 15 minutes or the small meatballs for 10 minutes. Rotate the sheet pan 180 degrees and continue to bake the large meatballs for about 15 minutes longer or the small meatballs for about 8 minutes longer. To check for doneness, insert an instant-read thermometer into the center of a meatball; it should register 140°F.

If you would like the meatballs more browned, turn on the broiler and broil for 1 to 2 minutes. If the meatballs will be used on a pizza or in a calzone, let them cool completely before crumbling or slicing. They can be wrapped in plastic wrap and refrigerated for up to 2 days.

MEATBALL GIGANTE

MAKES 1 MEATBALL; SERVES 2

1 (13-ounce/470-gram) Meatball
(page 287), at room temperature

1/2 cup (125 grams) Meatball Marinara
(page 290), at room temperature

Position a rack in the center of the oven and preheat the oven to 400°F.

Place the meatball in the center of an individual ovenproof serving dish. Pour the sauce over the top; it will pool in the bottom of the dish. Put in the oven for 10 to 15 minutes, until the meatball is hot. Garnish with one of the following variations.

Burrata: Top the meatball with a piece of *burrata*, a scattering of julienned fresh basil, a sprinkling of sea salt, and a drizzle of extra virgin olive oil.

Farm Egg: Top the meatball with an egg fried sunny-side-up and a pinch each of Maldon sea salt and freshly ground black pepper.

Honey: Drizzle honey over the top of the meatball and garnish with grated Parmesan cheese.

Mushroom Pancetta and Robiola Sauce: Spoon the sauce (page 291) over the top.

MEATBALL MARINARA

LARGE BATCH **MAKES 6 CUPS (1.5 KILOGRAMS)**
SMALL BATCH **MAKES 3 CUPS (755 GRAMS)**

Here is an intensely flavored red sauce in which to simmer the Meatballs on page 275. I've given you two batch sizes. The large batch makes enough to simmer a full recipe of the small meatballs. The small batch will give you enough to sauce a full recipe of the large meatballs.

If you are making the sauce to use immediately, combine all of the ingredients in a small stockpot and bring to a simmer over medium-low heat, stirring occasionally, then remove from the heat.

If you are making the sauce ahead, combine all of the ingredients in a large bowl, mix well, then cover and refrigerate for up to 3 days.

LARGE BATCH

2.4 pounds (1.1 kilograms/4½ cups) ground tomatoes, preferably 6 in 1 or DiNapoli

12 ounces (340 grams/1¼ cups plus 2 tablespoons) tomato paste, preferably SuperDolce

2 tablespoons (3.5 grams) dried oregano

1½ teaspoon (7 grams) fine sea salt

2 tablespoons (28 grams) extra virgin olive oil

1 fresh basil leaf, torn

SMALL BATCH

1.2 pounds (550 grams/2¼ cups) ground tomatoes, preferably 6 in 1 or DiNapoli

6 ounces (170 grams/½ cup plus 3 tablespoons) tomato paste, preferably SuperDolce

1 tablespoon (2 grams) dried oregano

¾ teaspoon (3.5 grams) fine sea salt

1 tablespoon (14 grams) extra virgin olive oil

1 small fresh basil leaf, torn

MUSHROOM, PANCETTA, AND ROBIOLA SAUCE

ENOUGH FOR 1 MEATBALL GIGANTE

5 ounces (140 grams) assorted mushrooms (such as pioppini, oyster, clamshell, and trumpet)

Olive oil, for sautéing

Fine sea salt and freshly ground black pepper

1 ounce (30 grams) thinly sliced pancetta, chopped

1/2 cup (120 grams) heavy cream

1 ounce (30 grams) robiola cheese, cut into small pieces

Robiola is a soft, creamy cheese from northern Italy. I use it to add flavor and a silky texture to this rich mushroom cream sauce. When you spoon it right over the marinara-drenched meatball, the two sauces mingle and it's a beautiful marriage. You might be tempted to use this sauce all on its own on pasta. You would be absolutely right.

Clean and trim the mushrooms so that they will all cook in about the same amount of time. Leave the pioppini and other small, delicate mushrooms whole. Slice the trumpets lengthwise into slices 1/8 inch thick.

Heat a generous film of oil in a skillet over medium-high heat until very hot. Add the larger mushroom pieces and sauté for about 30 seconds. Add the remaining mushrooms, season with salt and pepper, and sauté for another 30 seconds. Add the pancetta and continue to sauté, stirring often, for 2 to 3 minutes, until the mushrooms are golden brown and the pancetta is cooked but not crisp.

Stir in the cream, lower the heat to medium, and simmer for 1 1/2 to 2 minutes, until the cream is reduced by about one-third to a saucelike consistency. Add the cheese and stir constantly until just melted. Serve immediately.

Focaccia and Bread

A lot of people seem to be scared of baking bread. Guess what? Pizza dough is bread dough. And it can be your "gateway dough" to becoming a confident bread baker. Here's how to turn my Sicilian Dough into fantastic focaccia and ciabatta—and two of my favorite ways to use those homemade breads.

FOCACCIA

MAKES ONE 12 BY 18-INCH FOCACCIA

This is the rich, super-light, meltingly tender focaccia we serve in my restaurants. You can slice it into sticks to add to a bread basket or to serve as a nibble with drinks, or make larger slices for sandwiches, like Focaccina (page 297). Not an olive lover? You can swap in roasted cherry tomatoes with a little olive oil and salt (see page 206). Just add them as directed for the olives, after the dough has been pushed out the last time. Roasted Garlic Cloves (page 209) are another nice olive substitute.

1 (35-ounce/990-gram) ball Sicilian Dough Without Starter (page 120)

1/4 cup (56 grams) olive oil, for oiling the pan

15 black or green oil-cured olives, pitted and halved.

Extra virgin olive oil, for brushing and drizzling

2 teaspoons (6 grams) minced garlic

2 teaspoons (2 grams) chopped fresh rosemary

1/4 teaspoon (0.5 grams) red pepper flakes

Honey, for drizzling

Fleur de sel or Maldon sea salt

Follow the instructions for Parbaking Sicilian Dough (page 122) with the following additions: Once the dough has risen the first time (for 30 minutes) and has been pushed out in the pan a final time, use the tip of a paring knife to make a small opening in the dough. Push an olive into the opening, still allowing it to peek through. Continue with the remaining olives, spacing them evenly around the dough. Let the dough rise again as instructed (for 1 1/2 to 2 hours), then follow the baking instructions below.

While the dough rises, set up the oven with two pizza stones or baking steels and preheat to 450°F for 1 hour (see Getting Started, page 29).

Gently set the pan on the top stone and bake for 10 minutes. Rotate the pan 180 degrees and transfer it to the bottom stone. Bake for 5 minutes, until the top is a rich golden brown. Using a wide metal spatula, lift a corner of the focaccia to check the bottom. If you want to crisp the bottom further, move the pan to the top stone for 1 minute, rotate it 180 degrees, and continue baking for 1 minute more.

Take the pan out of the oven. Run the spatula around the edges of the focaccia to make sure it has not stuck in any area. If you suspect a problem, drizzle a bit of oil down the side of the pan and work slowly to loosen in that area. Then run the spatula under the entire focaccia to be sure it is completely released from the pan.

Brush the top of the focaccia with extra virgin oil and sprinkle with garlic, rosemary, and pepper flakes. Dip a brush in the extra virgin oil, hold it over the top of the focaccia, and rapidly move it backward and forward to drizzle the surface evenly. Dip a fork into the honey and repeat the motion. Sprinkle with *fleur de sel*.

FOCACCINA

MAKES 1 SANDWICH, SERVES 1 TO 2

This sandwich is the ultimate combo of salumi, cheese, veggies and creamy pesto mayo. It's great made with still-warm focaccia, and equally good made ahead of time for a picnic or a lunch at work. You'll find that even if the greens get a bit wilted, the way the flavors blend and soak into the bread as the sandwich sits is focaccing incredible.

2 tablespoons (26 grams) mayonnaise

1 tablespoon (10 grams) Basil Pesto (page 134)

1 (5-inch) square piece Focaccia (page 295)

4 thin slices (2.5 ounces/70 grams) provolone cheese

4 thin slices (2 ounces/55 grams) prosciutto

4 thin tomato slices

4 ounces (115 grams) fresh whole-milk mozzarella cheese, homemade (page 190) or store-bought fior di latte, thinly sliced and well drained

Fine sea salt and freshly ground black pepper

1 thin slice red onion

6 thin slices (1.5 ounces/45 grams) Genoa salami

Small handful of arugula leaves

2 (30 grams) Peppadew peppers, coarsely chopped

Balsamic vinegar, for drizzling

Extra virgin olive oil, for drizzling

Garlic Oil (page 29), for brushing

Chopped fresh rosemary, for sprinkling

Maldon sea salt

In a small bowl, stir together mayonnaise and pesto and set aside. Cut the focaccia in half horizontally.

Lay the provolone over the bottom half of the bread and top with the prosciutto, tomatoes, and mozzarella. Season the mozzarella with salt and pepper.

Separate the onion into rings. Continue layering with the onion, salami, arugula, and Peppadew peppers. Drizzle with balsamic vinegar and olive oil. Spread the pesto mayonnaise on the cut side of the top piece of bread and close the sandwich.

Brush the top of the sandwich with garlic oil and sprinkle with rosemary and Maldon salt. Cut the sandwich in half on the diagonal.

CIABATTA

MAKES 2 LOAVES

You're probably familiar with ciabatta, the long, flat Italian white bread, and I'm happy to tell you that it's quite easy to make using my Sicilian Dough with Starter. The name, Italian for "slipper," comes from the shape of the rustic hearth-baked loaf—a shape achieved with a slipper-fold technique that's pretty easy and forgiving. I spray the loaves in the oven after 10 minutes to moisten and soften the exterior, which allows the dough to rise a bit more before the crust sets and ultimately yields a crispier, more richly browned loaf. Ciabatta is a good choice for sandwiches, for serving with a meal, and, of course, for making a quick After-School Ciabatta Pizza (page 300).

2 (20-ounce/540-gram) balls Sicilian Dough with Starter (page 118), made with Poolish

3 parts semolina mixed with 1 part flour, for dusting

Remove the dough balls from the refrigerator and leave wrapped at room temperature until the dough warms to 60°F to 65°F (see Getting Started, page 29).

Dust the work surface with the dusting mixture, then move the dough to the surface and dust the top (see Transferring the Dough to the Work Surface, page 30).

The dough will be sticky, so dust your hands and push the dough open to a rectangle about 10 by 6 inches. Fold about 1 inch of each short end toward the center, and brush away any excess dusting mixture from the top of the folded edges. Fold in the long sides to meet in the center, and brush the top again. Pinch together the seam down the center of the dough, sealing well, and turn the folded dough over, seam side down.

Using your hands, gently coax the dough into a slipper shape about 12 by 4 inches. Sprinkle the top with the dusting mixture and cover with a damp dish towel.

Repeat with the other piece of dough. Let both loaves rest for 1½ hours to rise slightly.

Meanwhile, measure the depth of your baking stones. It's best to bake both loaves at the same time, with the loaves running vertically on the stone. Most stones are about 14 inches deep, and the loaves should be about 12 inches long. If your loaves are longer than your stone will allow for, bake one loaf at a time, placing it horizontally or diagonally on the stone. Set up the oven with two pizza stones or baking steels and preheat to 425°F for 1 hour (see Getting Started, page 29).

Sprinkle a wooden peel with the dusting mixture. Lift the loaf (loaves) gently and place on the peel. Shake the peel forward and backward to ensure the dough isn't sticking.

Using a razor blade, score the top of each loaf with 3 evenly spaced diagonal slits, each about 2 1/2 inches long and 1/4 inch deep.

Slide the loaf (loaves) onto the top stone (see Moving the Dough to the Oven, page 34). Bake for 10 minutes.

Meanwhile, fill a spray bottle with water. When the 10 minutes are up, quickly mist the loaf (loaves) with water and continue to bake for another 10 minutes.

Lift the loaf (loaves) onto the peel, rotate 180 degrees, and then transfer to the bottom stone. Bake for another 10 minutes. Quickly mist the loaf (loaves) once again, then bake for 6 minutes, until it is richly browned and sounds hollow when rapped with your knuckles. The internal temperature of the finished bread will be 200°F to 210°F.

Transfer the loaves to a cooling rack to rest for at least 2 hours before cutting. Once cool, they can be stored at room temperature tightly wrapped.

AFTER-SCHOOL CIABATTA PIZZA

MAKES 2 PIZZAS; 8 TO 10 PIECES

If you grew up any time after the 1960s, you're probably familiar with French bread pizza—an open-faced sandwich with pizza sauce and mozzarella, sometimes pepperoni, usually made in a toaster oven as an after-school snack. If you haven't tried it since childhood, this A+ version, made with my homemade ciabatta, will take you back, and it's an easy way to let your kids discover their inner *pizzaiolo*.

5 ounces (140 grams/²/₃ cup) ground tomatoes, preferably 7/11 or DiNapoli

5 ounces (140 grams/¹/₂ cup plus 1 tablespoon) tomato paste, preferably SuperDolce

Dried oregano, for seasoning and dusting

Fine sea salt and freshly ground black pepper

1 loaf Ciabatta (page 298)

Garlic Oil (page 29), for brushing

8 ounces (225 grams) whole-milk mozzarella cheese, shredded (2 cups)

2 ounces (55 grams) sliced pepperoni, preferably with natural casing (optional)

Grated Pecorino Romano cheese, for dusting

Extra virgin olive oil, for drizzling

Set up the oven with a pizza stone or baking steel on the center rack and preheat to 500°F for 1 hour (see Getting Started, page 29).

Combine the ground tomatoes, tomato paste, a generous pinch of oregano, and a pinch each of salt and pepper in a deep bowl or other deep container and puree with an immersion blender.

Cut the bread in half horizontally and put both halves cut side up on a half sheet pan.

Place the pan on the pizza stone for 2 to 3 minutes to dry the bread.

Remove the bread from the oven and brush the cut sides with garlic oil. Spoon half of the sauce on each piece and spread it evenly, covering the tops completely. Sprinkle both halves evenly with the mozzarella and arrange the pepperoni slices over the cheese.

Place the pan on the pizza stone for 4 to 6 minutes to melt the cheese and cook the pepperoni. Then, if you want to brown the top a bit more, turn on the broiler for about 1 minute.

Transfer the pizzas to a cutting board. Finish with a light dusting of pecorino and oregano and a drizzle of olive oil. Cut each pizza crosswise into 4 or 5 pieces.

BAKER'S PERCENTAGES CHART

	FLOUR	WATER	YEAST	MALT	SALT	HONEY	OIL	STARTER	TOTAL HYDRATION
Chicago Deep-Dish Dough*	100%	60	1	2	2	-	-	-	60
Cracker-Thin Dough with starter	100%	62	.5	2	2	-	-	20	65
Dough for Grilling without starter	100%	65	1	-	2	-	-	-	65
Einkorn Dough without starter	100%	60	.5	-	3	-	-	-	60
Khorasan Dough with starter	100%	62	.5	-	3	-	-	20	65
Master Dough without Starter	100%	65	1	2	2	-	1	-	65
Master Dough with Starter	100%	64	.5	2	2	-	1	20	65
Multigrain Dough with starter	100%	66	.5	2	3	-	1	5	67
Napoletana Dough with starter	100%	62	.5	2 home oven only	2	-	-	20	65
Organic Dough with starter	100%	60	.2	-	2	-	-	30	65
Romana Dough with starter	100%	66	.2	2	3	-	-	5	68.5
Sicilian Dough without Starter	100%	70	1	2	2	-	1	-	70
Sicilian Dough with Starter	100%	67	.5	2	2	-	1	20	70
Sprouted Wheat Dough	100%	35	.25	-	2	3	5	50	61

*This dough also contains 4% butter and 4% lard.

PRO TIP

If you're using a starter, be sure to take into account the extra flour weight it adds when calculating your percentages of salt, malt, and oil.

MEASUREMENT CONVERSION CHARTS

VOLUME

U.S.	IMPERIAL	METRIC
1 tablespoon	1/2 fl oz	15 ml
2 tablespoons	1 fl oz	30 ml
1/4 cup	2 fl oz	60 ml
1/3 cup	3 fl oz	90 ml
1/2 cup	4 fl oz	120 ml
2/3 cup	5 fl oz (1/4 pint)	150 ml
3/4 cup	6 fl oz	180 ml
1 cup	8 fl oz (1/3 pint)	240 ml
1 1/4 cups	10 fl oz (1/2 pint)	300 ml
2 cups (1 pint)	16 fl oz (2/3 pint)	480 ml
2 1/2 cups	20 fl oz (1 pint)	600 ml
1 quart	32 fl oz (1 2/3 pint)	1 l

WEIGHT

U.S./IMPERIAL	METRIC
1/2 oz	15 g
1 oz	30 g
2 oz	60 g
1/4 lb	115 g
1/3 lb	150 g
1/2 lb	225 g
3/4 lb	350 g
1 lb	450 g

LENGTH

INCH	METRIC
1/4 inch	6 mm
1/2 inch	1.25 cm
3/4 inch	2 cm
1 inch	2.5 cm
6 inches (1/2 foot)	15 cm
12 inches (1 foot)	30 cm

TEMPERATURE

FAHRENHEIT	CELSIUS/GAS MARK
250°F	120°C/gas mark 1/2
275°F	135°C/gas mark 1
300°F	150°C/gas mark 2
325°F	160°C/gas mark 3
350°F	180 or 175°C/gas mark 4
375°F	190°C/gas mark 5
400°F	200°C/gas mark 6
425°F	220°C/gas mark 7
450°F	230°C/gas mark 8
475°F	245°C/gas mark 9
500°F	260°C

SOURCES

Most ingredients and equipment can be found in specialty markets, cookware stores, and the following online sources. Thefind.com is an excellent source for locating hard to find items. Another favorite of mine is bakerybits.co.uk.

FOOD

Cheese and Butter

Brick
Comte
Dubliner
Greek Feta-water packed
Mozzarella Fresh Ovoline (fior di latte)
Mozzarella Curd
Mozzarella di Bufala
Mozzarella – Grande part-skim
Mozzarella – Grande whole milk
Manchego
Parmigiano, Reggiano
Pecorino, Fiore Sardo
Pecorino Romano, aged
Piave
Provolone, Grande Provo-Nello
Ricotta, Grande Sopraffina
Smoked Scamorza
Saint André
White Cheddar Cheese, Cabot
pennmac.com

Burrata alla Panna by Di Stefano
amazon.com and igourmet.com

Crescenza Stracchino Cheese
amazon.com or igourmet.com

Goat Cheese, Laura Chenel
laurachenel.com for a list of locations

Nicasio Reserve Cheese
nicasiocheese.com

Pecorino, Soft Romano
Pecorino, Soft Sardinian
Pecorino, Hard Sardinian
igourmet.com and dibruno.com

Fromage Blanc
amazon.com

Mozzarella, Dry
arthuravenue.com

Mt. Tam, Organic
cowgirlcreamery.com

Provel
amazon.com

Ricotta, Polly-O New York Style
italco.com

White Cheddar, Organic
sierranevadacheese.com

Butter, European style (at least 82% butterfat)
sierranevadacheese.com and plugra.com

Flours, Grains, Malts, and Starters

Power Unbleached Flour (Pendleton Flour Mills)
amazon.com

All Trump's Flour (General Mills)
amazon.com

Caputo 00 Flour and San Felice 00 Flour
amazon.com, chefcentral.com and fgpizza.com

Bran, Organic Bakers Brand
Cornmeal, medium grind
Malt, Diastatic
Organic Dark Rye Flour
Organic High Mountain Hi-Protein Flour
Organic Type 70 Malted Flour
Organic White Khorasan Flour
Sprouted Wheat
Organic Whole Wheat Medium Flour
centralmilling.com

Ceresota All Purpose Flour
heckersceresota.com and amazon.com

Einkorn Flour
jovialfoods.com, amazon.com and Whole Foods Market

Harvest King Flour (General Mills)
amazon.com

High Performer High Protein Unbleached by Giustos
giustos.com and mugnaini.com

Sir Lancelot Unbleached Hi-Gluten Flour (King Arthur)
kingarthurflour.com and chefcentral.com

Starters, Ed Woods International Sourdoughs
sourdo.com

Meats

Bottom Beef Round Flat, Snake River Farms
Corned Beef Brisket, Snake River Farms
snakeriverfarms.com

Chorizo, raw, bulk sausage
fontanini.com

Chorizo, cured
Genoa Salami
Guanciale
Mortadella
Pancetta, smoked
Proscuitto Cotto
Proscuitto di Parma
Sopressata Piccante
framani.com, arthuravenue.com, amazon.com and creminelli.com

Lardo
Jamón Serrano
tienda.com

Pepperoni, natural casing by Ezzo
pennmac.com

Pepperoni, natural casing by Swiss American Sausage Company
burkecorp.com

Seasonings

Maldon Salt
amazon.com and Whole Foods Markets

Nora Peppers, ground
tienda.com

Oregano Stems, dried by Tutto Calabria
fgpizza.com and mugnaini.com

Crushed Hot Chile Peppers by Tutto Calabria
tuttocalabria.com and amazon.com

Sweet Smoked Spanish Paprika
tienda.com

Spices
wholespice.com and amazon.com

Speciality Items

Amarena Cherries
amazon.com

Anchovies, Oil-Packed
Anchovies, Salt-Packed
agostinorecca.com and amazon.com

Anchovies – Calabrese
tuttocalabria.com

Black Truffle Paste
amazon.com

Blood Orange Syrup, Torani
amazon.com

Fig Jam by Dalmatia
amazon.com and Whole Foods Market

Giardiniera–Hot
fontanini.com

Hog casing–32 mm
amazon.com

Olive Oil, Filippo Berio (Pure and Extra Virgin)
Olive Oil, Corto
Olive Oil, Sagra Extra Virgin
amazon.com

Olive Oil, Siloro Extra Virgin (for finishing)
casadecase.com

Olives, Castelvetrano, Cerignola and Pugliese
pennmac.com

Peppadew Peppers
pennmac.com and amazon.com
Whole Foods Market

Truffle Oil, white
amazon.com and Whole Foods Market

Quail Eggs
amazon.com

Tomato Products

Strianese San Marzano Tomatoes
fgpizza.com and mugnaini.com

Bianco di Napoli Organic Tomatoes
pizzeriabianco.com and fgpizza.com

Escalon 6 in 1 Ground Tomatoes
Escalon Bontá Tomato Paste
Escalon Christina's Certified Organic
   Ground Tomatoes
Stanislaus Valoroso
Stanislaus Alta Cucina
Stanislaus 7/11
Stanislaus Tomato Magic
Stanislaus Saporito
Stanislaus Super Dolce
escalon.net or pennmac.com

EQUIPMENT

Baking Steel
bakingsteel.com

Barrels
barrelsonline.com

Bowl Scraper
amazon.com

Brush, heatproof
amazon.com

Dough Cutter, no scratch from GI Metal
gimetalusa.com or fgpizza.com

Dough Scraper from Epicurean
epicureancs.com

Dough Docker
fgpizza.com and amazon.com

Dough Trays and Lid, Artisan by DoughMate
doughmate.com

Grill Cleaning Brick
amazon.com

King Cube Ice Trays
amazon.com

Meat Slicers
edgecraft.com

Oil Can, Oliera Tradizionale
artisanpizzasolutions.com or fgpizza.com

Cast Iron Skillet, 12-inch by Lodge
lodgemfg.com

Chicago Deep-Dish Pan, 13-inch black steel
Sicilian Pan – 12 by 18-inch black steel pan
Quattro Forni Pan, 8-inch square
fgpizza.com

Detroit Pan, seasoned pan by Detroit Style Pizza
Detroitstylepizza.com

Wood Peel, 16 by 18-inch with 24-inch handle
by Allied Metal
amazon.com

Aluminum Perforated Pizza Peel, 16-inches with
20-inch handle by GI Metal
gimetalusa.com

Natural Pizza Peel, 4 by 23-inches
by Epicurean
epicureancs.com

Pizza Stand, 12 by 12-inch stand by American
Metalcraft
amazon.com

Pizza Stones
amazon.com

Neapolitan Pizza Plate, 13-inch
artisanpizzasolutions.com

Rock-n-Roll Pizza Cutter, 20-inch by
Dexter-Russell
amazon.com

Scales, My Weigh iBalance and Palm scales
amazon.com

Wood-fired Ovens and Accessories:
Ash Scraper, Floor Brush, Log Grate,
Infrared Thermometer Gun, Palino,
14-inch Wood Peels
mugnaini.com

Acknowledgments

A BIG, HAPPY SHOUT OUT TO EVERYONE WHO HELPED ME CREATE THIS BOOK OVER THE LAST TWO YEARS.

Our book team: Susie Heller, producer/writer (recipes), Steve Siegelman, writer (text); and Janet Mumford, designer. You are true models of what it means to respect the craft.

Everyone at Tony's Pizza Napoletana, Capo's, Tony's Coal Fired Pizza, Tony's of North Beach, Tony's Slice House, Pizza Rock Sacramento, and Pizza Rock Las Vegas, especially Laura Meyer, Thiago Vasconcelos, Mario Abruzzo, Matt Molina, Elmer Mejicanos, and Luis Valadez for sharing their time, their recipes, and their friendship and support, day after day.

Our photography team: Sara Remington, photographer; Erin Quon, food stylist; Dani Fisher and Jen Ryan, prop stylists; Nicole Rejwan and Luaren Janney, photo assistants; and Lori Nunokawa, food styling assistant for keeping it real and beautiful at the same time.

The gang at Ten Speed Press: Aaron Wehner, Jenny Wapner, Hannah Rahill, Emma Campion, Natalie Mulford, Ashley Matuszak, and Daniel Wikey for taking us on so enthusiastically and supporting us all the way.

Amy Vogler for expert testing, proofing and good counsel, Sharon Silva for savvy copy editing; Rebecca Willis, Jorge Velazquez, and Blair Scott for their hard work and support during the testing process; and Renée Harcourt for working her design magic on the cover art.

My industry friends who supplied ingredients, equipment and advice as we tested our recipes: Nicky Giusto of Central Milling, Daryl Gormley of Grande Cheese, Andrea Mugnaini of Mugnaini Wood Fired Ovens, my friends at Stanislaus Food Products, Snake River Farms, and GI Metal, and Chef Curtis Di Fede, Carol Blymire, and Clay McLachlan.

I also want to thank my mom, Eileen, and my father, Frank.

And most of all, thank you Julie and Lucy for loving me and my pizzas so much.

INDEX

Published in the United States by Ten Speed Press, an imprint of the Crown Publishing Group, a division of Random House LLC, New York, a Penguin Random House Company.
www.crownpublishing.com
www.tenspeed.com

Ten Speed Press and the Ten Speed Press colophon are registered trademarks of Random House LLC.

Library of Congress Cataloging-in-Publication Data

Gemignani, Tony.
The pizza bible : the world's favorite pizza styles, from Neapolitan, deep-dish, wood-fired, Sicilian, calzones and focaccia to New York, New Haven, Detroit, and more / Tony Gemignani.
pages cm
1. Pizza. I. Title.
TX770.P58G45 2014
641.82'48—dc23
2014015999

Hardcover ISBN: 978-1-60774-605-8
eBook ISBN: 978-1-60774-606-5

Printed in China

Design by Janet Mumford

20 19

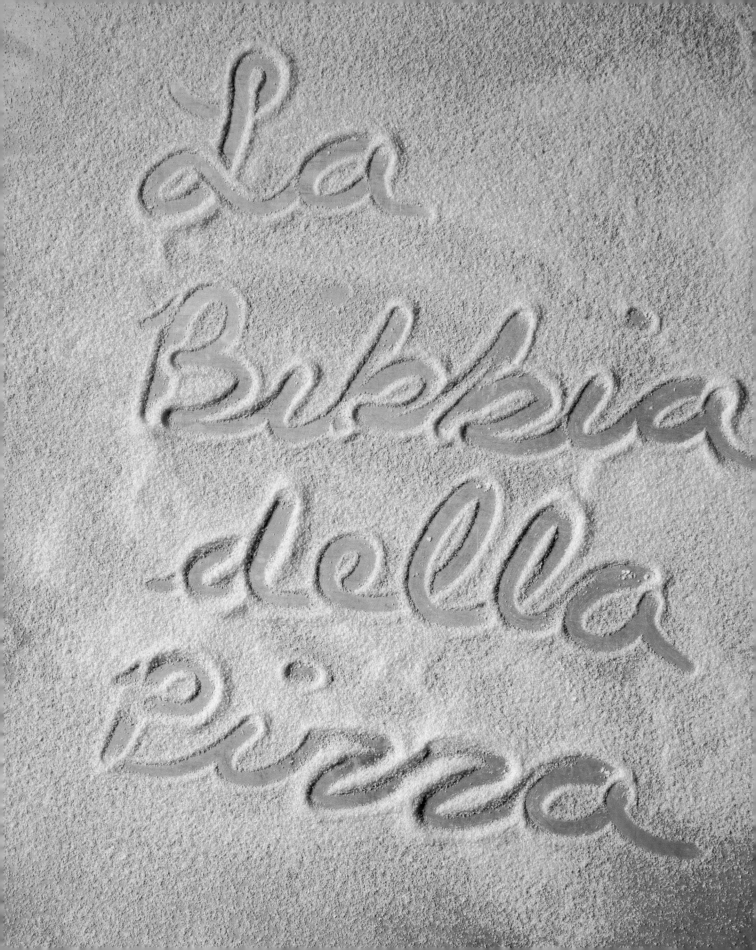